D1369250

IBN SA'UD'S WARRIORS
OF ISLAM

SOCIAL, ECONOMIC AND POLITICAL STUDIES OF THE MIDDLE EAST

ÉTUDES SOCIALES, ÉCONOMIQUES ET POLITIQUES DU MOYEN ORIENT

VOLUME XXVII

JOHN S. HABIB

IBN SA'UD'S WARRIORS OF ISLAM

LEIDEN
E. J. BRILL
1978

IBN SA'UD'S WARRIORS
OF ISLAM

*The Ikhwan of Najd and Their Role in the Creation
of the Sa'udi Kingdom, 1910-1930*

BY

JOHN S. HABIB

LEIDEN
E. J. BRILL
1978

Le but de la collection est de faciliter la communication entre le grand public international et les spécialistes des sciences sociales étudiant le Moyen-Orient, et notamment ceux qui y résident. Les ouvrages sélectionnés porteront sur les phéno- mènes et problèmes contemporains: sociaux, culturels, économiques et administra- tifs. Leurs principales orientations relevèront de la théorie générale, de probléma- tiques plus précises, et de la politologie: aménagement des institutions et admini- stration des affaires publiques.

The series is designed to serve as a link between the international reading public and social scientists studying the contemporary Middle East, notably those living in the area. Works to be included will be characterized by their relevance to actual phenomena and problems: whether social, cultural, economic, political or admini- strative. They will be theory-oriented, problem-oriented or policy-oriented.

ISBN 90 04 05757 9

Dedicated
to my father,
Sasin Habib Khoury-Hannah,
and to my mother
Mary Backus Saad
and to the memory of
Faysal ibn Abd-al-Aziz Al Sa'ud,
truly a King

TABLE OF CONTENTS

LIST OF TABLES

LIST OF ILLUSTRATIONS

Plates 1-7 between pages 64 and 65

1. An Akh dressed in typical Ikhwan garb.
   Photographed in Al-Artawiyah, March 1968

2. Sultan ibn 'Abd-al-Rahman al-Dawish, Governor of Al-Artawiyah, holding a bullet-ridden Ikhwan war banner

3. Abandoned houses in Al-Ghat Ghat

4. Several residents of Al-Artawiyah demonstrating the use of primitive hand weapons which some Ikhwan used during battles and raids

PREFACE

This is an historical study of the Ikhwan movement which arose in Najd around 1910, reached its peak in the 1920's, and declined in the early 1930's, a movement which molded members of various nomadic tribes, ignorant of the fundamentals of Islam, and unaccustomed to the control of central authority, into a fanatically religious, para-military force that played a decisive role in the creation of the present kingdom-state known as Sa'udi Arabia, and left an indelible mark on the character of that nation. Simply stated, this study is directed to the questions: Who are the Ikhwan? How did they come into existence? Why? What role did they play in the political unification of the greater part of the Arabian peninsula under the suzerainty of 'Abd-al-'Aziz ibn 'Abd-al-Rahman Al Sa'ud (Ibn Sa'ud), the founder of modern Sa'udi Arabia.

The religious and social implications of the Ikhwan movement, the economic-social disruptions which may have resulted from the settlement of these bedouin on the land, the challenges to the orthodoxy of their religious beliefs and practices, are all problems which are peripheral to this study, and therefore considered only within the context of the movement's origin and development as a military-political instrument of Ibn Sa'ud. Similarly, while a complete study can be dedicated to the many battles which the Ikhwan fought for and against Ibn Sa'ud, only two battles, those at Turaba and Sabila, will be considered in this work because of their particular relevance to the rise and fall of the movement.

Residence in Sa'udi Arabia afforded me the unique opportunity to study the Ikhwan in their native land, more particularly Najd. This included visits to the two original Ikhwan settlements of Al-Artawiyah and to Al-Ghat Ghat, and other settlements such as Al-Hayathim. During my stay in Arabia, I had the good fortune to meet with several Ikhwan and Wahhabi leaders who personally participated in the Ikhwan drama, namely Muhammad ibn 'Abd-al-'Aziz al-Sahabi, former governor of Ta'if after its fall to the Ikhwan, and a direct descendant of the reformer, Muhammad ibn 'Abd-al-Wahhab, and with Majid ibn Khathila, present governor of Al-Ghat Ghat, the *hijrah* of the 'Utaybah, and formerly the senior lieutenant for his relative, Sultan ibn Bijad, the prominent Ikhwan leader and rebel. Other Ikhwan personalities included 'Abd-al-Rahman al-Dawish, former governor of Al-Artawiya, the *hijrah* of the Mutayr tribe. His mother, Walha, was the sister of the indomitable Ikhwan leader Faysal al-Dawish, and it was she who pleaded with Ibn Sa'ud for her brother's life; and Sultan ibn 'Abd-al-Rahman al-Dawish, the son of 'Abd-al-Rahman, and present governor of Al-Artawiyah. All of the above took much of their time to answer questions about the Ikhwan, and to escort the writer around Al-Artawiyah and Al-Ghat Ghat. It was in Sultan al-Dawish's *majlis* (sitting room) that this writer had the opportunity to meet rank and file Ikhwan who participated in different battles and who obliged him by bringing out old weapons, rifles, knives, and various types of shoes which the Ikhwan used on their raids. Among these old timers were Mutlaq Abu Ras who gave his age as 83, and Marzuk ibn Miflah who said that he was 70.

H.R.H. 'Abdullah ibn 'Abd-al-Rahman, Ibn Sa'ud's brother, gratiously provided me with an interview in his home, during which he provided forthright and unequivocal answers to many sensitive issues surrounding the origin and later demise of the Ikhwan; his son, Prince 'Abd-al-Rahman was also very helpful.

Much of the information contained herein was acquired through research in the Public Record Office, Chancery Lane, London, during the course of three separate visits to England in the spring and summer of 1968, and the summer of 1969. A short, but interesting interview with Sir John Bagot Glubb in London in the summer of 1968 offered the pleasant experience of meeting and discussing the Ikhwan movement with the man who, more than any other non-Arab, was responsible for the creation of the military-political conditions which resulted in the collapse of the movement. In several personal letters to this writer, he offered significant insights on the attitude and character of the Ikhwan.

In extending thanks to those Sa'udi Arabians who assisted me, special mention is due to Mr. Fu'ad Anqawi of the Saudi Arabian Ministry of Information for his direct help in arranging the first indigenous contacts when it appeared that the obstacles to serious historical research in the Kingdom were insurmountable, and to his colleague, Mr. Ghalib Abu Farraj. Through them, I was introduced to 'Abdullah ibn Khamis, the Director of the Water Department. A scholar in his own right, 'Abdullah invited me to his home several times to discuss poetry, Arab History and Islamic civilization. After several visits, he took special interest in the project, and then the doors to research began to open slowly but continuously. 'Abd-al-'Aziz al-Khuwaytir, the vice-rector of Riyadh University, at the time, offered me the use of the library facilities and access to its valuable collection of Umm al-Qura news-papers.

Sheikh Ibrahim al-'Anqari, deputy director of the Ministry of Interior, at the time, arranged for me to visit the *hijrah* of Al-Ghat Ghat and to be received by the governor, Sheikh Majid ibn Khathila; and also to visit the *hijrah* of Al-'Artawiyah, where I was received by the governor who escorted me personally to the battlefield at Sabila, where the final drama of the Ikhwan played itself out. Sheikh Ibrahim provided a four wheel drive vehicle, plus provisions, a driver, and an escort to ensure that the trip was comfortable and without complications.

I wish to thank here Mr. William Mulligan of the Arabian Affairs Department of ARAMCO, Miss Annette Matthews, the librarian there, at the time, Mr. Mike Ameen, ARAMCO company representative in Riyadh, while I was there, and Mr. Malcolm Quint, also of ARAMCO. All of them assisted me in acquiring and using the resources of ARAMCO's technical library in Dhahran. Special thanks is also owed to three persons without whose continuous help over the past years, this work could not have been started: William Schorger, and Richard P. Mitchell, my professors at the University of Michigan and my mother for her constant but quiet encouragement. Dr. George Rentz of Stanford University read the manuscript, and I am indebted to him for his comments and valuable suggestions.

Finally, I must mention the late King Faysal, without whose tacit permission this work could not have been carried out in Sau'di Arabia. After completing the manuscript in the United States, I sent the King a bound copy, and he kindly responded with a letter of thanks.

Any shortcomings in this work which may have occurred in spite of the above mentioned assistance are, of course, my own responsibility.

Thousand Oaks
California
March 1977

NOTE ON TRANSLITERATION OF ARABIC WORDS

It is difficult to decide on a translation system that meets the requirements of accuracy and yet provides an easily readible text for the person who is not trained in the Arabic language. The difficulty is compounded further because not all Arabists agree on one system.

I have decided to use a system based on a simplified rendition of each letter for Arabic words when they appear in the text, and a more scientific rendition for the same words when they appear in the index. In places where direct quotes from other writers or from manuscripts are cited the spellings are given as in the original text.

Arabic words and place names such as Mecca and Medina which are commonly used in the English language have been retained in their Anglicized form.

Arabic Letter	English Equivalent	
	Text	Index
ا	a	a
ب	b	b
ت	t	t
ث	th	th
ج	j	j
ح	h	ḥ
خ	kh	kh
د	d	d
ذ	dh	dh
ر	r	r
ز	z	z
س	s	s
ش	sh	sh
ص	s	ṣ
ض	dh	ḍ
ط	t	ṭ

Arabic Letter	English Equivalent	
	Text	Index
ظ	z	z
ع	'	'
غ	gh	gh
ف	f	f
ق	q	q
ك	k	k
ل	l	l
م	m	m
ن	n	n
ه	h	h
و	w	w
ى	y	y

PART ONE

THE RISE OF THE MOVEMENT

CHAPTER ONE

INTRODUCTION

When Muhammad ibn Sa'ud, a minor princeling of Najd and ruler of Al-Dar'iya, decided in 1744 to champion the religious revival preached by the Najdi reformer, Muhammad ibn 'Abd al-Wahhab, a religious teacher expelled from his native village of Al-'Uyanah, [1] all of what is known today as Sa'udi Arabia was little more than a loosely knit patchwork of independent towns and villages and tribal grazing grounds inhabited by quarreling townsmen and undisciplined tribesmen, and ruled by feuding princes and jealous tribal sheikhs. Orthodox Islam, especially among the bedouin of Najd, had degenerated into a multitude of superstitious practices, cults of tree and stone worship; tribal and customary law, for the most part, prevailed among the bedouin and sedentary population, respectively, and had eroded the influence and primacy of Islamic Law know as *shari'a*. Tribe raided tribe; village made war on village; [2] some bedouin looted merchant caravans [3] while others robbed travellers and intimidated pilgrims on their way to Mecca. Sometimes whole segments of tribes sustained themselves economically through such violence and theft. [4]

'Abd-al-Wahhab's call to return to the practice of true Islam based on the Qur'an and the *sunna* [5] as interpreted by the strict Hanbali school was sustained and championed throughout the peninsula by Muhammad ibn Sa'ud and his partisans. So thorough was the conversion of the Najdi people that they became intense devotees of 'Abd-al-Wahhab and thereafter became known in different parts of Arabia and the outside world as Wahhabis. Actually, however, they referred to themselves as *muwahhidun* or *ahl al-tawhid*, that is, unitarians, or

---

[1] Al-Dar'iya is located about ten miles north of present day Riyadh. Al-'Uyanah is located about twenty miles northwest of Riyadh.

[2] *Umm Al-Qura*, number 289, 20 June 1930.

[3] Hafiz Wahbah, *Al-Jazirat Al-'Arabiyah Fi Al-Qarn Al-'Ashrin* (*Arabia in the Twentieth Century*) (Cairo: Maktabat Al-Nahdhat Al-Masriyah 1961), p. 295.

[4] Interview with Muhammad ibn Majid ibn Khathila, son of the governor of Al-Ghat Ghat, March 1968. See also Philip P. Graves (ed.). *Memoirs of King Abdullah of Transjordan* (London: Jonathan Cape, 1950, pp. 71-72.

[5] This refers to the sum total of the traditions and practices of the Prophet Muhammad as set down by the six medieval compilers of these tradition. They are now standard and authoritative.

people of unity, a term which emphasized their belief in the oneness of God. [6] The combined power of religion and the sword introduced an almost absolute degree of public security and centralization of governmental authority and universality of religious practice into that part of the peninsula that came under their control. After the collapse of the First Wahhabi Empire, conditions of anarchy and violence prevailed in most areas until Ibn Sa'ud restored security to the lands which he captured.

The rise of the House of Sa'ud was simultaneous with the ascendancy of the House of 'Abd-al-Wahhab. Together they shared victory and defeat, success and failure. By 1811 their successive military victories in the peninsula, in Syria and in Iraq caused the Ottoman Sultan to order his Albanian vassal in Egypt, Muhammad 'Ali, to send a military expedition to crush Wahhabi power at its source. This objective was finally achieved with the destruction of Al-Dar'iya, the Wahhabi capital in the summer of 1819. With the Wahhabis defeated and various members of the House of Sa'ud taken hostage, killed, or exiled, Najd once again reverted to conditions of intertribal feuding and village rivalry in the vacuum created by the breakdown of central authority. Although a few members of the House of Sa'ud in the following few decades succeeded in extending their control over small areas, nevertheless by the close of the 19th century their loss of Najd was complete. By 1900 Riyadh was governed by 'Ajlan al-Shammari in the name of the great rival of the Sa'ud family, Muhammad ibn Rashid. The Hashemite princes governed the Hijaz for the Ottoman Sultan, while the Ottomans themselves controlled Al-Hasa, the eastern province. Najd once again fell into the backwater of the international scene, and when Europe turned its eyes toward Arabia it now focused on the Hijaz.

To the casual observer of the Arabian scene, then, it may be surprising that the unification of the greater part of the Arabian peninsula, between the years 1901-1925, from the frontiers of Jordan in the north to the borders of Yemen in the south, was achieved through the efforts of a lesser known family of Najd, the Al Sa'ud, rather than through the leadership of the Sharifian Hashemite dynasty in the Hijaz which gained international prominence through the romance of Lawrence and the Arab Revolt. Boasting Jidda, a seaport and the

---

[6] R. Bayly Winder, *Saudi Arabia in the Nineteenth Century* (London: Macmillan 1965), p. 1 (footnote).

political seat of the Hashemite Government, a city relatively sophisticated through long contact with the Ottoman Turks, foreign legations,
and hundreds of thousands of pilgrims from all parts of the world
containing Mecca, the holiest shrine of Islam; Medina, the City of
the Prophet ,and Ta'if, that mountain resort tucked away in the moun-
tains southeast of Jidda, the Hijaz contained the principal cities of
Arabia which could be expected to spawn the man or men who could
unite the peninsula. Yet Mecca, guarded by a relatively modern army,
the jewel in the crown of the self-styled Calif of Islam, proved to be
the weakest link in the chain of cities. When it finally capitulated
to the Ikhwan it did so without the shot of a gun. Not even a symbolic
clash of swords echoed its final days. The threat of the Ikhwan, ready
to be unleashed against the city, was sufficient to cause its surrender,
while Jidda was spared largely because of the presence of foreign
legations.

Najd's inherent superior capacity to re-unify the peninsula, on the
other hand, rested on the solid political, religious foundations laid
there two hundred years earlier by Muhammad ibn 'Abd-al-Wahhab
and Muhammad ibn Sa'ud, foundations which by 1900 had become
buried, so to speak, under the shifting sands or Najd, but which were,
nonetheless, extant.

The figure of King Husayn, self proclaimed leader of the Arabs
yet unable to rule his own estate, contrasts markedly with that of Ibn
Sa'ud who, dedicating his life and talents to the reclamation of his
family holdings, [7] began in 1901 the formidable task of clearing away
the sands and laying bare the Wahhabi infrastructure, and rebuilt on it
a new Wahhabi kingdom. Seen in this light, Ibn Sa'ud's re-unification
of Najd with the Hijaz and with 'Asir was a calculated repetition, not
an accident, of history. Within three decades of his capture of Riyadh
he was proclaimed King of the Hijaz and Najd.

Ibn Sa'ud dominated the events in Arabia from that moment when
he and his forty companions captured Riyadh in 1902 until his death
in 1953. A Najdi, having only the very fundamentals of a religious
education, [8] bred to toughness in exile with his father among the Al
Murrah bedouin, [9] that most deprived and primitive of the peninsular

---

[7] Amin Al-Rihani, *Najd wa Mulhaqatihu* (*Najd and Its Dependencies*) (Beirut:
Dar Al-Rihani Publishing Company, Third Edition, 1964), pp. 114-115.

[8] Muhammad Mughayribi Futayih Al-Madani, *Firqat Al-Ikhwan Al-Islamiyah bi
Najd* (The Islamic Brotherhood in Najd), 1923, no publisher given, pp. 19-20.

[9] H. R. P. Dickson, *Kuwait and Her Neighbours* (London: George Allen and
Unwin Ltd., 1956) p. 93. Al Murrah tribesmen are said to drink only camel's milk,
water of their grazing area being too saline for human consumption.

nomads, he had never been to the Hijaz until 1925 when he went there to claim what others had conquered first in God's name and then in his.

Ibn Sa'ud's genius is neither found in his ability to gather the bedouin under his banner through magnanimity or coercion—the bedouin had been won over by different leaders many times in the annals of peninsular history—nor in his lighting conquest of Najd and his subsequent victories in the Hijaz and 'Asir. These conquests too had been achieved previously by other Arabian leaders. Rather his genius reflects itself in the creation of the Ikhwan movement, formed by preaching an Islamic revival among the bedouin and by persuading them to settle in semiregious-military-agricultural communities called *hujar*. [10] Created and fostered over the objections of many of his closest family members and friends, [11] the Ikhwan provided a unique solution to the military, political problems which the bedouin had posed for centuries to those who would conquer and rule the peninsula, a solution which had eluded his illustrious ancestors and no less a genius than the Prophet Muhammad, himself. Although it caused Ibn Sa'ud many serious problems during its short span of life, the Ikhwan movement ultimately vindicated his vision of it as his principal instrument to unify the peninsula.

The villagers of Najd were the most loyal citizens and most reliable soldiers, but they could not leave their fields and shops for extended military service in campaigns far from their homes; on the other hand, the bedouin in their nomadic state were too opportunistic and fickle in their loyalties to provide the dependability which an Arabian leader required for distant, long range conquests. The Ikhwan, however, provided him with an ascetic, military force which could be mobilized and demobilized swiftly and which combined the mobility of the bedouin with the political reliability and loyalty of the villager.

Having left their nomadic pursuits to follow a sedentary life, the Ikhwan, while docile in the *hujar*, became invincible warriors when set against Ibn Sa'ud's enemies. They became the conquerors of Ha'il, the Hijaz, and Jawf. Yet at the height of their success and power, many of them, led by their most able chiefs, rebelled against him with the same wrath previously reserved for his enemies and the infidels. Prohibited by Ibn Sa'ud from raiding Iraq, Jordan and Kuwait, areas

---

[10] Singular: *hijrah.*

[11] Hafiz Wahbah, *Arabian Days* (London: Arthur Barker Limited), 1964, pp. 132-133.

which they had been taught were the abodes of infidels and therefore legitimate targets, the Ikhwan were frustrated by the lack of targets on which to unleash the militancy which their intense religious fervor had generated. Further, they objected to Ibn Sa'ud's introducing into the Kingdom modern devices such as the telephone, the telegraph, the automobile, instruments which they considered to be satanic innovations. They objected to his increasing contact, and cooperation with the British. Accusing him of betraying the letter and the spirit of the very doctrines which he, himself, had fostered among them, they challenged him either to lead them against the infidels in Iraq or to face them in battle. In March of 1929, the Ikhwan once again met Ibn Sa'ud on the battlefield but this time as his adversaries. Their defeat at the battle of Sabila rang the death knell of the movement as a meaningful military power and as a vital force guiding the development of the new state. The Ikhwan rebellion was the final effort of fanatical bedouin led by traditional tribal chiefs to continue their influence and control over the new, rising nation. It was intended to stave off the fate that they had sensed Ibn Sa'ud had decreed for them; instead, it succeeded only in advancing the date of their own destruction. The Ikhwan were punished for disloyalty; the chief leaders were sent to prison where some later died. The rank and file remained on their *hujar* collecting their subsidies from the central government, but their direct influence on the affairs of state had ceased. They were no longer the dominant military power in the country. Yet their ascetic existence, their extreme attention to religious detail and their high-spirited nationalism continued to influence and bolster the character of the nation which they helped to create.

CHAPTER TWO

NAJD 1900-1912

The Arabian peninsula is known in Arabic as *Jazirat Al-'Arab* (the island of the Arabs) bounded as it is by sea on three sides, and the vast Syrian desert to the north. Najd is, in a sense, the island within this island. The home of 'Unayzah, Buraydah, Riyadh, and a myriad of other towns and villages such as Majma' and Zilfi, it is hemmed in on all sides by the forbidding sand deserts or the rock lava bed wastes. Within this desert dotted with villages and palm oases lived the great nomadic tribes of Najd: Harb, Qahtan, Mutayr, 'Utaybah, Shammar, and Dawasir [1] whose members in their endless migrations through the desert wove, as it were, the desert and the town into a common fabric. Using the towns and oases as social centers, supply imporia, and fountains of religious nourishment, the tribes through these contacts, and often through individuals who elected to remain there, forged cultural and blood ties and infused the town folk with desert blood once again, thereby strengthening the common bonds between desert dwellers and some of their weaker kin who earlier surrendered to the prisons of walled towns.

The village and town dwellers of Najd developed a peculiar view of the world: isolationist, austere and frugal. Their great joy was the moderate rain which nurtured their meager crops and caused their date palms to thrive. Yet extremes of rainless years and severe deluges reduced them to misery, caused great loss of life and destruction of property. Life in the towns of Najd was ascetic with pleasures few and fleeting. [2] No music gladdened their festivities, if indeed their puritanical holidays could be described as celebrations, and no pipes of tobacco or cups of wine relieved the tensions of the day. Recitations from the Qur'an and from the *hadith* (compilations of the Prophet Muhammad's sayings) were the high-points of the puritan ceremonies which united them in marriage or commended them to unmarked graves. Today on the verge of starvation, tomorrow waxing fat, this was the shared fate of the townsmen and the bedouin.

---

[1] Mustafa Murad Al-Dabbagh, *Al-Jazirat Al-'Arabiyah* (The Arabian Peninsula), (Beirut: Dar Al-Tali'a, 1963), pp. 141-142.

[2] Paul W. Harrison, "Al Riyadh, the Capital of Najd," *Moslem World*, Vol. 8 (1918), pp. 412-419 (p. 418).

If the mentality of the Najdi bedouin and the villagers differed when compared, this difference faded dramatically when contrasted with that of the other Arabs who inhabited the peninsula: the city people of the Hijaz, the northern tribes, and the oases dwellers of Al-Hasa.

The people of Najd, bedouin and sedentary alike, considered the inhabitants of the Hijaz as racially impure and religiously suspect. More than a thousand years of pilgrimages had introduced a mixture of various races and Islamic creeds there, the intermarriage of which created a new people, whose manners, customs, religious practices and attitudes marked them as a separate people, and doomed them to a lower social status in the eyes of the humblest Najdi.

The Arabs of northern Najd, especially the Shammar of Ha'il and Al-Ruwalah of the Jawf reflected the characteristics of the pre-Islamic Arab. Quick to make war and poetry, flaunting death in a flash of gallantry, they wore the mantle of religion lightly on their shoulders. A less severe people who looked north to the fleshpots of Syria and Jordan where many emigrated annually with the flocks, for them life was happier than the dour, triste existence of their southern Wahhabi neighbors. Although they were Muslims, to them Islam was only one aspect of the Arab genius together with the hunt, the falcon, the romantic ode and the raid.

Al-Hasa on the east coast was cut off from the Hijaz by almost one thousand miles of uninterrupted desert. This distance perpetuated the different religious and historical experiences of its people. Although Al-Hasa is geographically contiguous to Najd, an abyss of mutual religious and tribal prejudice separated their peoples as effectively as the desert which yawned between the Hijaz and the eastern province. As the abode of the *shi'a* [3] sect of Islam, Al-Hasa concerned the Najdis only because of the danger posed by the Turkish garrisons stationed there, and because of the small, but unruly and powerful 'Ujman tribe which called it home.

In contrast with the merchants of the large towns in the Hijaz who prospered on the pilgrimage trade, gouged the pilgrims, exploited them (few pilgrims ever returned a second time), the traders of the desert towns of Najd treated the bedouin well. Revisiting these towns during the seasonal migrations, the bedouin bought their frugal needs from the shops and in turn provided the townsmen with camels, livestock

---

[3] This sect is one of the two major denominations of Islam.

and, in good years, milk products. For all the difference in the modes of daily life, the town dweller and the occupant of the black hair tents lived a remarkably similar life. Sedentary or nomadic, the inhabitants of Najd were tough and rough hewn, chiseled as it were from the same rock, and together they formed the most united, homogeneous interactive community in the peninsula.

Najd then, more particularly that area called Al-'Aridh, formed the core of the peninsula, and loyalty to the Wahhabi tradition ran through it like a vein of granite, and this was the secret of its past strength and future renaissance. [4]

To be sure, the strict practice of the Wahhabi faith had faded here and there in Najd, to some extent among the townspeople, but mostly among the bedouin. Crossing the barren wastes without benefit of religious teachers, medical doctors, or other formal assistance, the bedouin reverted to superstitious practices, charms, and amulets, which the original Wahhabi reformer thought he had obliterated forever. Once religious instruction was provided, however, the bedouin returned to the Wahhabi fold and became as dedicated and as militant as their ancestors.

The fundamental cause of the internal religious and political deterioration in Najd, after the fall of Al-Dar'iya, is not hard to find. In 1744 a success formula, consecrated by oaths, had been very simply devised between Muhammad ibn 'Abd-al-Wahhab, the reformer, and Muhammad ibn Sa'ud, the empire builder: the sphere of religion would belong to 'Abd-al-Wahhab while that of politics would be Muhammad ibn Sa'ud's. [5] This religious-political union generated the momentum which produced the First Wahhabi empire, and the offspring of the subsequent marital unions of these two families produced the leaders who, in later years, harnessed and exploited it. So strong was this leadership and so loyal were the people of Najd to this leadership that neither the Egyptian-Ottoman expedition against Najd, which dethroned the Sa'ud dynasty and destroyed their capital, nor the tragic intra-family feud which ultimately sapped the family's strength and caused it to lose all of Najd to the Rashid family could alienate completely the Wahhabi conscience of Najd.

---

[4] *Umm Al-Qura*, number 287 (6 June 1930). See also Uthman ibn Bishr, *'Anwan Al-Majd fi Tarikh Najd* (*Chapters of Glory in the History of Najd*) (Riyadh: Dar Banna lil Taba'a wa Tajlid, 1953), pp. 14-15 for his treatment of the superstitious practices to which the bedouin reverted prior to their becoming Ikhwan.

[5] Ibn Bishr, *op. cit.*, p. 20.

The Rashid conquest of Najd was made possible only through the intervention of an overwhelmingly powerful Egyptian military force which exhausted the resources of the Sa'ud family, generated, and then exploited inter-tribal and intra-family feuds. The people, as with any people subjected to long periods of war, wanted a stop to hostilities, almost at any price. A grove of palm trees cut down as sanctions against an insurgent village is not overnight resurrected come the peace; wells destroyed, stopped up or concealed as punishment to recalcitrant tribes are only with great difficulty restored or relocated, if ever. 6 Eight decades of internecine warfare gave Riyadh and Najd to the Rashid family and allowed the Turks to re-occupy Al-Hasa.

Once Ottoman political objectives had been achieved by the destruction of Al-Dar'iya, the Sublime Porte felt that Najd was best left to the quarreling tribes. Content to retain firm control over the peninsula's litorals: Hijaz, Yemen, Al-Hasa, none of which were challenged by a foreign power, the Sublime Porte cared little who ruled Najd as long as its hegemony was not challenged. While not desiring a dangerous revival of Wahhabi power through the restoration of the Sa'ud dynasty, neither did it want to eliminate that family completely as a political-military force, lest the tribal balance of power be upset, and the destruction of the Sa'udi monolith result only in its replacement by an equally dangerous and unchallenged power represented by the Rashid family.

The Rashids became the sole instrument of the Ottoman will in Najd not because of a natural alliance between these two groups, but because Ibn Sa'ud's father, 'Abd-al-Rahman who was the senior member of the family, refused to govern Riyadh even nominally in the name of the Sublime Porte. Sending his family and retainers to Kuwait for political asylum, 'Abd-al-Rahman took refuge with the Al-Murrah tribe in the Empty Quarter, and there reared his young son, Ibn Sa'ud, among those hearty bedouin. Later he joined the family in Kuwait. With Abd-al-Rahman absent through self-imposed exile in Kuwait and the rest of the Sa'ud family scattered, the Rashids' control was complete although superficial.

Even as the Sa'ud family fortunes revived after Ibn Sa'ud's capture of Riyadh in 1902, the Ottomans, judging from their failure to come to the immediate aid of the Rashids, did not fully appreciate or evaluate

---

6 The practice of cutting down palm trees which were an essential source of food and material was practiced late into the twentieth century, see Philip P. Graves, *op. cit.*, p. 182.

the threat that this posed to their position in Arabia. As for the British, the only other world power with an interest in the area, they were anxious not to do anything which would prejudice Ottoman control over Arabia. This was clearly spelled out in a reprimand message sent to Whitehall in London to the Government of India for the attention of Major General Sir Percy Z. Cox, the Political Resident in Bahrein. The cable dated 9 July 1913 noted:

> The Government of India was instructed by telegram on the 10th of June that His Majesty's Government policy is to consolidate the Turkish Government in Asia Minor, and to abstain as long as possible from intervention direct or indirect in Najd; that the political officer should hold as little communication as possible with Ibn Sa'ud; that His Majesty's Government desire above all things that nothing should be said or done at the present juncture to arouse suspicion in Turkey or elsewhere that they desire or will encourage disintegration of Turkish power in Asia. In view of these frequent and explicit orders, Lord Crewe does think it necessary to telegraph again. 7

So strictly was this policy applied that the journey of Captain Shakespeare required coordination at the highest echelons of Government as the following cable shows:

> Viceroy of India to the Foreign Office:
> From: Viceroy
> Date: 20 December 1913
> Foreign. Secret. Captain Shakespeare now political agent, Koweit, who is proceeding on leave early in January, has asked permission to attempt a journey through Central Arabia to the Red Sea. He has received an invitation from Bin Saud, who is a personal friend, to visit him at Riyarh and proposes to proceed thence in the direction of Hail. Shakespeare knows Arabic well, is personally acquainted with the tribes in Nejd, and is thus exceptionally well qualified to undertake a trip of this description. There is at present peace amongst tribes in his proposed route and we trust it may be possible if the political situation allows to grant him permission. His exploration would be most helpful, both for military, political, and geographical points of view. Possibly recent announcement that the Porte has decided to recognize Bin Saud a mutessarif of Nejd will enable journey to be made without offending Turkish susceptibilities or arousing suspicion. It will be unfortunate if

---

7 Telegram for Sir Percy Z. Cox, 9 July 1913, Public Record Office, MSS, Foreign Office, Turkey, Vol. 1820, Document Number 31610. (The telegram was paraphrased by this writer).

for political reasons, Englishmen are always to be excluded from exploration in Central Arabia while field is left open to foreigners. 8

Shakespeare's journey was finally approved, but such was British caution in the matter that it took the personal concurrence of Lord Crewe to sanction it. Yet even as the Sublime Porte was laying claim to Najd, and while the British were careful to respect this claim, Ibn Sa'ud was busy occupying it, and wresting control from the Turks.

After the capture of Riyadh in 1902, Ibn Sa'ud quickly aroused the interest and gained the support of the people in the towns and small oases around Riyadh, settlements which had traditionally supported the Sa'ud family. After annexing Kharj, Mahmal and Washm, he succeeded in eliminating his arch rival, 'Abd-al-'Aziz ibn Rashid in 1904. With the occupation of Buraydah in 1908 his threat to the Turks became vital. First only supplying military materiel to the Rashid ruler, then fighting side by side with him, the Turks ended up by fighting full scale battles with Ibn Sa'ud's levies. Unable to cope with the hit and run war which Ibn Sa'ud waged, the Turks gradually lost their grip. Finally Ibn Sa'ud compromised with the Turks and accepted their nominal suzerainty thereby giving them a facesaving formula to withdraw from Arabia. When the last Turkish troops evacuated Al-Hasa in April 1913, the Sublime Porte recognized Najd and Al-Hasa as areas officially under Ibn Sa'ud's rule, and he in turn acknowledged the nominal suzerainty of the Porte, but without allowing the slightest Turkish military presence in the land. Not content with these victories he planned to regain the peninsular territories lost by his forefathers. Toward this end he resolved to remold the bedouin and recast them in a form which had never before been attempted, and to use them as the spearhead of his campaign to unify the peninsula. 9

---

8 Letter from Viceroy to Foreign Office, 20 December 1913, Public Record Office, MSS, Foreign Office, Turkey, Vol. 1848, Document Number 57883. Clipped to the telegram as preserved in the official files is a newspaper item noting that a young Russian lady known as Countess Molitor planned a crossing in Arabia.

9 Al-Madani, op. cit., p. 23 .

CHAPTER THREE

ORIGINS OF THE IKHWAN MOVEMENT

The bedouin were traditionally known for their fickleness and their political unreliability, characteristics of their inherent individualism. [1] In the midst of battle they would quit, either individually or in groups, if they had acquired sufficient booty, if the battle was going against them or their leader, if the enemy was putting up a hard fight, [2] or if they were just tired of fighting. Al-Rihani, the Lebanese-American traveller and friend of Ibn Sa'ud described the opportunism of the bedouin eloquently: "Today a sword in the hand of the prince, a dagger in his back tomorrow." [3] Bedouin engaged in raids for sport and for loot, it being at once their method of diversion and of re-distributing wealth. [4] Hafiz Wahbah paraphrased them: "We wake up poor in the morning and retire rich in the evening, or we wake up rich and retire poor." "Wealth belongs to God, today it's mine, tomorrow yours." [5]

Desertion in battle was prudent, not cowardly. The point was not to kill or to be killed; the intention was not to decimate the enemy as it is in conventional warfare. Death only occurred as an unfortunate turn in the sport of raiding and collecting booty, except in those specific instances where battle was waged because of a blood vendetta but even many of these disputes were settled through the payment of blood money before they could become a source of serious dissension and the cause of extensive reciprocal killings.

The bedouin belonged only to themselves; the entire desert was their home. They used politically ambitious sheikhs [6] just as the latter used them: for convenience and for material gain. The bedouin were mercenaries in a sense, available to the highest bidder. Sanctions could not be placed against them: they owned no land, no homes, and only very little material wealth.

---

[1] Al-Rihani, *op. cit.*, pp. 260-261.

[2] Wahbah, *Al-Jazirat*, p. 295.

[3] Al-Rihani, *op. cit.*, p. 260.

[4] A. J. Toynbee, "A Problem of Arabian Statesmanship," *Journal of the Royal Institute of International Affairs*, Vol. 8 (1929), p. 367-375 (p. 368).

[5] Wahbah, *op. cit.*, p. 295.

[6] Hafiz Wahbah, "Wahhabism in Arabia: Past and Present," *Journal of the Central Asia Society*, Vol. XVI, 1929, Part IV, pp. 458-467, p. 465.

Taking their battles as sport and only rarely as serious welfare, the bedouin were not generally good fighters. Opportunistic and motivated by the need to fulfill a specific requirement, i.e. money, revenge, diversion, the bedouin were not a reliable element of an army.

In contrast, the townsmen of Najd loathed raids and inter-tribal fighting. Farmers, merchants, tradesmen, and teachers they preferred the routine pursuits of their peaceful existence to the sport of battle.

A sedentary people subject to a leader from whom they sought protection and to whom they pledged loyalty, once conscripted as soldiers they had the stable resolve of a home militia. Disciplined and determined, they followed the commands of their leader in order to preserve a vested interest in the land, or in goods, or to keep the caravan and trade routes open to send and receive merchandise. They fought with the bravery and courage of men who had much to lose and who were anxious to win the battle and return home.

The nucleus of the army with which Ibn Sa'ud originally expelled the Turks from Najd was composed of townsmen. Bedouin contingents participated only when it suited Ibn Sa'ud's particular needs and the corresponding whim and desire of the bedouin. As the Turks conceded the loss of each town, the inhabitants pledged loyalty to Ibn Sa'ud and provided for their own defense, thereby eliminating the need of a garrison. This also enabled Ibn Sa'ud to operate with a smaller force and to enjoy greater mobility in a large area friendly to him but hostile to his opopnent. As Ibn Sa'ud's arena of operation grew larger and more remote from Riyadh, however, it became apparent to him that the military force with which he won Najd was not suitable for the military conquests which he planned in more distant parts of the peninsula. The townsmen, while loyal to him, could not leave their fields, oases, and shops to do battle in the Hijaz or in the other provinces. What he needed was a fighting force that had the mobility of the bedouin and the loyalty, bravery, dedication and stability of the towsnmen. He neither could nor did he want to turn townsmen into a bedouin type para-military striking force. His only other human resources were the bedouin. Yet he well knew that they, in their traditional state, were too unreliable to trust on long marches far from Najd where they may suddenly desert, or join the opposition. Ibn Sa'ud fully understood the tragic effect of the Egyptian expedition against the Wahhabis in the early 19th century. Bedouin tribes of the Hijaz and Najd, originally loyal to the Sa'ud family, later defected and allied themselves to Ibrahim Pasha, the leader of the expedition,

and boldly guided the Egyptian troops across the desert to the very
walls of Al-Dar'iya. He also knew that the brave villagers of Najd
alone had delayed the Egyptian advance [7] and final onslaught until they
succumbed to the sheer superiority of military strength. The inhabitants
of Al-Dar'iyah refused to surrender and fought from house to house
against the Egyptians [8] until the city formally surrendered and even
then the end was quickened by the defection of a bedouin chief,
Ghasab al-Utaybi. [9] To resolve this dilemma, Ibn Sa'ud, using imagination and daring, transformed the bedouin within a few years so skill-
fully that they were mobile enough to cross the length and breadth
of the peninsula, and sedentary enough to be in a specific locality
when he needed them. He did this with so little fanfare that when they
first appeared on the Arabian stage it was as Ikhwan, [10] ready and
eager for war.

The term Ikhwan is the plural of the Arabic world *akh* which means
brother. Among Arabs today it is a very common form of address
applied equally to a stranger whose name may be unknown but who is
known to be an Arab, or to a close friend. The plural of the word may
also be correctly used to signify offspring of a common parent or a
person from the same tribe, religion, or even occupation. [11] The term,
as used by the Ikhwan of Najd, themselves, signifies the brotherhood
which they found through the common religion which they share, a
relationship which superseded family and tribal ties, and even past
animosities, as enjoined by the following Qur'anic exhortation:

> Cling all of you to the rope of God
>   and do not separate and
> Remember God's blessings, for you were enemies
>   and he joined your hearts together
> And you became, by the grace of God, brothers [12]

By definition, the Ikhwan of Najd are those bedouin who accepted
the fundamentals of Orthodox Islam of the Hanbali School as preached

---

[7] H. St. John Philby, *Sa'udi Arabia* (London: Ernest Benn Limited, 1955), p. 140.

[8] H. St. John Philby, *Arabia* (New York: Charles Scribner's Sons, 1930), p. 101.

[9] Ibn Bishr, *op. cit.*, p. 208.

[10] The Ikhwan of Najd are a phenomenon of Central Arabia and should not be
confused with the Muslim Brotherhood known as the *Ikhwan al-Muslimin* which
arose in Egypt.

[11] Majma' Al-Lughat Al-'Arabiyah, *Maja'im Alfaz al-Qur'an al-Karim* (Concordance
of the Qur'an) (al-Qahirah: al-Matabi'al-'Amiriyah, 1953, I. p. 30.

[12] Al-Quran, Surat al-'Umran, line 103. See also Wahbah, *Al-Jazirat*, p. 293; and
Ibn Bishr, *op. cit.*, pp. 10-11.

by 'Abd-al-Wahhab which their fathers and forefathers had forgotten or had perverted, and who, through the persuasion of the religious missionaries and with the material assistance of Ibn Sa'ud, abandoned their nomadic life to live in the *hujar* which were built by him for them: "The Ikhwan are those who migrated from nomadism to Islam and who openly showed this break with the past by wrapping a turban (*'immah*) around their headdress (*ghutrah*) in lieu of the black rope (*'iqal*)." [13] Hafiz Wahbah describes them as "a people of bedouin who left their bedouin life and who agree to fight for God and the raising of his word." [14]

Tied inseparably to the definition of the Ikhwan is the concept of "immigration" (*hijrah*). Instruction in the fundamentals of Islam alone does not qualify one to be a brother (*akh*); the believer must quit the nomadic life, sell his flocks and migrate to a *hijrah*. Simulating the Prophet Muhammad's flight from Mecca to Medina which signaled the dawn of the Islamic Era, the bedouin's *hijrah* symbolizes the irrevocable break with the nomadic past. Defining the *hujar*, al-Rihani writes: "Hujar is the plural of *hijrah* and *hijrah* in the dictionary means leaving the abode among the unbelievers and moving to the realm of Islam." [15] Finally, Wahbah combines the idea of the bedouin and of the *hijrah* into a definition of the Ikhwan:

> The term came to denote the bedouin population which left their abodes of tents and became settled in a special place, and build for their homes mud huts known as *hujar* as a sign that they left their own detestful life for another more beloved life. [16]

The central position which the concept *hijrah* enjoys in the settlement of the bedouin on the land may be attributed to the definition of the reformer, Muhammad ibn 'Abd-al-Wahhab, himself, that the "*Hijrah* is the move from the land of polytheism to the land of Islam." [17] 'Abd-al-Wahhab's use of the term *hijrah* here refers symbolically to the

---

[13] Interview with Muhammad al-Sahabi, former Governor of Al'Ta'if, after it fell to the Ikhwan. He is a member of the prominent Al al-Shaykh family, descendants of the reformer Muhammad ibn 'Abd-al-Wahhab. November 20, 1967, Riyadh.

[14] Wahbah, *Al-Jazirat*, p. 309.

[15] Al-Rihani, *op. cit.*, p. 261.

[16] Wahbah, *Al-Jazirat*, p. 293.

[17] Sheikh Muhammad ibn 'Abd-al-Wahhab, *Al-Usul Al-Thulathah wa Adilatuha*, (*The Three Principles and Their Proofs*), (Cairo: Dar Al-Tiba'a Al-Yusifiyah, no date given), p. 20.

flight of the Prophet Muhammad from Mecca to Medina as interpreted in Abd-al-Wahhab's book, Al-Usul Al-Thalatha wa Adilatuha
(*The Three Principles and Their Proofs*). This book was used by the
missionaries as a catechism during their preachings among the bedouins.
Hence the missionaries and later the Ikhwan likened their move from
nomadism to the sedentary life to Muhammad's flight to Medina and
their escape from the land of Polytheism to the land of Islam.

According to al-Rihani the first historical reference to a *hijrah* of
the Ikhwan is found in a letter from Prince 'Abdullah, the son of
King Husayn to Ibn Sa'ud: "If you wish well for the Muslims then
send back those whom you ordered to sell their flocks and for whom
you built *homes*" (italics mine). [18]

While all of the Ikhwan were Wahhabis to the extent that they
were taught the fundamentals of Islam as based on the writings, inter-
pretations and exhortations of the reformer 'Abd-al-Wahhab, not all
Wahhabis were Ikhwan. The overwhelming majority of the towns and
villages of Najd were inhabited by devoted adherents of Wahhabi
Islam; they were not, nor did they claim to be Ikhwan. They were
sedentary (*hadhr*) not nomads (*badu*). Significantly, it was from
among these Wahhabi villagers that Ibn Sa'ud ultimately formed the
nucleus of the posse which broke the back of the Ikhwan rebellion.
Conversely, the bedouin who were taught the fundamentals of Islam,
but who retained the nomadic form of life, were not Ikhwan because
they did not migrate to a *hijrah*. [19] Again, it was from among some
of these tribesmen that Ibn Sa'ud conscripted re-inforcements for his
force of villagers and loyal Ikhwan which clashed with the Ikhwan
rebels.

The appearance of the Ikhwan only after 1912 when Ibn Sa'ud had
already regained his ancestral fiefdom in Najd is understandable in
terms of his designs on the Hijaz. That the Ikhwan were indeed the
sword with which Ibn Sa'ud conquered the peninsula cannot be written
off as a corrolary or as incidental to another purpose, social or economic,
for creating the Ikhwan. Ibn Sa'ud himself considered almost the entire
peninsula [20] as former possessions of his family, all of which must be
recovered, and he made this quite evident to al-Rihani:

---

[18] Al-Rihani, *op. cit.*, p. 249 and p. 258.

[19] *Umm Al-Qura*, number 291 (4 July 1930).

[20] Hereafter the term peninsula will refer to what is now the Kingdom of Sa'udi
Arabia.

We shall not give up a pit stone of our rights; however, we will not
say about our enemies what they say about us. 21 We demand nothing
more than that which belonged to our fathers and grandfathers before
us. Our friends the English ought to understand this ... and also the
Sharif and his sons. 22

Ibn Sa'ud was referring in this particular conversation to King
Husayn's demand that Turaba and Khurma be returned to the Hijaz,
and that Ha'il should be returned to the Rashid family, but he may have
been thinking of the day when he would restore Sa'udi rule to Mecca
and Medina and to Jidda: "Bin Saud was said to have declared that
he will not rest until he has repeated his Grandfather's exploits at
Mecca." 23

While one may speculate that Ibn Sa'ud's creation of the Ikhwan was
primarily intended to improve the social-religious and economic welfare
of the bedouin, the establishment of numerous settlements soon after
his conquest of the Najd heartland when he was severely short of
funds was not a pressing necessity; similarly, it was out of character
for as politically astute a leader as Ibn Sa'ud to concentrate so much
armed power and military strength throughout the country which could
have easily challenged his authority—as eventually happened—without
a correspondingly greater objective to balance this risk. The fact was
that a militant spirit was fostered deliberately in the *hujar*, and the
religious indoctrination stressed the duty to fight the infidel. Since
there were no non-Muslims resident in Najd or the Hijaz, except for
an occasional Jewish merchant in Khaybar and since the people of
Najd were already practicing Wahhabis loyal to Ibn Sa'ud as the
religious leader (*imam*) and as their Sultan, the infidels which the
Ikhwan were encouraged to fight could only be the non-Wahhabi
Muslims of the Hijaz and Asir. 24 If the policy of bedouin rehabilita-
tion was altruistically formulated by Ibn Sa'ud to assist the
bedouin religiously and economically, one would have expected him to

---

21 The following passage from a letter sent by the Sharif's son, Prince 'Abdullah,
to Ibn Sa'ud in 1917 may clarify this remark: "I do not recall that anyone of us has
written anything about you or any other member of the Sa'ud family to the effect
that you are foreigners and not really true Muslims." al-Rihani, *op. cit.*, p. 248.

22 Amin al-Rihani, *Muluk Al-'Arab* (Bayrut: Dar al-Rihani lil Tiba'a wa al-Nashr,
1960), Vol. II, p. 59.

23 Cable from Sir R. Wingate in Cairo to the Foreign Office, 6 January 1919,
Public Record Office, MSS, Foreign Office, Vol. 4144, Document Number 3663.

24 Later at the Riyadh Conference of Notables, Ikhwan leaders openly identified
the Muslims of the Hijaz as legitimate targets of attack.

draw attention to them when speaking to foreigners. In fact, he made
no mention of them. While speaking to al-Rihani, he preferred to
discuss subjects quite remote from the controversial subject of the
Ikhwan. [25] Ibn Sa'ud steered clear of the subject because the creation
of the Ikhwan was based on his political-military ambitions in the
rest of the peninsula. This being true, he desired to conceal this
development from the English as long as possible because of their
support for King Husayn. To conceal the rapid rise and military
capability of the Ikhwan well served Ibn Sa'ud's purpose. In the
beginning during its growth he could disclaim any control [26] over the
Ikhwan, and when his connection with the movement could no longer
be denied, he could imply the threaat of an Ikhwan attack as leverage
with which to promote a given objective.

Because of the secrecy which enveloped the early beginnings of the
movement, its origins are clouded in mystery, confusion, and contradiction. Although the British Government began to get reports, both
from its own representatives in the area and from King Husayn's
Government in Jidda, about the Ikhwan, initially it did not have
sufficient information on the movement to understand fully its implications. Writing to the acting British Agent in Jidda on 18 September
1918, Husayn pleaded: "Therefore what concerns me above everything else ... is that H.M.G. should compel the Emir [27] to abolish
and disperse what he calls the 'IKHWAN'—the political society in
the cloak of religion..." [28]

On 4 December 1918 General Reginald Wingate, the British Resident in Cairo received the following message from Colonel C. Wilson
who passed on this concern: "King HUSSEIN appears to be really
nervous of the consequences of the present AKHWAN activity and to
this his appeal to British support is probably due. His statement GREAT
BRITAIN had agreed to support him is I understand not a fact..." [29]

On the same subject, General Wingate had written several months
earlier to the Right Honorable Arthur James Balfour noting "you will
observe that the King's (Husayn) distrust of the 'Ikhwan' sect is very

---

[25] Al-Rihani, *Muluk al-'Arab*, Vol. II, p. 43.

[26] W. F. Smalley, "The Wahabis and Ibn Saud," *The Moslem World*, Vol. 22,
No. 3, July, p. 245.

[27] Refers to Ibn Sa'ud who was known then as the Amir of Najd.

[28] Letter from King Husayn to the Acting British Agent, Jidda, 18 September 1918,
Public Record Office, MSS, Foreign Office, Vol. 3390, Document Number 161898.

[29] Dispatch from Colonel Wilson and a letter from Husayn, 15 December 1918,
Public Record Office, MSS, Foreign Office, Vol. 4144, Document Number 1181.

marked." [30] He then went on to express his opinions about the potential danger of the movement. One senior official of the Foreign Ministry wrote the following note on the cover sheet which forwarded Wingate's letter: "King Hussein would hardly be justified in demanding the suppression of the Ikhwan in Ibn Sa'ud's sphere, though he may take what measures he chose to exclude them from his own. As this is primarily a religious affair concerning independent Arabs, it would be difficult for HMG to take action." [31] From this, it is clear that as late as 1918 the British did not understand the purpose for which Ibn Sa'ud created the Ikhwan; conversely, King Husayn, with much more to lose correctly assessed its political overtones.

There are those who insist that Ibn Sa'ud did not form the Ikhwan, but rather that it existed and he merely exploited them for his own purpose. While there is some merit in this approach inasmuch as there is no evidence to prove that a religious revival, however small, was not going on at the time of Ibn Sa'ud's take over of Najd, this argument is not able to develop the religious movement from a small group of devotees into a highly organized, and highly disciplined military force. There are others who insist that Ibn Sa'ud did not form the Ikhwan with the intention of using them as a striking force to conquer the peninsula, and that this use of the Ikhwan came as an after thought. This argument does not provide the answer to the question of why, then, did he found the movement.

This writer finds that all the sources which he has located on the Ikhwan, whether primary, secondary, or information verbally received by him from contemporaries of Ibn Sa'ud, agree that he created the Ikhwan. The only exception to this is an apparent contradiction between what H. R. P. Dickson wrote when he was Political Officer in Kuwait in the early 1900s, and what he wrote several decades later. In his book *Kuwait and Her Neighbours*, Dickson wrote:

> (The Ikhwan movement) was started as far as one can tell by the religious divine Shaikh 'Abdul Karim Al-Maghrabi, at one time chief 'Alim to the late Faleh Pasha Al-Sa'dun, Shaikh of the Muntafiq confederation. He later became 'Alim to Miza'al Pasha Al-Sa'dun, father of the present Ibrahim Beg Al-Sa'dun. On leaving Miza'el Pasha's service he departed to Najd, where he ensconced himself as a religious

---

[30] Letter from King Husayn under cover of a letter sent by Wingate to Balfour, 3 October 1918, Public Record Office, MSS, Foreign Office, Vol. 3390, Document Number E 177596.

[31] *Ibid.* (See the original routing sheet attached to the document.)

teacher and reformer in the small township of 'Irtawiyah, then only a small nest of Wahabiism. There is a story that in the year 1899, he returned via Najd and on his way visited 'Irtawiyah. In place of a welcome, as he expected from his old friend, he was driven away by 'Abdul Karim, who cursed him for a *kafir* and a *mushrik*—an infidel and a polytheist. [32]

As will be shown later in this work during a discussion of the origins of Al-Artawiyah, no inhabited settlement existed at that site prior to 1912. It is possible that Dickson, an astute observer of the Arabian scene at the time, made an inadvertent error with the 19th century date.

The grandson of 'Abd-al-Karim al-Maghrabi told this writer in Riyadh in December 1968 that his grandfather emigrated to Al-Arta-wiyah only after that *hijrah* had been established. Majid ibn Khathila confirmed this and noted that al-Maghrabi, a pious immigrant from North Africa, settled in Al-Artawiyah because of its ascetic and religious reputation. [33]

The British Public Record Office preserves a report written by Dickson on 2 September 1929 while he was Political Agent in Kuwait. At the time he wrote:

> The Akhuan—*on the other hand were brought in to being by bin Sa'ud to fight his battles and win them in the name of religion.* (Italics mine). As bedouins they would never have been reliable, as Akhuan and inflamed by the "Din" (religion) they became well right invincible. They may be likened to Cromwell's "Ironsides" or the German Storm Troops. [34]

As for Ibn Sa'ud telling Dickson that he had nothing to do with the start of the Ikhwan, [35] Dickson himself wrote as early as 1920 to the Civil Commissioner in Baghdad that Ibn Sa'ud had told him "I am the Akhwan." [36] In that same message, Dickson wrote:

> On my recent visit to Hasa to meet Bin Sa'ud (January 29 to February 20) I went to pains to try to discover as much about the "Akhwan"

---

[32] Dickson, *op. cit.*, p. 149.

[33] Interview with Majid ibn Khathila in Al Ghat Ghat in Riyadh, Novemebr 1968.

[34] Disptach, from Lt. Colonel H. R. P. Dickson, Political Agent, Kuwait to the Political Resident in the Persian Gulf, 2 September 1929 Public Record Office, MSS, Foreign Office, Vol. 13740, Document No. 5154.

[35] Dickson, *op. cit.*, p. 149.

[36] Disptach, from Major H. R. P. Dickson, Political Agent, Bahrain to the Civil Commissioner, Baghdad, 5 March, 1920, Public Record Office, MSS, Foreign Office, Vol. 5062, Document No. (not given).

movement as possible. This, I found a rather difficult task as wherever I made enquiries I seemed to be looked upon with suspicion. It was obvious to me that people had been given the hint, by some one or other in authority, to give away as little as possible. One could not help but come to the conclusion that Bin Sa'ud himself was at the bottom of the matter. I believe now he had issued general instructions that as little as possible regarding the new movement should be divulged to strangers ... *he does not want it to be known that he himself is at the bottom of the whole thing, and is fostering and guiding the movement for his own ends.* [37] (Italics mine).

Colonel C. E. Wilson in a letter sent to Major Young wrote in 1919: (Ibn Sa'ud's) formation of the Akhwan was probably carried out with a view to political rather than religious aggrandisement, but we must take facts as they are and Ibn Sa'ud is the head of the really fanatical Akhwan, thus support given to him is really support given to the Akhwan movement." [38]

As a British Official of the Political Office, Baghdad, H. St. John Philby took a trip from 29 October 1917 to 1 November 1918 into Najd for the purpose of heading a British mission to meet with Ibn Sa'ud. At the conclusion of his mission, he wrote *Report on the Operations of the Najd Mission.*

This report describes the Ikhwan movement as Ibn Sa'ud's synthesis of the two elements which most accurately characterize Arabs: Islam and nomadism:

> In setting to work at the task of consolidation, by which he was confronted, Abdul Aziz cannot have failed to be impressed by two models from the history of Central Arabia. Muhammad Ibn Rashid had owed his strength to the peculiar characteristics, which made the Shammar what they have been and are—a Badawin tribe based on a Badawin city,—while his own great ancestor, Saud Ibn Saud had carried his conquering arms to the farthest corners of Arabia by reason of the judicious combination of religion and policy, to which he owed his power.
>
> Ibn Saud followed neither the one model nor the other in its entirety —he set to work to combine the two and the result was the Akhwan movement, whose essential characteristics are as follows:
>
> (1) it was restricted to the Badawin, who though nominally, for the most part, adherents of the Hanbali, or as they came to be called, the Wahabi doctrines were in practice divided into their alleigance between

[37] Dickson, Disptach, to Civil Commissioner, Baghdad, MSS, Vol. 5062, 5 March 1920.

[38] Disptach from Colonel C. E. Wilson to Major Young, 9 November 1919, Public Office, MSS, Foreign Office, Vol. 4147, Document No. 152998.

those doctrines and the codes of unwritten customary law, by which their lives were regulated; the townfolk of Najd, among whom the tyranny of public opinion in matters of religion is strong and well organized, are tacitly assumed to be devout Wahabis and, therefore, required no special attention...

(2) ...suitable sites were, as discovered, made available for the foundation of permanent settlements, and a number of villages have sprung up, during the last five or six years...

To sum up, we may say that the object of Ibn Saud in fostering the Akhwan movement has been to increase his military service over a greater number of his subjects, to minimise the weakness inherent in a Badawin state and a Badawin army and to economise his resources by substituting the hope of eeternal reward for more mercenary considerations. [39]

Philby's analysis given above corresponds very closely to the information provided by surviving Ikhwan personalities, Majid ibn Khathila of Al-Ghat Ghat, Muhammad al-Sahabi, and the Dushan of Al-Artawiyah, all of whom told this writer that one man and one man alone was responsible for the creation of the Ikhwan and ultimately for its downfall—Ibn Sa'ud. [40]

---

[39] Report on the Operations of the Najd Mission, 29 November 1918, Public Record Office, Foreign Office, Vol. 4144, Document No. 4370, p. 1.

[40] Ibid., p. 30.

CHAPTER FOUR

THE IKHWAN: MYTH AND REALITY

Emerging, as it were, out of nowhere to act out a brief drama on the stage of domestic, and, then later, international politics, the Ikhwan's appearance generated speculation and conjecture as to its real identity. This speculation was exacerbated, for the most part, by the dearth of factual reporting and information available to the public on the movement. Ibn Sa'ud, for reasons noted earlier, played down his involvement with the Ikhwan, and apparently had given instructions that Ikhwan activities should not be discussed with foreigners. Another reason was the geographic isolation of Najd and the lack of communications with the outside world. By the time news concerning the Ikhwan trickled out, it had been distorted, either through exaggeration in the telling, deliberate misrepresentation, or misinformation. We may never know how much, if any, responsibility falls on Ibn Sa'ud for the reputation of the Ikhwan as terrors best avoided, and as invincible fighters who always decimated their adversaries. Obviously such a reputation, if believed by the opposition, weakened the enemy and strengthened Ibn Sa'ud. On the other hand, it may never be known to what extent Ibn Sa'ud's enemies, themselves, exaggerated the Ikhwan danger and fanaticism in an attempt—which ultimately backfired—to disrupt the fast growing cooperation between Ibn Sa'ud and the British.

Equally an obstacle to information on the Ikhwan was their own attitude. Fundamentalist, taciturn, introverted, they themselves were not disposed to return the Islamic salutation, *salam 'alaykum* (peace to you) to those Muslims whom they considered infidels, much less discuss the fundamentals of their religious revival with the foreigner.

Only one attribute of the Ikhwan is found in all reports on them, whether friendly or inimical, namely, their religious fanaticism, more, their eagerness to die in battle on behalf of God and Islam. All other accurate information about their religious beliefs, practices, and origins must be gleaned from a morass of facts intermingled with fiction, exaggeration, and sometimes deliberate distortions.

The fundamental misconception about the Ikhwan is that they formed a secret movement with a mysterious ritual, covert membership, and other elements peculiar to a closed-knit clandestine society. Writing to the Rt. Honorable Arthur James Balfour on 3 October 1918, Reginald Wingate, the British High Commissioner in Egypt, pointed out:

> You will note that the King's (Husayn) distrust of the "Ikhwan" sect is very marked; and I think that this rather than a dislike to treat on equal terms with another Arab Chief, is at the root of his disagreement with Ibn Saud. I have not sufficient information about the power and aims of the Ikhwan to be able to appreciate to what extent his fear of their influence is well founded. But my experience in the Sudan has shown me the danger of a secret organization working under the cloak of religion 1 amongst an unsophisticated Moslem population. In times of stress this type of Moslem takes to religion as individuals of some Christian nations take to strong drink, and is prone to become tinder to the first spark of fanatical impulse which if fanned by unscrupulous or misguided leaders will produce a conflagration that is—at any rate for a time—impossible to control. 2

That same year an unidentified Foreign Office official in London scribbled the following note on the cover sheet of a document reporting on the situation in Arabia:

> ...the King's (Husayn) estimate of the Ikhwan is properly correct, and this society will be as hostile to civilization in Mesopotamia and Syria as in Medina. It is probably the result of Turkish propaganda. 3

This note sparked the following query from the Secretary of State for India to the Civil Commissioner on 1 October 1918:

> Secret. It has been suggested that Ikhwan movement among Bin Saud's subjects in Central Arabia has been worked up by the Turks for their own purposes. Do you consider there is any foundation to this view? 4

Baghdad telegrammed its answer:

> Your telegram of 1st October. We have no evidence to the effect and I doubt it because the Wahabis regard Turks as infidels. Central Arabia

---

1 It is interesting to note Wingate's choice of words, "under the cloak of religion," which were those used only three weeks earlier by King Husayn in his letter to the Acting British Agent in Jidda. See page 20 of this work.

2 Letter to the Rt. Honorable Arthur James Balfour from Reginald Wingate, British High Commissioner, 3 October 1918, Public Record Office, MSS, Vol. 3390, Document No. 177596.

3 Note on the cover heet of Document Number 161898 in Volume 3390, MSS, Public Record Office, 25 September 1918.

4 Telegram from the Secretary of State for India to the Civil Commissioner, Baghdad, 1 October 1918, Public Record Office, MSS, Foreign Office, Vol. 3399, Document No. 169854.

has always been a focus of Mohammedan fanaticism and present Ikhwan movement appears to me as the local expression of the political unrest which pervades whole Arabian continent. 5

On 12 May 1918 the Political Officer in Baghdad described the movement as a "socialist movement in that the rich have to divide their goods with the common herd. Several cases of a Sheikh owning camels which he had to hand over to his followers are on record." 6

King Husayn's son, Faysal, made a more extravagant attempt to associate the Ikhwan movement with the Bolshevik Revolution in Russia: "The case assumes a more threatening aspect," he wrote to General Allenby who was Special High Commissioner in Egypt at the time, "when compared with concomitant circumstances. The danger falls primarily on Great Britain, as much as ourselves and no wonder that it is so. The seditious movement in Afghanistan, Egypt, the restless state of India, and the boiling ferment in other Asiatic countries all show that there is a properly organised plan in operation."

> Why should not this Wahabite movement be an effective part of that plan?, or, why should it not be feared that this Wahabite movement should attract the attention of the organisers of this conspiracy who will use it as a nest for the propagation of intrigue and as a bridge from them to the sacred shrine of Islam so that the flaming result may be reached. We see the fire but the directing hand remains hidden... if the Western World considers Bolshevism as a social disease which endangers civilisation, why should not the Wahabite movement in the Near East be considered as such, in so far as it is brought forward by ignorance and fanaticism. 7

Sir Reginald Wingate also saw an element of "Bolshevism" in the Ikhwan and said so in a message to Sir James Balfour:

> ...Mr. Philby's reports and other indications have led me to think that there is very considerable religious excitement in parts of Central Arabia where the people have been incited against their co-religionists who have sold themselves to Christians, and, in particular (if our information here is correct), against King Hussein. If this is so, the latter—whose knowledge of the subject is certainly more extensive than ours even

---

5 Ibid.

6 Letter from the Political Officer, Muntafik Division, Nasariyah, to the Civil Commissioner, Baghdad, 12 May 1919, Public Record Office, MSS, Foreign Office, Vol. 4147, Document No. E 118698.

7 Letter from Prince Faysal to Sir General Allenby, Cairo, British Public Record Office, MSS, Foreign Office, Vol. 4146, Document No. 108194, 1919.

though his policy will be less disinterested—may have some reason for regarding Nejd as a "Bolshevik" factor in Arabian politics and for his belief in a secret propaganda working against him and us. [8]

The "Bolshevik" scare was spread further by Major G. W. Courtney in a report which found its way to the Director of Military Intelligence, War Office. Describing his source as one "El Sayed Hussein Moham-med el-Husseini el-Selafi of Mecca," Major Courtney said that the "Sayed" had told him that the Sheikh of Islam and the Muftis and judges in the Kazan and the Crimea had issued *fatwas* (religious rulings) which made a parallel between the principle of the nationaliza-tion of the public wealth and the principle of the *bayt al mal* of Islam (the public treasury):

> The Sayyed then expressed his own opinions on Bolshevism and said that he met in Constantinople with Russian Bolshevists and with Mo-hammedan Bolshevists (ex-prisoners of war in Russia) and they all tried to dissipate the calumnities of the Allied Press against Bolshevism. The Sayyed believes that the best way to propagate Bolshevism in Islamic countries is to propagate Wahabism which is an improved form of Islamic Bolshevism and which will be even more widespread than Bolshevism. [9]

As late as 1924 the brotherhood was described in an European newspaper as the "more or less Communist Ikhwan." [10]

Even as late as 1920 after Philby's report on the Najd Mission contained portions which clearly traced the origins and purposes and believes of the movement, provocative reports were still sent to the British Foreign Office by British officials in the peninsula:

> ...the gist of the King's (Husayn) message was that quite apart from the question of Nejd pilgrimage and danger arising thereof, he wished to impress as forcible as he could on His Majesty's Government the general dangers of the spread of Wahabism in Arabia. The Akhwan were like the Bolsheviks, and if they were not checked in their career it would mean that in the end we would see British troops being landed in Arabia to combat a movement which would end in setting the peninsula aflame and wipe out all progress for years. [11]

---

[8] British Public Record Office, Foreign Office, Volume 3390, Document No. E 177596, *loc. cit.*

[9] Report by Major Courtney to the Director of Military Intelligence, Public Record Office, MSS, Volume 4237, Document No. 13285. 3 September 1919.

[10] Dr. Wolfgang Von Weisl, "Islam's Iconoclasts at Mekka's Gates," *The Living Age* (Boston), Vol. 323, Oct.-Dec. 1924, p. 320.

[11] Extract of a report by Major W. Batten, Acting British Agent in Jidda, Public Record Office, Foreign Office, MSS, Vol. 5243, Document No. 11363.

Other myths about the Ikhwan were perpetuated also. In a report dated 20 February 1920 well after the Ikhwan had become a force with which to reckon, a British Rear-Admiral wrote, apparently in good faith:

> Their methods are very brutal, and they besmear their bodies and faces with the blood of their victims as a sign of their meritorious deed. They shave their upper lip and ... both sides of their beard and grow it in the center. They wear a white kerchief in place of the agal. [12]

Not even the wildest atrocity stories carried to Mecca by the refugees from Ta'if after its capture by the Ikhwan contained such unfounded accusations about blood smearing. When this writer queried Majid ibn Khathila in Al-Ghat Ghat about this allegation, he dismissed it with a wave of the hand, not deigning to comment on it as he had been willing to do on the question of atrocities.

The variety, the intensity, and the exaggeration of the misconceptions about the Ikhwan only enhance the simplicity of the real, as apposed to the mythological, Ikhwan. They were neither members of a new Islamic sect nor adherents of a new school. They considered themselves —and in the light of their actual beliefs and practices they must so be considered—adherents of the Hanbali School as refined and interpreted by Muhammad ibn 'Abd-al-Wahhab. No new religious practices, rituals, prohibitions or prescriptions were introduced by them as *fundamentals*, although certain codes of public and private behavior which they endorsed and enforced, such as the prohibition against cigarette smoking, are peculiar to them. The difference in piety between Wahhabism and the Ikhwan is one only of intensity, the Ikhwan requiring "more rigorous religious standards than Wahabism, and greater self-denial..." [13]

As defined earlier in this work, the Ikhwan are those bedouin who left their nomadic way of life, migrated to a *hijrah*, and there led a life consonant with Islamic teaching and practices. The method by which these bedouin were induced to abandon nomadism are two: first, certain individuals inspired by the new religious spirit which Ibn Sa'ud's Wahhabi missionaries enkindled among them set out to live a community life, having been promised material support by Ibn Sa'ud;

---

[12] Report from Rear-Admiral, Egypt, 20 February 1920, Public Record Office, MSS, Foreign Office, Vol. 5144, Document No. 2236.

[13] Reginald Hugh Kiernan, *The Unveiling of Arabia: The Story of Arabian Travel and Discovery*, (London: George C. Harriet & Co., Ltd., 1937), p. 290.

secondly, tribes that were not anxious to abandon nomadism were persuaded in the following way:

> ...He would send for the Shaikh and tell him in blunt terms that his tribe had no religion and that they were all "Juhl." [14] He next ordered the Shaikh to attend the local school of 'Ulama, [15] which was attached to the great mosque in Riyadh, and there undergo a course of instruction in religion. At the same time half a dozen 'Ulama, attended by some genuinely fanatical Akhwan, such as Al Duwaish the Shaikh of the Mutair were sent off to the tribe itself. These held daily classes teaching the people all about Islam in its original simplicity...
>
> ...When the Shaikh of the tribe was supposed to have received sufficient religious instruction, he was invited to build a house in Riyadh and remain in attendance on the Imam. This again was part of the control scheme... [16]

In both situations the emphasis was on *juhl*, ignorance of Islam. The bedouin, then, really considered themselves in their pre-Ikhwan days as, at best, nominal Muslims and, at worst, infidels. Sultan al-Dawish the Governor of Al-Artawiya, told this writer that the Islam practiced by the bedouin was "Islam al-'Uruba" (Islam of Arabism) in which the basic precepts were not known, hence not practiced. Majid ibn Khathila also told this writer that the bedouin did not even know the correct religious postures for prayer, and that customary and tribal law were practiced along side with popular medicine and trial by fire and ordeal. [17] According to Ibn Sa'ud, before the Ikhwan movement began, more than ninety per cent of the bedouin had never heard of religion, their marriages were never solemized, and circumcision was not practiced. [18]

This concept of Muslims in Arabia in the post Islamic period being referred to as "non-Muslims" is not new. The term was used by the early Wahhabis and even Muhammad ibn Sa'ud, the first member of the Sa'ud family to support and champion the Wahhabi Reformer, was considered *'jahil'* (ignorant) prior to his becoming a Wahhabi. [19] In conversations with this writer both Muhammad al-Sahabi and Majid

---

[14] This is the Arabic word for ignorance. *Al-Jahaliyah* refers to the pre-Islamic days which the Muslims called "the time of ignorance."

[15] Singular of this world is *'alim*, literally erudite here, religious scholar.

[16] Dickson, Report to the Civil Commissioner, MSS, Foreign Office, Vol. 5062.

[17] Interview with Majid ibn Khathila in Al-Ghat Ghat, March 1968.

[18] Dickson, Report to the Civil Commissioner, Vol. 5062.

[19] Husayn ibn Ghunnam, *Tarikh Najd* (*History of Najd*) (Cairo: Matba'a Mustafa al-Babi al-Halabi, 1949, First Edition), Volume II, page 3.

ibn Khathila used the phrase "when I became a Muslim," when talking about their "conversion to Islam." When asked what they were prior to becoming Muslims, the answer invariably was '*jahil*', implying that prior to their religious training by the Wahhabi teachers whom Ibn Sa'ud had sent to teach them, they were not Muslims. Thus, rather than considering themselves as the proponents of a new sect of Islam, the Ikhwan felt that they had embraced Islam much as had their fore-fathers almost fifteen hundred years earlier, and their submission to it was no less complete and no less enthusiastic.

As with both Sunni and Shi'a Islam, the precepts of the Ikhwan beliefs rested on the same five pillars:

a) The *shihada*: There is only one God and Muhammad is His Prophet.
b) Fasting: During the Month of Ramadan.
c) *Zakat*: Payment of Taxes to the Islamic Treasury.
d) Pilgrimage: To Mecca once in a lifetime if possible.
e) Prayer: At the five prescribed times, daily.

There were no secret rituals, codes, signs, or other trappings of a closed society; they did prohibit the use of pork and liquor, injunctions against their consumption enjoined by the Qur'an. Smoking was considered to be a grievous sin; it was prohibited throughout the realm. The use of silk clothes was banned. The only luxury appeared to be the use of incense [20] or coffee, or tea. Gambling, fortune telling and similar types of diversions were condemned. The Ikhwan did not return the Islamic salutation "salam alaykum" (peace to you) to non-Ikhwan. Close confidants and other friends of Ibn Sa'ud record that the religious scholars ('*ulama*') and the enforcers of Wahhabi precepts (the *mutawa'in*), who would have been their social peers and who would have moved with them in the same social circles had they not been 'infidels, avoided them, and that they only saw each other "by an accident—passing in a corridor..." [21] Another Ikhwan habit was to cover their faces rather than look at an infidel. [22]

As former bedouin, the Ikhwan were most noteworthy for their renunciation of tribal loyalty and even family ties in favor of the bonds

---

[20] Kiernan, *Ibid.*
[21] Gerald De Gaury, *Arabia Phoenix* (London: George G. Harrap & Co., Ltd., 1946), p. 93.
[22] Dickson, Report to the Civil Commissioner, Vol. 5062.

of brotherhood. In a desert, tribal society where the family was an individual's security, identity, and legitimacy, the renunciation of all this was no light matter. It underscored the degree to which Ibn Sa'ud was able to substitute the brotherhood of Islam domiciled in the *hijrah* for the protection, security, and identity which they surrendered when they left the tribe.

The simplicity of Ikhwan life was symbolized by the unadorned, domeless mosques, the exterior and interior of which were void of even the most abstract decoration. Vows [23] were prohibited, and the taking of oaths in other than God's name was blasphemy. Even the Prophet Muhammad, who was given great respect, was stressed as a mortal like all men. [24] Some writers have incorrectly interpreted this as meaning that the Ikhwan denigrated the Prophet. Others claim that the portion "and Muhammad is His Prophet" of the *shihadah* was omitted. [25] The fact, however, that the entire formula appears on the Ikhwan war banners disproves this allegation. (See plate 5).

Sulayman ibn Samhan al-Najdi, an *'alim*, who authored the book, *Al-Hudiyah Al-Sunniyah* (*The Orthodox Path*), one of the books which the missionaries to the bedouin used as an instruction manual, made the Prophet Muhammad's favored role in Islam among all Muslims very clear:

> ...and what we believe is that the rank of our Prophet Muhammad, on him be peace and prayers, is absolutely the highest of all created beings ... and it is permissible for the Muslim to say "peace be on him" and to visit the mosque where he is buried but the visit to the mosque must be incidental to the primary purpose, i.e. prayer. [26]

Nor did the Ikhwan appreciate any less the early companions of the Prophet and the holy men (*al-awliya'*) who first put Islam on the road to success. [27] What they did, however, was return to pure Islam which Muhammad had preached. Worship is due to God alone. The practices of popular religion in which men and saints were revered or worshipped, and in which saints were asked to intercede with God on behalf of ordinary believers, were diametrically opposed to the prin-

---

[23] This refers specifically to the practice of promising to donate a gift to a mosque if, through the intercession of a saint, the request of the person making the vow is granted.

[24] Harrison, *op. cit.*, p. 417.

[25] Letter from the Political Officer, Muntafik Division, Public Record Office, MSS, 12 May 1918, Vol. 4147, Document No. E 118698.

[26] Al-Madani, *op. cit.*, p. 24.

[27] *Ibid.*

ciple that no intermediary, not even the Prophet Muhammad, stood between God and man.

Visits to the saints' tombs where vows were made were prohibited because they were considered as *shirk*, [28] and as attributing divine powers to ordinary mortals. By extension, the building of domes over the tombs of these saints was a tacit acknowledgement that in death they were more than ordinary mortals. By so honoring the saints, the total reverence and homage due to God alone was being shared with finite creatures, and hence contrary to true Islam.

While the Ikhwan did not form a secret society in any sense of the word, there were secondary characteristics of their movement which made them a distinguishable group, the most important four being: (1) dress (2) fanaticism (3) forced conversion and (4) economic subsidization.

(1) *Dress*: The costume of the Ikhwan was a slight adaptation of the traditional garb worn by the bedouin and village-town dwellers alike. This consisted of a veil-like kerchief sometimes worn over a skull cap. The kerchief fell behind the back of the head and over the houlders. This kerchief is called a *ghutrah*, the skull cap a *taqiyah*. In ordinary dress the kerchief was bound to the head by a rope-like band, almost always black, placed on top of the head. This rope is called an *'iqal* and it kept the kerchief from slipping off the head. A one piece night shirt-type garment called a *thawb* covered the body. Over this was worn a cloak, called a *mishlah*. Shoes could be rustic sandals made either of camel or goat leather. The Ikhwan adaptation of this costume was as follows:

(a) the *ghutrah* was made of red and white checkered material, worn winter and summer, although among some bedouin and townfolk the checkered headdress is worn in the winter and the white in summer. The Ikhwan utilized the red and white type cloth because it was the most common, and least expensive material, and it avoided any possible affectation and preoccupation with change of dress. [29]

(b) the *'iqal*: instead of using the black rope-like band, the Ikhwan used the *'immah*, which is a turban, because they regarded the *'iqal* as an anachronism of the pre-Islamic era, and as a symbol of nomadic ways. They claimed that the Prophet Muhammad wore the *'immah*, therefore, it was only appropriate that they do the same. The Ikhwan, however, wrapped their turban in a peculiar way. It was folded into a

---

[28] Literally, to share or to associate, hence polytheism.
[29] Ikhwan rarely wore the white *ghutra*.

long sash about three to four inches wide, and wrapped around the head just above the ears, until the material was used up, the end piece being tucked under the base to secure it firmly in place. The result was that the crown of the head, covered by the red and white checkered *ghutrah*, was visible with the *'immah* outlining it something like an exaggerated halo. (See plate 1).

(c) the *thawb*: instead of allowing the *thawb* to brush the ground, the Ikhwan wore it approximately at ankle length. The Ikhwan believed that the Prophet Muhammad wore his *thawb* only to the ankle which was sufficient to cover the body and legs, the excess material being deemed a waste and an affectation.

(d) *shoes*: the Ikhwan rarely used conventional shoes, wearing instead a very basic form of sandal, if any foot covering at all was utilized. During military raids, however, they would wear the *zambul* which were leather slippers to which was sewn a woollen sock which came up several inches over the ankle.

(e) the *staff*: completing the Ikhwan outfit was the omnipresent bamboo stick with which they caned, quite conveniently, unbelievers who were unfortunate enough to incur their wrath or cross their path.

In general, then, the Ikhwan felt that their dress conformed to the costume worn by the Prophet, himself, and therefore was the most desirable form of apparel.

With regard to personal grooming, the Ikhwan permitted the head hair to grow long, and sometimes it fell over their foreheads and down around their shoulders, giving them a ferocious, wild appearance. A mustache was grown but carefully clipped to reveal the upper lip, and a beard on their chin was carefully cropped below the lower lip. [30]

During a military alert or mobilization the Ikhwan warriors wore a cartridge belt filled with the bullets which, to them, were very precious because of their high cost; a rifle was slung over the shoulder and a knife or dagger was tucked into their waist belts. (See plate 1).

Various descriptions of the Ikhwan costume as worn in their hey day of power are extant [31] and in large part it conforms to the Ikhwan dress as seen today in the *hujar* and in and about Riyadh; however, today, many Ikhwan have abandoned the *'immah* [32] and now wear the old style black rope (*'iqal*).

---

[30] Report from Rear-Admiral, *op. cit.*

[31] Philby, The Ikhwan and the Wahhabis. F. O. 371-4144, Document No. 7615.

[32] Dickson, Report to the Civil Commission, Vol. 5062. As early as 1920 Dickson could write that Ibn Sa'ud ordered that the wearing of the *'immah* was not necessary, but "the custom continues among all newly converted Akhwan."

With regard to cleanliness, some sources describe them as preferring to remain dirty. Notably among these sources are Philby and Chessman, both of whom are generally sympathetic to the bedouin. Dickson wrote: "...most Ikhwan present a ragged appearance. [33] Chessman wrote: "The washing of clothes is not one of the compulsory articles of the creed, it seems to be numbered among the pomps and vanities." [34]

It is really an oversimplification to say that the Ikhwan were deliberately dirty and did not care to wash, although such habits do exist among some religious ascetics, in the Near East who find that daily grooming is a chore that is not essential to religious contemplation. Judging from the Ikhwan who are observable today some appear to be impeccably clean and others appear to be unnecessarily unkempt. Financial standing, education and training have much to do with cleanliness. Also, inasmuch as the Ikhwan were recruited completely from among the bedouin who were not known for their personal cleanliness, one can understand why it would appear to be a trait peculiar to the Ikhwan, whereas in reality it was a bedouin trait which had carried over. With regard to the bedouin the fundamental question on cleanliness was the availability of water, the lack of which oftimes made the decision for them. Al-Rihani notes: "as for their cloak, they wear it for a time, then wash it once or twice, and then wear it inside out..." He has them asking, "how should we wash, and we need the water to drink?" [35] Persons familiar with the lack of water in the Arabian desert can fully appreciate the other essential uses to which the sparse supply of water can be put other than washing one's clothes and body. Al-Rihani's observation does not refer specifically to the Ikhwan but to the bedouin. Actually the bedouin's conversion to Islam taught them cleanliness. Nevertheless, the habits learned in their original desert home continued with them and conditioned them to use water very sparingly.

The Ikhwan could be easily identified by their dress and the sight of the 'immah was often the signal for pedestrians to change their route to avoid a direct confrontation with an akh, because the wrath of the Ikhwan could be incurred by the slightest deviation from the Wahabbi creed, and the akh felt that he was ordained by God to see that His law was implemented. To the akh this was dedication; to their victims this was fanaticism.

---

[33] *Ibid.*

[34] R. E. Chessman, *In Unknown Arabia* (London: Macmillan Company, 1926), pp. 25-26.

[35] Al-Rihani, *Najd,* p. 259.

(2) *Fanaticism*: The fanaticism of the Ikhwan is well known and true. It has been preserved in stories among the people of the Hijaz: Ta'if, Mecca, Medina, and among the people of Iraq and Kuwait, and even among the Ikhwan themselves. The Ikhwan knew that they were fanatical, that is to say that they were uncompromising and literal in their application of religion, but they considered this to be virtuous. To these zealots, tolerance in religion was tantamount to indifference. They could not understand why an individual or a group of people or a tribe, given the opportunity to become true Muslims would refuse this chance unless they were anti-God, in which case they deserved to die. By killing them, the Ikhwan felt that they were rendering a service to Islam, and at the same time putting another paving stone in their own road to heaven, even if these stones were, in fact, the bones of their victims. While this is harsh judgement, it is true, although there are mitigating circumsetances which lessen the culpability of the Ikhwan if not the magnitude of their misdeeds. The question to ask is not so much "were the Ikhwan fanatics?" but "why were they fanatics?" Ikhwan attitudes can only be understood against the original background of these bedouin who, originally indifferent to religion in general and Islam in particular, were deliberately and consciously inculcated with religious indoctrination that did not allow for compromise or tolerance. The unalterable fact is that they did what they did not out of inherent cruelty and maliciousness, but as the logical result of their religious training at the hands of people who should have and probably did know better.

Ikhwan fanaticism was not directed against any particular race, creed, or color. It was directed against all those persons, whether they be blood relatives, fellow tribesmen, or fellow countrymen, who, when judged by Ikhwan standards, did not measure up to being true Muslims. Examples of families split down the middle, segments of tribes disowning others, father and son turned enemy, are not rare. If members of one branch of a tribe became Ikhwan, they would more than likely want to share this "blessing" with another branch, and would invite them to become Ikhwan. If the offer was refused the first time, two subsequent invitations would be issued. If these were rejected, then the Ikhwan members of the tribe would move against their non-Ikhwan tribesmen with all the ferocity and force available to them. [36]

The religious students and teachers who were sent from Riyadh

---

[36] Interview with Muhammad ibn Jab'a al-Dawish, in Riyadh, November 1968.

by the religious authorities to teach the bedouin knew only too well that they were preaching to a group of primitive people, who, once they accepted an idea, could be expected to implement it literally. [37] The bedouin were told that in their unconverted state each was *jahil*, and that for Muslims the wealth and even the life of the unbeliever was legitimate (*halal*). Hence the wealth of the infidel neighbor became the proper and legal objective of the bedouin.

The atrocities which the Ikhwan committed against innocent people who were merely "guilty" of smoking tobacco is typical of the Ikhwan desire to impose their own moral standards on the masses even though smoking tobacco itself was not prohibited by the *sunna*. The beating of women who wore silk garments, the verbal and oftimes physical abuse of citizens arriving late to prayers or not observing the Ramadan fast minutely are other examples of Ikhwan brutality in meting out swift punishment to those Muslims who did not follow their rules of religious piety. In some parts of the country such Ikhwan behavior was more often the rule than the exception.

It became increasingly clear to Ibn Sa'ud that the Ikhwan were becoming uncontrollable and arrogant. Occupying a choice place, as they did, in the Riyadh regime, conscious of their power, their organization, and their zealousness, the Ikhwan took it on themselves to enforce religious law and sometimes raided "infidels" in the name of Ibn Sa'ud without his specific permission. It is certain that Ibn Sa'ud did not personally approve of the more exaggeratetd aspects of Ikhwan fanaticism; also, he was unable to be the omnipresent overseer of Ikhwan conduct in the more remote parts of the kingdom. Finally, as Ikhwan power increased they used it as leverage against Ibn Sa'ud, and in the last analysis, if a choice had to be made by him either to reprimand the Ikhwan or turn his back on their abuse of power, he preferred for the time being to overlook the abuse. He never forgot it, however, and at the appropriate time he made them pay dearly for their arrogance.

No such inhibitions restricted his severe cousin, 'Abdullah ibn Jiluwi, who was one of the original companions who accompanied Ibn Sa'ud on the raid which resulted in the capture of Riyadh. King of Al-Hasa in all but title, the name of Ibn Jiluwi evoked as much fear as that of the Ikhwan, [38] and in that man the Ikhwan met their match. Known

---

[37] For Ibn Sa'ud's view on this as recorded by Dickson, see Memorandum to the Civil Commissioner, Volume 5062.

[38] George Kheirallah, *Arabia Reborn*, (Albuquerque: Univerity of New Mexico Press, 1952, p. 142.

for his unequivocal justice, whether it meant severely punishing his own son for a misdemeanor committed against a commoner, or lashing out against a recalcitrant tribe, Ibn Jiluwi tamed the Ikhwan, as the following incidents, recorded in confidential memoirs dated 23-26 April 1920 by the British political agent in Bahrain show:

(a) In Hufuf on 10 April (1920) Ibn Jiluwi's sister-in-law, a girl of the Subay' tribe, was wearing a colorful silk dress during a visit with her sister in town. An Ikhwan bedouin sitting at the gate beat the girl senseless, since silk was anathema to the Ikhwan. Ibn Jiluwi rounded up all the Ikhwan in Hufuf who were connected with the man, confiscated their camels and flogged the culprit.

(b) At Qatif on 14 April some Ikhwan saw a Shiite girl on the beach "immodestly" dressed and beat her; her relatives intervened, a riot ensued, and Ibn Jiluwi jailed thirty of the men.

(c) At Jubayl some Ikhwan from Maj'ma came to buy rice in the town. They objected to a man from Bahrain wearing a long mustache but no beard. They seized him, cut off the mustache. The people of the town intervened and fought with the Ikhwan killing two of them. [39]

In another province, the governor and the people would not have dared to turn on the Ikhwan, however great the provocation may have been. In Al-Hasa Ibn Jiluwi's reputation fo combatting the Ikhwan was probably enhanced by the belief widely prevalent at the time that he had warned Ibn Sa'ud very early that the Ikhwan would get out of hand and cause him much trouble.

(3) *Forced Conversion*: Conversion of the bedouin in the very early days was carried out through the efforts of trained Wahhabi missionaries, who used manuals specially written for the bedouin's mentality. At the height of the movement, forced conversions occurred to a lesser degree due to the intervention of Ibn Sa'ud, and the complaints lodged with Ibn Sa'ud by the British. Forced conversion, then, appears to be a phenomenon of the early period when the Ikhwan were increasing in number and influence, but not yet center stage in the peninsula. Dickson described the situation as follows:

> Forcible proselytising was an article of faith among the Ikhwan up to a short time ago. It was their methods in this matter which caused such consternation among the people of Hijaz and surrounding countries. Bin Sa'ud tells me he never countenanced these acts at all from the first

---

[39] Confidential Memo from the Political Agent, Bahrain to the Civil Commissioner, Baghdad, 23/26 April 1920, Public Record Office, MSS, Foreign Office, Vol. 5261, Document No. E 8538.

but was unable to stop them till the end of 1919. Today all forcible conversion of spreading of the faith by the sword has been definitely abandoned. 40

Forced conversion was carried out largely by the Ikhwan without Ibn Sa'ud's permission, but inasmuch as he benefited enormously through the new converts, he may not have opposed forced conversion to the full extent of his capability. It was only after it came clear that such activity damaged his own image abroad that Ibn Sa'ud began to put meaningful pressure on the Ikhwan to desist in this type of zealotry. On the other hand, he authorized his cousin Prince Ahmad Thunayan to deny to the British that the Ikhwan had engaged in forced conversions. 41

Since the Ikhwan believed that they alone possessed the secret of religious truth, they wanted to share it with everyone, either through peaceful persuasion, or by threats of force, and then, if needs be by the application of force. As they carried out this belief, reports of forced conversion gradually trickled into the offices of the British political agencies from all parts of the peninsula. Captain Garland wrote:

> The tenets of the Ikhwan creed are very similar to those of Wahabism, though its followers are without doubt more fanatical. To the non-Moslem, however, it is the brutal methods of effecting conversions and of punishing sinners, rather than the principles of the creed itself, that appear objectionable. There is no doubt whatever that the Bedouin are systematically terrorised into conversion, and those two refuse are done to death. In war, the Ikhwan are said to take no prisoners, but to cut the throats of all who fall into their hands. 42

The Political Agent in Kuwait wrote:

> Large bodies of Bedouins now in Koweit are seen to have adopted the white head-dress of the Ikhwan, but it has been ascertained that the change of head-dress has been occasioned by fear rather than any change in their religious ideas. Many of them confess that they are wearing this head-dress merely to protect themselves from attack by the Ikhwan and their enjoying a quiet cigarette seems proof of their words. 43

---

40 Dickson, Memorandum to the Civil Commissioner, Volume 5062.

41 Ahmad Thunayan Denial to Captain Bray, 1920, Public Record Office, MSS, Foreign Office, Vol. 5060, Document No. 1154.

42 Note by Captain Garland of the Arab Bureau, 11 June 1919, Public Record Office, MSS, Foreign Office, Vol. No. 4146, Document No. E 91521.

43 From Officiating Civil Commissioner of Baghdad, 9 May 1919 Public Record Office, MSS, Foreign Office, Vol. No. 4147.

Examples of alleged forced conversions exist in British records, and verbal sources in Riyadh today confirm that "invitations" were sent to non-Ikhwan to join and if they did not become Ikhwan, they were put to death. [44] These pointed invitations were terse:

"Letter No. 1

In the Name of the Most Merciful God.
From THIAB EL DAHASY to SULTAN and MOHAMED EL ABBUD.
Peace be upon him who shall follow the true direction.
We colicit peace for you and those who will come to us shall obtain the safety of God and his family and property as well.
Those who come (to us) will resign themselves to God and will enjoy protection of SULTAN IBN HAMAYID and the AKHWAN.

Letter No.

In the Name of the Most Merciful God.
From THIAB EL DAHASY to MISFIR IBN SAMRAN EL DAHASY.
After all we solicit peace for you all male and female.
He who comes (to us) will enjoy the safety of his property and his family and will really resign himself to God and should be protected by SULTAN IBN HAMAYID and the AKHWAN, and you O MISFIR and SHAILY, if you come to the Islam you both will take your camels and be in the safety of God.

Letter No. 3

From THIAB EL DAHASY to EL DAHASAH.
We invite you to come to Islam and he who will come (to us) from amongst you will be in the safety of God and will resign himself to God and will enjoy the protection of SULTAN IBN BIJAD and the AKHWAN. " [45]

A note on the Foreign Office cover sheet for the document contains the following handwritten notation: "The letters were apparently sent to the Agent at Jeddah in original and there would seem no reason to doubt their authenticity. The propaganda is not merely religious but political, involving change of allegiance." [46]

The above three letters did not use the name of Ibn Sa'ud. The

---

[44] Interview with Muhammad ibn Jab'a al-Dawih in Riyadh, November 1968.

[45] Letter and enclosures from Reginald Wingate to Arthur James Balfour, 20 December 1918, Public Record Office, MSS, Foreign Office, Volume No. 4144, Document No. 3059.

[46] *Ibid.*

following letter is particularly interesting because it claims to have been written at the express order of Ibn Sa'ud:

Assaf ben Hussein el Mansur to Brother Rcheidren Smeir
  In the Name of God the Compassionate

Greetings!

YOU are aware that the Sultan of all the Arabs, Al Imam 'Abdul Aziz-ben Abdul, Rahman-el-Faical, has ordered me to remain at Djauf.

He has, however, ordered me to write you this letter to inform you that you must let me know by special messenger whether you are following the Moslem creed of Abdul Aziz. Safety is for those who understand.

You are asked this question by the Imam and all good Moslems. You have been warned. You have only yourselves to blame. That is all.

Greetings to those dear to you. Our brothers greet you.

28 Bil Kaade 1340
  (17 July 1922)   ASSAF-BEN HUSSEIN [47]

Whereas the first three letters written in the name of Ibn Humayd have the ring of authenticity, since he was known for his directness and lack of tact, the letter of Assaf-Ben-Hussein reads like a forgery. Ibn Sa'ud was far too clever a person to allow his name to be associated with such a self-damning letter, especially when there was no need for a written warning containing his name. For example, a letter from Ibn Humayd inviting a tribe to join the Ikhwan was indirectly an invitation from Ibn Sa'ud ,since Ibn Humayd was known to be one of Ibn Humayd's chief lieutenants. Also, some Dushan of Al-Arta-wiyah and members of the Khathila family of Al-Ghat Ghat have told this writer that Ibn Sa'ud hardly ever wrote letters or notes, preferring to contract all of his business verbally, and that if a written letter were necessary it would be of a type that never compromised him. Ibn Sa'ud preferred to send messengers, and his verbal messages whether a threat of war or a promise of presents were carefully studied by the recipient. [48] Finally, in view of Ibn Sa'ud's denials of forced conversions which he made to the British officials via his trusted aide Prince Ahmad

---

[47] Transmittal of documents by Field-Marshal Viscount Allenby to the Marquess Curzon of Kedleston, 17 October 1922, Public Record Office, MSS, Foreign Office, Vol. 7715, Document No. E 11186/248/91.

[48] In such cases the messenger was detained with the sheikh who sent his own messenger to Ibn Sa'ud to confirm that in fact the detained messenger was his. (Interview with Muhammad ibn Jab'a al-Dawish in Riyadh, November 1968.)

ibn Thunayyan, it is not likely that such a letter as that signed by
Assaf would be authentic inasmuch as it could be easily produced
as evidence against Ibn Sa'ud, something which he would have for-
seen. [49]

There can be little doubt that the Ikhwan engaged in forced conversion; there is even less doubt that Ibn Sa'ud knew about this
activity, and in some cases tacitly sanctioned it, and in others felt unable
to do anything about it without incurring the wrath of the Ikhwan.
In any case Ibn Sa'ud's political and territorical expansionist objectives
had not been fully achieved, and until they were he was not ready
to call off the Ikhwan unless an overriding necessity made this essential.
For all his farsightedness and wisdom, Ibn Sa'ud apparently did not
anticipate such fanaticism and zelousness among the Ikhwan when
he conceived of them as an implement to unify the peninsula. Once
having created them, however, he was far too prudent to challenge
them at a time not of his own choosing. Ibn Sa'ud bided his time—
patience being another of his virtues—and confronted them only when
they had outlived their usefulness.

(4) *Subsidized existence*: Having been obliged to sell their camels,
sheep and goats—the mainstay of their economic existence—the Ikhwan
were dependent, in large part, on subsidies from the *bayt al mal* for
daily subsistence. This was especially true at the beginning of the
movement, particularly when a new *hijrah* was established. Then, even
the seeds for the first season's crops were provided by the state; even
so the subsidies continued long after the *hujar* became operative. These
subsidies were necessary not only because the Ikhwan had no other
means of support, but because of the very nature of their existence as
a para-military organization which required that they be ready to
mobilize for war at any moment and precluded their involvement in full
time activities such as farming, trading, and commerce. Hence, while
government support is in a true sense a subsidy, it was not a payment
for idleness but for fulfilling a vital requirement of the state, namely
military preparedness and almost instant mobility. These subsidies are
known collectively as *Al-'Atiyat* [50] (givings) and were of four kinds:

---

[49] The Assaf-ben-Hussein letter was only transmitted by Allenby. It was originally
an attachment to a report on the Ikhwan written by the "French Army of the Levant,"
according to the description on the document source. The French, not having very good
intelligence sources in the peninsula, the ben-Hussein letter appears to be all the more
apocraphyl. See cover sheet of document E 1187/248/91 in Vol. 7715, Public Record
Office.

[50] *Umm Al-Qura*, number 291, 4 July 1930.

(a) *al-sharba* (b) *al-qa'idah* (c) *al-barwa* and (d) *al-mu'awnah*, but only one of these, namely *al-qa'idah* was restricted to the Ikhwan, while they, on the other hand, partook of the other three.

(a) *al-sharba*: was a form of financial help given to those persons, but usually tribal chiefs and heads of *hujar*, who would make special visits to Ibn Sa'ud as *imam*. The recipient would spend several days as Ibn Sa'ud's guest either in one of the guesthouses or in his own tent, but he would eat at Ibn Sa'ud's table. During this time he would have registered his name in a special book which was later shown to the King who indicated in writing next to each name the amount or type of gift which the King decided to give.

(b) *al-qa'idah*: this was a monetary gift given annually to every person in the *hujar* who registered his name in the King's register which was usually reserved for those in the *hujar* called to war. This amount was pre-fixed. People throughout the Kingdom received the same amount. This money was paid automatically each year, without new permission from the King. The person collected directly from the *bayt al-mal* and payment was never stopped except by special order from the King to the *bayt al-mal* as punishment or as a warning to the affected individual.

(c) *al-barwah*: this was a gift in the form of rice, coffee, tea, sugar or other similar commodities distributed from certain special centers located in fixed geographical areas, such as Al-Hasa, Qatif, Jubayl. The *barwah* differed from the *al-qa'idah* in that the former was a one time gift, whereas the latter was annual. One could ask each year for the *barwah* but each time the request went through the King's special office (*diwan*) for his approval. Usually the request was approved and the requester (*talib*) was given the same amount as he received the previous year.

(d) *al-mu'awnah*: this was usually given at the time of the *sharba*. The person verbally asked the King for special assistance. The requester was then told to register his specific need at the *diwan*. This request usually took the form of help for marriage, price of a riding horse, or a camel, construction of a home, or payment of a loan. These requests were handled through the *diwan*, and the King personally decided on the merit of each case.

In a real sense, then, the Ikhwan constituted something of a privileged class in the new state. They considered themselves the guardians of the state's security and morals, and their increased political and military power generated among their ranks an arrogance and class consciousness that began to wear thin on the other vested interest groups such as the *'ulema'* and the elite of the towns and villages. Ibn Sa'ud had his hands full satisfying the needs of all groups, and assuaging the real and imagined injuries sustained by the non-Ikhwan groups at the hands of these bedouin turned religious zealots.

PART TWO

THE DEVELOPMENT OF THE MOVEMENT

CHAPTER FIVE

THE RISE OF IKHWAN COMMUNITIES

The re-conversion of the bedouin to Wahhabi Islam was the first step of Ibn Sa'ud's plan to harness them as the vanguard of his military force which would bring northern Najd, Jawf and Asir as well as the Hijaz under his sway. The creation of small agricultural communities in which to settle them was the second step.

Sometime between the period of his conquest of Riyadh and the year 1912, the date of the establishment of the first *hijrah* Ibn Sa'ud began to implement his scheme to convert and settle the bedouin. Scores of young religious teachers spread out among the bedouin teaching them the word of God and the sayings (*hadith*) of the Prophet Muhammad. They painted very vividly the evils of sin, hell fire, the wrath of God, punishment, pestilence, and other plagues, all of which inflamed the imaginations of the bedouin. It was not so much the negative or punitive aspects of the teachings that inspired them to become Muslims; it was the positive promise of a better life. Become Muslims! Fight on behalf of God (*fi sabil Allah*), and all the riches of the world will pale before the blessings of the Lord, they were told. The bedouin visualized a paradise of palm trees, of flowing water, and maidens of paradise (*huriyat*) to help them pass the days of eternal bliss. Their mean, miserable life provided for very few pleasures; it was little wonder that they sought martyrdom on the field of battle and thereby guarantee themselves a place in heaven. And the price of this was only that they adopt the heritage which their ancestors lost because of their lack of contact with Islamic civilization. Their nomadic life had weaned them away from their heritage and caused them to lapse into "ignorance." The new religious teachings did not fundamentally change any aspect of their life; even raiding was not prohibited. Their life style was only remolded, re-shaped to fit a different set of circumstances. Raiding true Muslims and other Ikhwan was prohibited. Now all the energies of raiding were to be channeled into one rushing course, against the infidels; raiding would not be sport alone, but the execution of God's will. Instead of treking across the deserts to eke out a living husbanding camels, goats and sheep, they would live in small agricultural communities where food, if not abundant, was adequate. There, the blessings of Islamic learning would be showered upon them by the religious teachers who would live in the communities to protect them against lapsing once again into ignorance.

While the missionaries were busy converting the bedouin, powerful tribal leaders were brought to Riyadh as personal guests of Ibn Sa'ud. If the strong tribal leader refused to accept this hospitality, or if Ibn Sa'ud felt that a certain tribal leader was not fully receptive to his requests, a lesser tribal chief would be invited. There in Riyadh, under the tutelage of the Wahhabi *'ulema'*, the chiefs were instructed in the fundamentals of Islam. In Riyadh, these chiefs would have an opportunity to witness Ibn Sa'ud's power; the English representatives sitting in his *majlis*; the chiefs of other larger, more powerful tribes pledging allegaince to him; the hundreds of people who daily shared his table; the many hundreds that returned to their tribe with a new set of clothes; or gold sovereigns, or promises of aid. These chiefs, when they returned to their tribes, could describe Ibn Sa'ud as the man of the future, and convince their tribesmen that their well-being was served by throwing in their lot with Ibn Sa'ud. Once the tribal leader and the elders of the tribe acknowledged Ibn Sa'ud's leadership through the oath of allegiance, then any reversal of this allegiance would rightfully bring down Ibn Sa'ud's wrath upon them since they would be insurgents against legitimate authority.

It was under these circumstances that the first *hujar* came into being. A group of bedouin having taken the message of the missionaries to heart, proceeded to the town of Harma where they sought more information on religion. There among the settled Arabs of the town, they clashed, because of their fanaticism, with the townsmen. Consequently they left Harma and migrated to a site called Al-Artawiyah, located at the extreme east corner of Sudayr province; it was a place known for its water and as a place where caravans on their way to Kuwait stopped to replenish their water supplies and to rest. Shortly after the establishment of this *hijrah*, the second was established in the place now called Al-Ghat Ghat, located south-east of Riyadh. The fame of these two *hujar*, inhabited as they were by the two powerful tribes of Najd, Mutayr ,and 'Utaybah respectively, sparked a race by other tribes of Najd to have their own *hijrah,* their piece of Islamic paradise on earth.

Although Dickson describes it as existing in 1899, the evidence of travelers to the site of Al-Artawiyah after 1899 and prior to 1912 proves that no settled site existed there prior to 1912. Philby writes:

Barclay Raunkaier was apparently the last European to pass this spot, and that was in 1912, when, it would seem, the first house had not yet been built. Only six and a half years had passed and there had grown up a town of not less than 10,000 inhabitants, which I was the first European to look upon from afar. [1]

In another work Philby added further:

...the Dutch (sic) traveler, Barclay Raunkaier, visited the locality in the course of a journey from Kuwait to Buraida some months before the foundation of the colony, and appears to have been unaware of the plan for the conversion of the well area into a militant religious cantonment. Not many months later a famous English traveler Captain G. E. Leachman, went down from Baghdad through Buraida to Riyadh, where he made a fleeting contact with Ibn Saud; continuing his journey eastward to the Hasa, which was still in Turkish occupation, though soon to change hands. He also failed to sense the atmosphere of change which was beginning to pervade the desert in consequence of the still incipient Ikhwan movement. Nor did Shakespeare, when traveling across Arabia in the winter of 1913/1914 appreciate the potentialities of an idea which was already beginning to galvanize the nomad tribes into the semblance of a viable state. [2]

The first bedouin immigrants appear to have arrived, then, sometime after the visit of the Danish and British travelers, but probably in the same year.

The site of Al-Artawiyah had long been known for its abundant water, and it had became the pastureland of the Mutayr tribal chief, Faysal al-Dawish. According to al-Rihani [3] the name of the first Ikhwan settlement is derived from the Arabic word for pasture, Artawi, hence, Al-Artawiyah. Lorimer's *Gazeteer of the Persian Gulf*, published in 1908 which included all information available to the British Government on Central Najd as of that date makes no mention of Al-Arta-wiyah, although the location geographically falls in the major route between Riyadh and Kuwait. Even for the minor routes, the Gazeteer routes the traveler as follows: "Zilfi in Sidair direct desert route leads to Laqut near Kuwait and that desert route from Juma' and Riyadh converge at Wabrah on the way to Kuwait." [4] Only eight years later, however, the British Admiralty handbook, citing as its sources Shake-

---

[1] H. St. John Philby, *Arabia of the Wahhabis*, (London: Constable & Co. Ltd., 1928), pp. 352-352.

[2] H. St. John Philby, *Arabian Jubilee*, (London: Robert Hale Ltd., 1952), p. 39.

[3] Al-Rihani, *Najd*, p. 263.

[4] Lorimer, *Gazeteer of the Persian Gulf*, Vol. II, (1908), p. 1313.

speare (1910) and Barclay Raunkaier (1912) described the site as "wells in an extreme hollow with mounds about them; that measured by Raunkiaer was about twenty feet deep. Water is nearby always plentiful." [5] Yet the Admiralty book makes no mention of a settlement.

During this writer's trip to Al-Artawiyah in March 1968, Sultan al-Dawish, the town governor, pointed out the original well which the Ikhwan first dug at the site, and it was around this well that the *hijrah* was built and occupied by Mutayr tribesmen.

With regard to the founding of the *hijrah* at Al-Artawiyah, Ibn Nasir, the Najdi historian writes: "Sa'ad ibn Muthib and his brother Radhi, Salih ibn Fa'iz al-Harbi, Jiluwi al-Ashqar and his family, and Fahd ibn Fuhayd and his group from Mutayr and others" [6] founded the settlement in 1912 having left the town of Harma because of a dispute with the local people there involving their religious zeal. Both Majid ibn Khathila and Muhammad al-Sahabi told this writer during various interviews that Sa'ad ibn Muthib was the founder of Al-Artawiyah. While escorting this writer around Al-Artawiyah in March 1968, Sultan al-Dawish, said that the town was founded by 'Abd-al-Mushin ibn 'Abdullah ibn 'Abd-al-Karim al-Tamimi who first came to the site with about thirty people who dug the first of the two original wells at the site.

Dickson's mention of 'Abd-al-Karim al-Maghrabi as the founder of Al-Artawiyah in 1899 was explained to this writer in October 1968 during a discussion with Sultan al-Dawish and with the grandson of 'Abd-al-Karim al-Maghrabi who referred to his grandfather as al-Darwish (the mendicant). First, they both agreed that Al-Artawiyah was founded in 1912 and that there was no settlement at the site prior to the establishment of the *hijrah*, Second, they said that Dickson confused two different 'Abd-al-Karims, both of whom did live in Al-Artawiyah, and both of whom had gained prominence. The founder of the *hijrah*, they said, was 'Abd-al-Muhsin ibn 'Abd-al-Karim, a Najdi, who led the first group of emigrants to the site, among whom was Sa'ad ibn Muthib. The 'Abd-al-Karim to whom Dickson refers, they said, was not really known as al-Maghrabi but as al-Darwish, because of his reputation for religious fanaticism, asceticism, and his

---

[5] *A Handbook of Arabia*, Admiralty War Staff, Intelligence Division, 1916, Vol. 1, p. 97.

[6] 'Abd-al-Rahman Ibn Nasir, *'Unwan al-Sa'ad wa al-Majd*, Manuscript, Photostatic copy in possession of this writer, p. 114. See also Fu'ad Hamza, *Qalb Jazirat Al-'Arab*, (Cairo: Al-Salafiyah Press, 1933), p. 379.

renunciation of all worldly goods. They concluded by saying that other than these two 'Abd-al-Karims they could not identify anyone who could be the al-Maghrabi mentioned by Dickson.

In December 1968 Majid ibn Khathila verified the substance of this story. He agreed that there were two 'Abd-al-Karims and that in any case the al-Maghrabi mentioned by Dickson was not the founder of the *hijrah*. Majid said that the person called al-Maghrabi immigrated from North Africa in 1918, visited Mecca and Medina and then settled in Al-Artawiyah because of its reputation for piety and asceticism. That date would put him there about six years after the establishment of the *hijrah*. Majid gave the following as being the first to immigrate to Al-Artawiyah. Sa'ad ibn Muthib, 'Abd-al-Muhsin ibn 'Abd-al-Karim; Sittam al-Khuwaytiri, Man' ibn Fadliyah, 'Abdullah ibn Jasir al-'Utaybi, 'Abdullah ibn Fa'iz al-Harbi, and Abu Siday al-Khuwaytiri.

In a personal letter to this writer dated 5 January 1969 Lt. General John Glubb wrote:

> I looked up the reference to Irtawiyah or Artawiyah in Dickson's book on Kuwait. He only mentions that Abdul Kerim Al-Mughrabi established himself as a religious teacher in Artawiyah. I think that Dickson was certainly wrong in calling Irtawiyah a township in 1899. I certainly always heard that the place was started by 'Abdul Aziz ibn Saud. I also believe that Abdul Aziz started the Ikhwan movement. [7]

Within two years of its founding in 1912, control of Al-Artawiyah fell to Faysal al-Dawish, the paramount chief of the Mutayr tribe, who had once been an avowed enemy of Ibn Sa'ud but who later became an *akh* and dedicated his sword and his influence to championing Ibn Sa'ud's cause. The most prominent leader in the colony at the time of its founding was Hasan Al al-Shaykh, a member of the prominent Al al-Shaykh family. [8] According to the present governor of Al-Artawiyah, that colony under Faysal al-Dawish's dynamic leadership grew to a town of 35,000 persons. [9] Philby, however, estimated that at the maximum the town contained no more than 10,000 or 12,000 persons. Most other western sources agree with Philby's figure. On the other hand, Colonel Hamilton, the British Political Agent in Kuwait, who

---

[7] Personal letter to this writer dated 5 January 1969 from Lt. General John Glubb, Mayfield, Sussex.

[8] Known as The Sheikh (tribal elder or learned person), Muhammad ibn 'Abd al-Wahhab's family is now known as Al al-Shaykh, the family of the Sheikh, to the present day.

[9] Personal interview with Sultan Al-Dawish in Al-Artawiyah in March 1968.

passed near Al-Artawiyah in October 1917 cited the figure of 35,000
as being the population of the town at the time. Oddly enough, this
figure corresponds to the same estimate given by the present governor
of the *hijrah* as noted above. [10] Philby disputes this figure:

> Colonel Hamilton, on his journey to Riyadh in October 1917 had
> occasion to pass within a day's journey of Artawiya, one of the centres
> of the new Wahhabi movement associated with the name of the Akhwan
> brotherhood. He was impressed with what he heard regarding the
> tenets of this fanatical sect, and without enquiry, accepted as probably
> correct a local estimate, which gave the town a population of 35,000
> souls. A little reflection would, I am convinced, have deterred Colonel
> Hamilton from reporting what he had heard without further inves-
> tigation, and it is not improbable that he did not expect his report
> to be taken seriously. In the first place, it was *prima facie* improbable
> that a town twice as big as the biggest town in Central Arabia, could
> have sprung up in the space of a few years; in the second place—and
> this point is to my mind conclusive—native estimates of population
> are notoriously unreliable. Doughty's plan of reducing all such estimates
> by 90 per cent might have been usefully resorted to in this case. I saw
> the town, from a safe distance, in October, 1918, and I am satisfied
> that its population cannot exceed from 10,000 to 12,000 souls. [11]

Philby's "safe distance" was a distance of three or four miles and
he was using binoculars, [12] hence he was not in a very good position
to accurately estimate the size of the town.

This writer attempted to reach the correct population of Al-Artawiyah
by comparing the relative sizes of Al-Ghat Ghat and Al-Artawiyah.
In December 1968 a professional city planner [13] accompanied this writer
to Al-Ghat Ghat and made a quick examination of the town. From a
perch at the top of the minaret of the main mosque located in the
ruined town he made an approximate house count of 500 and from that
derived a population of about 3,500 persons. On the other hand, the
present governor of Al-Ghat Ghat estimated the original population
of the town as 10,000. Assuming that the professional town planner's
estimate is correct, and estimating that Al-Artawiyah is three times as
large as Al-Ghat Ghat, Al-Artawiyah would have had a population
of between 10,000 and 12,000 persons.

---

[10] It is interesting that sixty-one years after Hamilton passed near Al-Artawiyah,
at which time he was given 35,000 as the town's population, the present governor cites
the same number. It is obviously a figure which tradition has honored as correct.
Umm Al-Qura, number 218 (1 March 1929) placed the population at 30,000.

[11] Philby, Najd Mission, MSS, Public Record Office, Vol. 4144.

[12] Philby, *Arabia of the Wahhabis*, p. 353.

[13] Mr. Christos A. Antachopoulos of Doxiades Associates, Inc., Athens, Greece.

Unlike Al-Ghat Ghat, Al-Artawiyah was not destroyed after the abortive Ikhwan rebellion in 1929, therefore, during this writer's visit it was possible to see the town completely intact, although many houses had been abandoned by their owners and had fallen into disrepair, after Faysal al-Dawish fled the town in 1929.

Al-Artawiyah was built on the basic plan of a wheel with the mosque and the village square forming the center of the town. A mud wall approximately twelve feet high surrounded the town—and for the most part it is still intact—with entry and exit governed by four gates on the east, west, south, and north. As appropriate to a military canton-ment, horse stables and fodder bins were located conspicuously in the center of town near the square. It was at the square that the Ikhwan war banner (*bayraq*) was raised as a sign that a raiding call had been issued. The houses are all one storey [14] and are lined up contiguous with each other along winding, narrow lanes barely wide enough for a cart to navigate. The buildings are made of mud and have a rust brown color. Except for an occasional white washing around the windows and doors, there were no embellishments or decorations on the houses. Most of the houses are two or three room structures, one room being the 'coffee room' with a hearth peculiar to Najd. Each house had its own well because Ikhwan womenfolk were not allowed to use a public well.

The original large mosque of the *hijrah* has been torn down and replaced by a modern form of a Najdi type mosque, but there are several smaller, original mosques still extant and used by the local population. Several mosques have a subterranean mosque under the floor level to accomodate worshipers in the winter, a feature peculiar to mosques in other parts of Najd. The mosques are void of any decoration.

Faysal al-Dawish's original house is still in excellent condition, and unlike the other houses has some architectural virtue. The interior of the *majlis* (sitting room) is embellished with crude but interesting calligraphic motifs and verses from the Qur'an and with Arabic proverbs. The house is not inhabited.

Al-Artawiyah is located in a wadi (dry river bed) of the same name. When intense rains hit the area, the *wadi* is turned into a rushing river. The townspeople have tried to preserve some of this water by building a small, crude but functional, dam which stops up a consider-

---

14 Dickson reported that multi-storey houses were prohibited. Memorandum to the Civil Commissioner, Public Record Office, MSS, Volume 5062.

able amount of water. The original wells dug by the first immigrants still contain water but are not used. Large gardens to the west of the town, consisting mostly of date bearing palm trees give something of a verdant atmosphere to the town, which otherwise is set in an unattractive, greybrown plain devoid of natural beauty. Off on the horizon to the west looms a plateau on which four conical towers were constructed by the inhabitants of the town to provide an early warning of a hostile attack. [15]

Although Al-Artawiyah today is a sleepy town on the fringe of Najd, almost forgotten, and although it no longer claims the importance that it once had, its name still evokes a glint of pride and a flash of a smile when mentioned in the presence of an old *akh*. But in its heyday, the name alone struck terror in the hearts of Hijazis and awe among the Najdis. Its reputation for fanaticism and militancy was Al-Artawiyah's stock in trade, and even today the ring of its name among certain Hijazis familiar with peninsula history raises eyebrows. Such was the reputation of the town that on 7 December 1918 Colonel Hamilton wrote: "Everyone appears to be against our going to Artawiyah, which is said to be a hotbed of Muhammadan puritanism, not only is the foreigner unwelcome, but all outsiders are put in quarantine for various periods until their orthodoxy is ascertained." [16] The governor of Al-Artawiyah told this writer that visitors from Kuwait, specifically, were put into quarantine prior to being admitted to the town, even residents from Al-Artawiyah who had gone to Kuwait, until it could be proven that they were not defiled by their visit to that city. This writer was also told that the same month that he visited the *hijrah* a young woman who had brough coffee beans with her from Kuwait had consulted the local religious sheikh to ascertain whether or not the coffee beans were legitimate (*halal*) for use. Even today no woman is allowed in the market [17] to shop. Instead, the women congregate at the steps of the large mosque where the merchants bring their wares, and then take orders. The merchants deliver the merchandise to the customers' homes. Even today the sound of a woman's voice is not allowed to be heard in the streets, and when one woman desires to call the attention of

---

[15] At all of the towns in Wadi Hanifa, Wadi Huraymila, and others, towers (*burj/pl. abraj*) are located on the high bluffs.

[16] Report by Lt. Col. R. E. A. Hamilton, Political Agent, Kuwait, 7 December 1918, Public Record Office, MSS, Foreign Office, Vol. 3390, Document No. 20419.

[17] Interview with the governor of Al-Artawiyah in that town, March 1968.

another in public, she claps her hands. [18] Smoking in public is also prohibited.

Even Philby would not chance a visit to the town, and he described his observations of the town through binoculars saying that he and his party had decided to "avoid Artawiyah like the plague ... having not the slightest intention of risking my skin in Artawiyah." He continued: "The town ... was a landmark in history, already at this time dreaded through the length and breadth of Arabia, avoided even by Muslims professing the tenets of Wahhabism in its broader aspects.... [19]

Al-Artawiyah is still a traditional, Ikhwan town with all its pre-juidices and drawbacks. Yet Philby's description of this town and its inhabitants, a description which is true and accurate, fails to paint the human side of the picture. It is, therefore, Dickson's final summation of his attitude toward the Ikhwan which this writer took away with him from his visits to those settlements:

> Though much has been written also about Ikhwan cruelty and fright-fulness, I must record the opinion that this was carefully exaggerated to suit political ends at the time. I always had a sneaking admiration for the Ikhwan, this possibly because there is a curious charm about men who are truthful, are earnest believers in God, and, according to their lights, are out to cleanse religion of abuse. I confess that, once I got to know individual Ikhwan, I found very little difference between them and other good types of Badawin Arab elsewhere. They were just as fond of their women, their children, their camels, their mares as others were, while their attractive ladies had the same delightful characteristics as one finds among their sisters all over Arabia if one genuinely cares to study them. [20]

Unlike the establishment of Al-Artawiyah, the founding of the second *hijrah*, Al-Ghat Ghat of the 'Utaybah tribe, is not historicially controversial as to the date of its founding. All sources which this writer has located, verbal or written, agree that the town was founded in 1912, and Majid ibn Khathila, one of the original founders of the town, has been a generous source of information. In many interviews

---

[18] The governor of Al-Artawiyah told this writer in March 1968 that one of former King Sa'ud's daughters was forcibly prohibited from entering the town market, and that the truck in which she was riding was damaged by the crowd that turned her back; also, that King Sa'ud sustained the action of the people of Al-Artawiyah and reprimanded his daughter for attempting to break with tradition.

[19] Philby, *Arabia of the Wahhabites*, p. 352.

[20] Dickson, *Kuwait*, p. 148 .

between the period of March 1968 and January 1970, Majid ibn Khathila told this writer that the town was founded in 1912, and that the original immigration consisted of about one hundred persons, forming a community of about fifty tents. All, except ten persons from the Qahtan tribe, were 'Utaybah tribesmen. According to Majid, the original immigrants were led by Dughaylib ibn Kamhan, Fayath al-Habra, Muqham ibn Rumayzan, Husayn ibn Ghusham. These were followed nine months later by Majid ibn Khathila and Alush ibn Humayd. One year later Sultan ibn Bijad ibn Humayd arrived and assumed control over the *hijrah*. With the latter in charge, the town grew, according to Majid, until it reached a population of from 10,000 to 12,000 persons. However, as noted earlier in this work, judging from the present ruins of Al-Ghat Ghat, the total would appear to have been considerably less based on the estimate that the entire town contained only five-hundred houses located in an area of about ninety acres. [21]

Al-Ghat Ghat is located approximately fifty miles southwest of Riyadh and about two miles from the old sedentary oasis of Al-Muzahi-miyah. The red-brown plateau of Jabal Tuwayq forms a dramatic background to the town on one side, while the golden sands of the Dahna provide a striking contrast on the other. Unlike Al-Artawiyah, the geographical location of Al-Ghat Ghat, if not beautiful, is quite scenic.

The old town is completely ruined, having been deliberately destroyed in 1929 after the abortive Ikhwan rebellion which Ibn Sa'ud put down at the battle of Sabila; nevertheless enough houses are relatively intact to give the vistor an idea of the type of stark existence its inhabitants lived. Except for one or two houses, namely those of Sultan ibn Bijad and Majid ibn Khathila, all of the dwellings were two or three room structures similar to those at Al-Artawiyah. All were one-storey. Each house had its own well, [22] most of which are still visible in the old town, and all of which have since dried up. The town plan was similar to that of Al-Artawiyah: a large mosque dominated the center of the town, and the main square contained shops, stables, and fodder bins.

---

[21] Estimate of Mr. Christo A. Antachopoulos, December 1968.

[22] Uninvited visitors are not welcome in Al-Ghat Ghat. A visitor, however, should be very careful where he walks, since a network of uncovered wells riddle the old town. The wells have dried up, and many of them are more than forty feet deep; they are unmarked, appear only as large holes in the ground, and are hazardous.

It was in the town square that the *bayraq* [23] was raised calling the brothers to war. There is no trace of a wall around the town, but most likely such a wall existed since they were typical of all Najdi towns.

Judging from the completeness of the destruction, one would surmise that the town was bombarded by artillery or was razed by fire. Majid, however, told this writer that when Ibn Sa'ud ordered the town's destruction, he invited the people of neighboring Al-Muzahimiyah to loot the town, which they did. They stripped the valuable wood from the houses. Since the houses were made of clay and straw, and since the roofs were supported by wooden beams, when the beams were removed the houses collapsed. The wooden beams rested on rather crude pillars, which were formed from a series of circular pieces of hard stone cut about twenty inches in diameter, and about five to eight inches high. Laid one upon the other, looking much like a giant vertebrae, the individual pieces were cemented together, and the surface given a stucco-like finish. When the beams were removed, the pillars collapsed. The shell of each house has at least one collapsed pillar. Thus Al-Ghat Ghat remains today a grouping of roofless houses, many of the walls of which are still intact. Much of the ruins, nevertheless, have suffered the ravages of wind, rain, and other natural attrition.

Ibn Sa'ud ordered the town to remain unoccupied, but in 1956 the present governor, Majid ibn Khathila, was allowed to return with a group of former residents. They were authorized to build on the fringe of the town, but not within the old town itself. The original mosque in the center of the old town has been razed, and a new structure has been built on the same spot. It is the only building in the old town which may be used.

Together with Al-Artawiyah, Al-Ghat Ghat earned the reputation of being one of the most fanatical and militant Ikhwan centers. It was from here that the first Ikhwan military probe into territory claimed by King Husayn set out. Sultan ibn Bijad, the governor of the town, was the man who personally led the raid against Taif which led to its conquest and to the Ikhwan terror looming over Jidda, Mecca, and Medina. Finally, here Sultan ibn Bijad planned his opposition to Ibn Sa'ud which ultimately resulted in the Ikhwan rebellion, and the subsequent destruction of the *hijrah* because of the part it played in that rebellion.

With the establishment of Al-Artawiyah on the north-east fringe of

---

[23] A war standard.

Central Najd, and the founding of Al-Ghat Ghat to the southeast of Riyadh, important elements of two of the most turbulent tribes of Najd, the Mutayr and the 'Utaybah, were fully committed to the standards of Ibn Sa'ud. The groupings of these tribes that remained nomadic were too insignificant to change by themselves the course of their tribes' involvement in the Ikhwan experiment. From the military-political standpoint this commitment of Fraysal al-Dawish, the traditional enemy of the Rashid Family, severely limited the latter's capability against Ibn Sa'ud, since the full weight of the Mutayr was now directed against the Rashid capital at Ha'il. Similarly, the 'Utaybah under Sultan ibn Bijad at Al-Ghat Ghat protected the western flank from attacks which could possibly originate in the Hijaz. Both centers, strategically located as they were, served as Ikhwan beacons, flashing a message of a revived Islam, with all the enthusiasm of a neophyte, militarily successful movement. Tribe after tribe flocked to Ibn Sa'ud's standard and sent their leaders to Riyadh [24] to seek his support for the establishment of a *hijrah* for their tribes. The privileged position of Al-Artawiyah and Al-Ghat Ghat was not lost on them: abundant water, seed, arms, and almost immediate access to the most powerful man in the peninsula: Ibn Sa'ud at Riyadh.

Within a decade and a half of the founding of the first two, more than two hundred *hujar* were established. Although most of the *hujar* were located in Najd, some were founded on the fringes of the Hijaz, others in the north country populated by the Al-Ruwalah and Shammar tribes near the Syrian-Jordanian border, and still others on the edge of the Rub' al-Khali. Two were located at the west end of the Qatar peninsula, namely, Sikak and Ambaq. [25]

Thit writer has been able to identify 222 *hujar*. Although this number may not be definitive, it probably represents the majority of those that existed for any reasonable length of time, since some *hujar* were abandoned shortly after their establishment due to the lack of water and other serious problems. Based on the names of *hujar* collected from various sources, including documents from the British Public Record Office, Arabic manuscripts, Arabic historical works, and western authors who lived in Arabia at the time, the *hujar* may be identified by name and by tribe as follows:

---

[24] Ibn Nasir, *op. cit.*, p. 115.

[25] J. B. Kelley, *Eastern Arabian Frontiers*, (London: Faber and Faber, 1964), p. 125. Also see H. St. John Philby, *The Empty Quarter* (New York: Henry Holt & Co., 1923), p. 50.

Tribe	*Number of Hujar*
Yam	1
Mutayr	27
'Utaybah	25
Harb	38
Shammar	23
'Anza	7
Hutaym	6
Qahtan	11
Dawasir	4
'Ajman	19
'Awazim	4
Kharj Area (mixed)	5
Bani Hajir	5
	175

Some *hujar* are not listed because the identity of the tribe could not be made.

The geographical distribution of Ikhwan colonies enabled the striking arm of Ibn Sa'ud to be flexed in such a way that no part of the peninsula was more than day's march from the Ikhwan. The tribal distribution provided links to all the major tribes of Najd. Ibn Sa'ud had, therefore, a network of military cantonments which served as outposts of loyalty and collection points of intelligence at the farthest distances from Riyadh during peace; in war, they became centers of mobilization and springboards of attack against specific targets. Ikhwan troops marching from the farthest corners of Najd could find brothers-in-arms in the *hujar* of the Hijaz and Jawf, and in between these two points, they could find *hujar* which would give them provisions, water, intelligence, and other essentials. The *hujar* served as military bases, supply bases, and religious outposts, [26] and since many of them were located close to the traditionally sedentary places—such as Al-Ghat Ghat's location in relation to Al-Muzahimiyah—they acted as a disciplinary influence on those towns, keeping them safely within the Wahhabi fold.

In the early days of the *hujar* the bedouin, once ensconced in their new town, dedicated themselves totally to religious pursuits, shunning work, avoiding farming, and business, and basking in the bliss that certain salvation awaited them now that they had become brothers and had renounced their old ways. Part of this attitude was the result of

---

26 Fu'ad Hamza, *Qalb Jazirat*, p. 378.

laziness, and part was the result of their lack of basic skills. But the overwhelming reason was their genuine conviction that the pursuit of wealth was inconsistent with their total dedication to the things of God. Ibn Sa'ud moved quickly to correct this attitude by dispatching religious teachers once gain to quote the Qur'an and the *hadith* as proof that making money was not only desirable but virtuous, and that rich Muslims were far more pleasing to the Lord than impoverished ones. Only then did the *hujar* take on the tempo and activity that is typical of life in an organized settlement. There were merchants, farmers, shepherds, religious teachers, all contributing their share to the welfare of the community. Shops, austere by almost any standard, provided the basic needs of the unsophisticated bedouin: pots, pans, coffee, dates, rice, sugar, and salt. Looming prominently over the entire settlement was the paternal figure of Ibn Sa'ud fostering his Ikhwan, and ready to step in with whatever material aid they required.

Daily life in the *hujar* was similar to that type of existence peculiar to any religiously puritanical society. It was a life dedicated to prayer and contemplation when it was not geared for a raid; a life broken only by the excitement generated by the arrival of a courier with news from Riyadh, or, as the occasion warranted, by the raising of the war standard in the town square, a signal to the warriors to mobilize for war. Life was devoid of music, dancing, sports, and even children's games were discouraged. The one pleasure which the Ikhwan enjoyed was their women. They married young, and often.

The very absence of the other diversions seemed to ferment the religious fanaticism of the people. Their entire preoccupation was religion, and as they focused their attention on Islam, as they understood it, they could only view the world and its inhabitants in terms of black or white: those who differed from them were obviously wrong, hence deserving of their wrath. Those who worshipped like them were Ikhwan, hence their brothers. This almost childlike simplicity was born of their limited experience and education. Viewed in the context of their isolation on the *hujar*, isolated not only from the stream of developments in the European world, but even from the larger Islamic-Arab world of which they were a part, the Ikhwan of the *hujar* could hardly be expected to carry on in a manner other than which they did. In short, they were victims of geographic isolation, living as they were in the Arabian peninsula, and even within the peninsula, they were isolated in their remote, desolate settlements.

As with other areas which Ibn Sa'ud ruled, each *hijrah* was governed by an *amir* and a *hakim*, the former being responsible for the promulgation, application, and execution of the decrees emanating from the Consultative Council (*majlis al-shura*) which were signed by Ibn Sa'ud. [27] As for the *hakim* he was responsible for the application of the *shari'a*. The *amir* was tied directly to Ibn Sa'ud and participated in the election of the Consultative Council, and in the confirmation of the newly elected central ruler (*imam*), [28] who in this case was, of course, Ibn Sa'ud. The *hakim* was tied indirectly to the chief Islamic religious leader (*Shaykh Al-Islam*). In actual practice, however, since there was no fundamental distinction between secular and religious authority, both the *amir* and the *hakim* were responsible directly to Ibn Sa'ud. He was, in a very real sense, however, limited in his power by the precepts of Islamic Law as interpreted, defined, and refined through the medieval scholars, and the four schools of Orthodox Sunni Islam.

According to Dickson, there were two "governors" appointed by Ibn Sa'ud whose duties "were the preservation of order and the collection of taxes (*zakat*) which followed a fixed formula, a certain percentage for land, cattle, etc. On the other hand, the elected *amir* was responsible for keeping law and order [29] and he was assisted in these endeavors by a treasurer (*ma'mur bayt al-mal*) and about ten persons for mail and police activities. [30] The taxes, paid to the Imam, were collected twice yearly, and were distributed according to the provisions of Islamic Law. The balance went to the *bayt al mal*.

Religious power and authority rested largely in the hands of the descendants of Muhammad ibn 'Abd-al-Wahhab. The religious hierarchy was based in Riyadh, and the general education and religious administration of the areas under Ibn Sa'ud's control were entrusted to a body of religious scholars, the *'ulema'*. According to Philby [31] who was writing in 1922 there were six *'ulema'* in Riyadh, three in the Qasim, three in Al-Hasa, and one each in the other districts of Najd, approximately twenty in all. The decisions of the *'ulema'* were binding

---

[27] Al-Madani, *Firqat*, p. 42.

[28] This title signified his primacy as religious and secular leader.

[29] Report to the Civil Commissioner, Public Record Office, MSS, Vol. 5062 (5 March 1920).

[30] Al-Madani, *Firqat*, p. 42.

[31] St. John Philby, *The Heart of Arabia*, (London: Constable and Company, 1922. 2 Vols.), p. 297.

on the provincial *umara'* [32] who "merely signed and executed" the order. The *'ulema'* also provided the training and direction of the *mutawwi'in* who enjoyed no special administrative or judicial function, but who were entrusted with the religious instruction of the bedouin, and enforced their attendance at prayers, the closing of shops at prayer time, and in general enforced public morality. The ratio of *mutawwi'-in* to the bedouin was one for every fifty; under the *mutawwi'in* came the *tilmidh*, [33] the student who aspired to the the position of *mutawwi'*.

The organized structure of the Ikhwan made them an almost unique institution in the peninsula which was characterized by the Arab-bedouin penchant for independent action, and loose organization. The rapid spread of the Ikhwan movement, and the increasing number of *hujar* presented Ibn Sa'ud with a problem that became apparent all too soon: the Ikhwan, impelled by their deep religious conviction, under almost constant motivation by the *'ulema'* and the *mutawwi'in*, totally preoccupied with religion for lack of other interests or diversion, posed a threat not only to the power and authority of Ibn Sa'ud but to the Islamic Community in the larger sense. Very early in the reporting of British political agents, the warning that Ibn Sa'ud was losing, or had lost control over the Ikhwan became a regular theme, [34] and the warnings increased in number directly in proportion to the growth of Ikhwan military strength.

---

[32] Plural of *amir*.

[33] H. St. John Philby, *The Heart of Arabia*, p. 297.

[34] From Captain Bray to the India Office, 28 July 1919, MSS, Public Record Office, F. O. 371-4147, Document No. 129678. Also see Report on the Ikhwan, 13 May 1919, MSS, Public Record Office, Vol. 371-4146, Document No. E 94390.

CHAPTER SIX

MILITARY CHARACTERISTICS
OF THE IKHWAN

After the founding of Al-Artawiyah in 1912 Ikhwan colonies mush-roomed throughout the peninsula. No tribe was without converts; no city was devoid of Ikhwan adherents. As Ibn Sa'ud's missionaries made their way across the country preaching among the various tribes, they made converts and inroads among the bedouin to the extent that whole tribes were divided in their loyalties, some looking to the traditional tribal leadership, others looking to Ibn Sa'ud as religious *imam* and temporal ruler. By the time Ibn Sa'ud decided to make a final strike against the Rashids, many of the Shammar had already become Ikhwan. [1] In Khurma, the *amir* Khalid ibn Luwai, a Sharif himself, had embraced the Ikhwan doctrine and pledged his loyalty to Ibn Sa'ud. These Ikhwan minorities in a sense acted as spies, providing the forces of Ibn Sa'ud with information on troop numbers, their weapons, state of alert, and their morale, and the local rulers dared not raise a hand against them lest they incur the wrath of Ibn Sa'ud and his Ikhwan and provide a pretext for attack.

The appearance of the Ikhwan contingents in the battle of Jirab in 1914 [2] marked their first participation as a cohesive fighting force, thereby radically altering the balance of power in the peninsula. In the Hijaz, King Husayn relied militarily on a regular army that had had some Turkish and British training; it was officered by some Syrians, and was re-inforced by bedouin levies from the Hijaz tribes. To the north, the Rashids' rule was backed by the Shammar bedouin forces supplied with Turkish arms and gold. In Najd proper, Ibn Sa'ud depended on a combined military force composed of a) the people of *'Aridh*, b) the townsmen, c) the Ikhwan poised in the *hujar* and d) the bedouin: [3]

a) *The people of 'Aridh*: were generally regarded as the most loyal supporters of the Sa'ud family and were considered to be the strongest pillar propping the state's security. Proud of their reputation for bravery

---

[1] Armstrong, *op. cit.*, p. 144.

[2] Armstrong, *op. cit.*, p. 88.

[3] *Umm al-Qura*, number 287 (6 June 1930).

and rarely ever retreating in battle, they were known to revert to the use of the sword when they had used up all the ammunition in their rifles. The people of *'Aridh* constituted the inhabitants of Riyadh proper, the people of the towns surrounding Riyadh, and the semi-nomadic bedouin living in the vicinity. The bedouin were mostly Suhul-Subay' tribesmen. Due to their proximity to Riyadh these nomads did not look to one *amir* but rather attached themselves to the King or other members of the Royal family as part of their "staff."

b) *The townsmen (hadhr)*: these are the inhabitants of the different villages in Najd. Each settlement was required to provide a certain number of soldiers to serve four months per year and to provide their own food, rifles, mounts, and fodder for this period. The time limit was required because the townsmen were obliged to tend to their daily tasks of farming, commerce and trade which they could not leave for long periods of time unless there was an extreme emergency. If the raid or mobilization period took longer than four months, the soldiers were paid for their food from the *bayt al mal*. If there was no war, the villagers were obliged to pay to the *bayt al mal* the amount of money which the levy of soldiers for four months would have cost if it had been called up.

c) *The Ikhwan*: these warriors were always prepared for war, and the total mobilization of the men in the *hujar* did not significantly disturb any type of casual farming, commerce or trade which they may have been conducting. Unlike the townsmen who served for a specific time under a compulsory system, the Ikhwan "compells himself" (*yilzim nafsu*). When the call went out for war, any person who carried arms was expected to respond, and none remained behind unless he was physically confined to the sick bed or for any other legal reasons for which the person was individually excused. Anyone who did not respond and remained behind was reviled by the women, and was either severely punished or killed as an example to others. [4] Males joined the ranks of warriors at age fifteen [5] although cases of youths aged eight and nine years old are recorded as actually having participated in raids. Males as old as seventy years old were also expected to fight. [6]

d) *The bedouin*: each tribe was split, ideologically, into those that accepted settlement on the *hujar* and became Ikhwan and those that

---

[4] *Umm Al-Qura*, number 291 (4 July 1930).

[5] Interview with the Governor of Al-Artawiyah in that *hijrah*, March 1968.

[6] *Umm Al-Qura*, number 287 (6 June 1930).

Plate 1. An *akh* dressed in typical Ikhwan fashion. Photographed by this writer in Al-Artawiyah in March 1968.

Plate 2. Amir Sultan bin 'Abd-al-Rahman al-Dawish, Amir of Al-Artawiyah, holding a bulletriddled Ikhwan war banner.

Plate 3. Abandoned houses in Al-Ghat Ghat.

Plate 4. Several residents of Al-Artawiyah demonstrating the use of primitive hand weapons which some of the Ikhwan used in their raids and battles for lack of a rifle or other type of weapon.

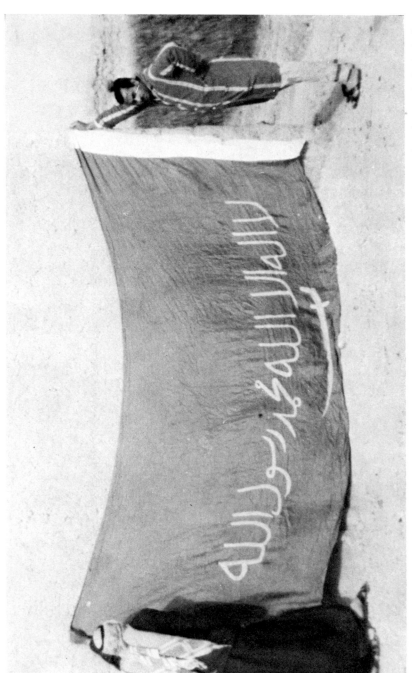

Plate 5. An old Ikhwan war banner that saw many raids and battles, photographed in Al-Artawiyah. The banner (*bayrak*) is riddled with bullets.

Plate 6. The small hillock at Sabila where Ibn Sa'ud planted his war banners to face the rebellious Ikhwan.

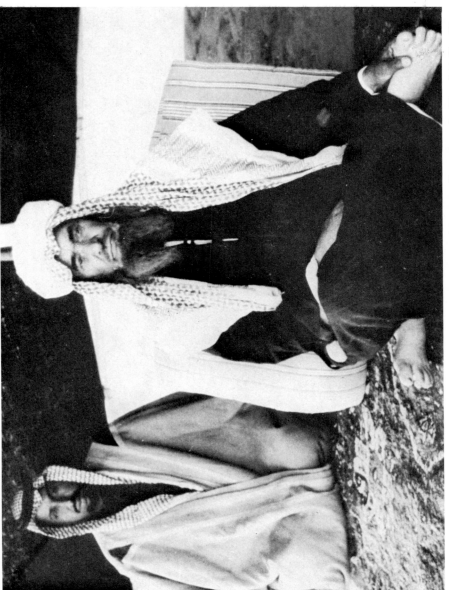

Plate 7. Majïd bin Khathila, Amir of Al-Ghat Ghat, seated in a tent several kilometers distant from the *hijra* of Al-Ghat Ghat.

chose to remain nomadic while embracing the tenets of Wahabbism. [7] The character of both parties was basically the same since they were all originally bedouin. The bedouin made good fighters in defense of their property, women, and other matters of value to them, but they were disposed to plunder even those with whom they were fighting if it appeared that their allies were losing the battle on the rationale that it is better to take your friend's property than to let it fall in the hands of the enemy. These bedouin were valuable as re-inforcements for a more reliable, disciplined army.

While Ibn Sa'ud made use of each of the above fighting arms at the appropriate time, he relied in the main on the Ikhwan. In a sense the Ikhwan played the role of modern type guerrillas, waging an unconventional war against the conventional army commanded by King Husayn. As for the Rashids and Shammar they were prepared to fight a traditional bedouin-Arab battle but the Ikhwan had already penetrated their ranks through religious conversion of part of the Shammar subjects—substituting tribal and family ties with ideological and religious loyalties.

King Husayn's modern army [8] to the contrary, and the nationalistic, tribal loyalties of the Shammar aside, neither the Sharifs of the Hijaz nor the Rashids could put into the field of battle anything remotely resembling the military machine represented by the Ikhwan. The Ikhwan provided Ibn Sa'ud with a striking force that could mobilize in hours or days, depending on the size of the raid, a force that could travel great distances on almost uninterrupted marches, endure in battle on the most meager of diets, and plunge into the battle seeking death and paradise. No other ruler could match it!

Military battles were fought by bedouin at this time in the same fashion that they had been fought for centuries. The Ikhwan made only slight improvisations in these types of raids which are known as *al-sabah, al-ghara, al-ruhah,* and *al-hijad,* [9] names based on the hours of the day when the raids occur.

a) *Al-Sabah*: also known as *al-tasbih*. This type of raid occurs at first dawn. The attackers do not know if the adversary is still sleeping, and proceed to their target under the cover of night to arrive at their destination as dawn breaks.

---

[7] Smalley, *op. cit.*, p. 245.

[8] The Sharifian army had acquired some artillery and some cannon, and later several aircraft which were piloted by mercenaries.

[9] *Umm Al-Qura*, number 302 (19 September 1930).

b) *Al-Ghara*: also known as *Al-Laqwah* when it comes at forenoon (late morning). This method is used by powerful forces that do not fear the enemy and do not fear being detected.

c) *Al-Ruhah*: also known as *Al-Tarawih* takes place in the afternoon, and requires the same degree of military strength and striking power as the *Al-Sabah*.

d) *Al-Hijad*: also known as *Al-Muhjad*, this raid takes place anytime from the setting of the sun to dawn the next morning. It is the most difficult type of raid because it occurs in the darkness when it is difficult to distinguish friend from foe, and can be quite confusing unless the raid is led by an exceptional leader. Ibn Sa'ud was skilled at this type of battle because in his early days his forces were so small that he had to rely on surprise. The most important battle which Ibn Sa'ud fought in *al-hijad* fashion was the battle at Rawdah (between Zilfi and Buraydah); the Ikhwan raid at Turaba was also an example of this type of daring raid.

These battles were fought with rifles, but many Ikhwan were still armed only with spears and knives. In any case the rifle [10] may have given some longer range, but it did not significantly change the scenario from what it had been hundreds of years earlier. There still were no roads, no telephonic-telegraphic communications lines, no logistical supply lines, no administrative organization backing up the fighting force. Battles were short and decisive and best fought as close to one's home as possible. Heat, rainfall, the previous year's rainfall were all calculated in considering the time and place of battle. The abundance or lack of scrub vegetation was a significant factor; the camels and horses required food and water, the warriors being capable of carrying only their own meager provisions. [11] Other considerations were religious: Ramadan (the fasting month) and the *hajj* season both put a damper on hostilities. While the scene remained the same, the cast of characters changed only slightly. Yet the Ikhwan did introduce several new tactics:

a) The long march for a short hit and run raid.
b) The desire for martyrdom on the field of battle.
c) Slaying all males in the enemy camps, including the children and sometimes the females.

---

[10] According to Dickson, the regular soldier ('askar) used rifles that had the small bore magazine type (mauzer mostly), whereas the bedouin used every type of rifle, the majority being of the bore magazine type, mainly 303, mauzer, and maulichers. Report to the Civil Commissioner, F. O. 371-5062.

[11] John Bagot Glubb, personal letter to this writer, 5 January 1969.

These new tactics threw the whole concept of warfare in the peninsula out of line. Contemporary Ikhwan speak of almost non-stop marches from Central Najd into Transjordan, and from Al-Artawiyah deep into Iraq. On these long marches, the Ikhwan usually continued all through the night arriving at the enemy camp at nightfall and swarming down upon the unsuspecting enemy just before dawn. Night marches allowed them to approach the camp undetected. During the battle, the Ikhwan would seek death; sometimes the casualties were high because of their blind, uninhibited plunge into the fray; they were known to charge cannons which were being fired. [12] But what underlined the Ikhwan reputation for ferocity was their habit of indiscriminate killing among the enemy. Many times Ibn Sa'ud had to take them to task for such conduct and behavior, and Ibn Sa'ud's opposition to it was one of the elements which caused the rift between him and the Ikhwan.

The Ikhwan raided in groups of various sizes, some as small as fifty, others as large as two thousand and, according to some reports, even twenty thousand. Few horses were used, the riding camel (*zalul*) providing the most common form of transportation, although during the large raids most of the troops went on foot. Generally two persons would share one camel, each taking turns to ride; [13] in some raids, such as those against Khurma and Ta'if, as many as five persons would share one camel. [14] Each *akh* brought along his own provisions, which usually consisted of a handful or two of dates; a small sack of flour, and a canteen of water. [15] He provided his own arms and ammunition, and sometimes he went into battle armed only with a knife or sword, and there are instances where he joined a raiding party without any type of weapon, but only with the hope that in the heat of battle he would capture a weapon from the enemy. [16] (See plate 4).

Mutlaq ibn Ras who identified himself as being eighty-three years old, and Marzuk ibn Miflah, who said he was seventy years old, both told this writer in Al-Artawiyah in March 1968 that they had participated in an Ikhwan raid deep into Iraq. They said that it took them

---

[12] Majid ibn Khathila told this writer that during the battle at Ta'if many Ikhwan charged the artillery directly, although they were armed only with swords, and that the sight of these zealous Ikhwan so frightened the artillerymen that they turned and fled. See also Ameen Rihani, *Ibn Sa'ud of Arabia*, (London: Constable & Co., Ltd., 1928), p. 158.

[13] Interview with Sultan al-Dawish in Riyadh, December 1968.

[14] Interview with Muhammad ibn Jab'a Al-Dawish in Riyadh, January 1969.

[15] *Umm Al-Qura*, number 291 (4 July 1930).

[16] Interview with Muhammad ibn Majid ibn Khathila in Riyadh, January 1969.

ten days to reach there; that between the two of them they killed one-hundred persons. The march took place during the day, and they slept only three hours. Their food consisted of dates, bread, and coffee. A handful of dates, they said, would last two months. The last statement may be an exaggeration, but in this connection it is interesting to note what Ibn Sa'ud said one evening to al-Rihani while discussing the Ikhwan:

> They come to us in peace time and we give them whatever they need in terms of clothes, rations, or money. But in wartime they do not ask anything from us. During war each one gets a cartridge, runs to his rifle, then rides the camel to war, taking with him a little money and a few dates ... a little with us takes the place of much with others ... we used to march for three days without food. *From time to time one would take a date and freshen his mouth with it* (italics mine). Yes, it used to be that the villager was more sure-footed and braver than the bedouin. But now the settled bedouin, the people of the hujar, are more stable in war and more anxious to seek martyrdom. [17]

The general tactics of battle were surprise and a concentrated blow or strike with no thought given to surrender or withdrawal. If the attack were a surprise, the Ikhwan would descend on the target as a wild mixture of men on horses, camels, and infantrymen wreaking havoc with the enemy camp and slaying the soldiers and people therein with no compassion or mercy. The Ikhwan discounted the enemies' numbers or his weapons content to match overwhelming odds with their fervor and dedication. Ibn Sa'ud described the Battle of Turaba, [18] to Sa'ud ibn 'Abd al-'Aziz Al Rashid as follows:

> The Sherif had with him four thousand Turkish soldiers who were at Medina and 7,000 men of Hejaz, together with 20 guns, 40 machine guns and provisions and ammunition on ten thousand camels, while our Ikhwan numbered only 2,000 and of these 500 were even without any arms except swords and knives. The Sherif had made trenches as deep as the height of a man, and fortifications, and had placed guns and machine guns in every position. The "Ikhwan" started their advance at midnight, and when they said their morning prayers they sought, against the Sherif and his guns, the help of "la ilah illa Allah" (There is no God but Allah) and attacked him from morning and the battle lasted all day and the next night until the Sherif and his men were defeated and ran away until they reached el-Baida, near Al-Taif with 200 camels and horsemen. The rest were killed by the "Ikhwan" who

---

[17] Al-Rihani, *Najd*, p. 264.
[18] This battle was of the Al-Hijad type.

also won their (enemy's) possessions and forwarded to me the good
news when I had just left el-Qunsuliyah. 19

If the battle was a match between two different forces grouped on
a battlefield, one waiting for the other to charge, the Ikhwan used the
following formation: a standard bearer holding aloft the great green
and white Ikhwan banner (plate 5) was positioned several paces in
front of the commanding chief Ikhwan. On either side of the chief
were the Ikhwan mounted on horses, acting somewhat in the capacity
of modern armor to drive a spearhead into the ranks of the enemy.
Behind them were the Ikhwan on camels, prepared to give one great
push once the wedge was made; rushing in behind the camel corps
were the infantry, waving spears or rifles, or both, and heading for
the enemy.

During the battle the Ikhwan used various war cries, the most famous
being:

> The Winds of Paradise are blowing!
> Where are You, Who seek it. 20

or:

> I am a Knight of Unity
> Brother of He who Obeys God.
> Show your head, oh enemy! 21

or:

> People of Unity! People of Unity!
> People of Awja! People of Awja! 22

At the attack, the Ikhwan would often shout: "It is You Whom we
Adore and You From Whom we seek help! 23 All of these battle cries
replaced the old tribal war slogans that had been used by individual
Arab tribes throughout the ages.

In addition to their frequent use of dawn attacks and night marches,
the Ikhwan used such tactics as flank and rear attacks. Dismounting
from their camels and horses, they would advance shoulder to shoulder

---

19 Letter from 'Abd-al-'Aziz ibn 'Abd-al-Rahman Al-Faysal to Sa'ud ibn 'Abd-al-
'Aziz Al Rashid, Public Record Office, MSS, Foreign Office, No. 371-4146, Document
No. 117487, 2 August 1919.

20 Wahbah, *Al-Jazirat*, p. 295 .

21 Al-Rihani, *Maluk*, vol. II, p. 82.

22 Al-Rihani, *Najd*, p. 222. (Awja is another name for Riyadh).

23 This is the fourth line of Surah I of the Qur'an.

in infantry style. [24] The Ikhwan may have been a primitive fighting force, but they had a definite objective, simplicity of plan, offensive action, speed of movement and tactical surprise. [25] For this they needed intelligence information which they acquired by sending strong reconnaisance parties, each consisting of perhaps thirty or forty camelmen, who would sometimes creep up under cover of darkness and count the camp fires. [26] In collecting intelligence the Ikhwan were even bolder than this:

> A most valuable device to advancing Ikhwan raiders was to send a spy to sit in the camps which they intended to attack. Assuming a suitable disguise, this man would endeavour to stay in the Iraqi tent as a guest until the day before that fixed for the attack. He would then try to slip away, probably under cover of darkness and meeting the advancing raiders at a pre-arranged rendezvous, a few hours before that chosen for the attack to inform them of the eleventh-hour dispositions of the camps. [27]

In spite of its great effectiveness, the Ikhwan were not led by a military hierarchy or administered from a general or central headquarters. The Ikhwan were governed by personalities, the chief being, of course, Ibn Sa'ud. He was the supreme commander in the sense that all Ikhwan—until the abortive revolt—looked to him for ultimate leadership and guidance. But he did not administer the Ikhwan as a modern army. Instead, the Ikhwan rested on the two great *hujar* of Al-Artawiyah and Al-Ghat Ghat. Faysal al-Dawish was the chief Ikhwan leader after Ibn Sa'ud, and Sultan ibn Bijad followed a close second. Other Ikhwan leaders such as Muhsin al-Firm of the Al-Ruwalah and Dhidan ibn Hithlain of the 'Ujman tribe played significant roles, but they were secondary to those of al-Dawish and Ibn Bijad. Both of the latter exercised ingenuity and imagination in carrying out raids, selecting targets, and whipping up enthusiasm for the call. Both had sufficient individual prestige and authority among their own tribes to act, at times, independently of Ibn Sa'ud, as did Ibn Bijad against Ta'if, and Faysal al-Dawish against Iraq.

When the Ikhwan leaders decided to carry out a raid, they would

---

[24] Dickson, Public Records Office, MSS, Foreign Office, No. 371-13740, Document No. E 5154.

[25] Sir John Bagot Glubb, *War in the Desert*, (London: Hodder & Stoughton, 1960), p. 231.

[26] *Ibid.*

[27] *Ibid.*

order the Ikhwan *bayraq* planted in the village square. Volunteers would line up for the raid, bringing with them their own provisions, weapons, and a horse or camel, if they had one. There were no specific numbers required by each tribe or each *hijrah* the presumption being that since they were all warriors there would be more than enough recruits. Among the larger tribes located in the *hujar*, however, tribal customed prevailed, and in some instances the volunteers would offer themselves as part of the *bayraq*, or standard, of a sub-tribe within the larger tribe. For example, if the 'Utaybah tribe of Al-Ghat Ghat decreed a raid, the volunteers would go out carrying several standards (*bayraq*). The volunteers under one standard would be from one branch (*fakhdh*) of the 'Utaybah tribe, for example, from the Al-Da'ajin, Al-Daghalibah, Al-Asha, Al-Shayabin, Al-Qumazah, or Al-Hawain, or any of the fifteen or twenty branches of this tribe. [28] In Al-Artawiyah, a group of men from each *harat*, or quarter of the town, would form one bayraq. [29] This was the extent to which there was any type of organizational, or regimental pattern to the Ikhwan method of mobilization. In any case, this is how the Ikhwan operated as a practical matter. Al-Rihani records a general system of mobilization which may have existed during Ibn Sa'ud's time, but to this writer's knowledge it was never used. Theoretically there were three types of mobilization: the *jihad* (holy war), and when this was proclaimed, the professional soldiers of the *hujar* who were always militarily prepared went out to battle. In more serious cases of mobilization the *radif* (reserve) was called out. This group consisted of those Ikhwan who may have been engaged in some type of religious, commercial, or educational activity within the *hijrah*. Finally, the *nafir* or general alarm was called in states of national emergency, and under these circumstances all able bodied men and boys flocked to the war banner. [30] According to al-Rihani only the *'ulema'* could call up the *nafir*, but inasmuch as the *imam* was the chief religious leader, his recommendation would be followed by the *'ulema'*. There is no recorded instance which this writer has been able to locate, or information which he was able to acquire from his verbal sources, wherein a *nafir* was called. Not even during the Ikhwan rebellion or the conquest of the Hijaz was there even a secondary mobilization of forces.

---

[28] Interview with Muhammad ibn Majid ibn Khathila in Riyadh, January 1969.

[29] Interview with Sultan ibn 'Abd-al-Rahman al-Dawish in Al-Artawiyah, March 1968.

[30] Al-Rihani, *Najd*, p. 264. See also Umm Al-Qura, number 291, (4 July 1939).

Al-Madani records an even more ambitious organization of Ikhwan forces, and has them divided into five groups:

a) *Northeast Sector*: at the Iraq border. Its headquarters were at Lina and Umm Al-Radmah headed by Ibn Jabril and Ibn Thunayyan respectively. Its responsibilities were to bring into the Ikhwan fold the following tribes of Ibn Hadhdhal of the 'Anayzah confederation: Al-Saqur, Al-'Amarat and the Al-Sadid which are along the Iraqi border, in addition to the Al-Jarba and the Al-Hadi. Also to bring into line the following Shammar tribes which were not early disposed to following Ikhwan creed: Al-Jazira and the Al-Zafir of Ibn Suwayt.

b) *Northwest Sector*: at the Syrian border. Its headquarters were at Al-Juba, headed by Ibn 'Aqil and Ibn Dughmi. Its general responsibilities were concerned with the bedouin of Syria as far as Ma'an, and to bring into the Ikhwan fold the Al-Ruwalah tribe of the Sha'alans and the Al-Shararat as well as such persons as Ibn Jandal, Ibn Milhim, Sultan Al-Tayyar, Ibn Samir, and Ibn Mahid and others of the Al-Saba' and the Al-Fad'an who emigrated beyond Aleppo; also, the banu Sakhr, banu 'Atiyah and finally to bring the Al-Huwaytat tribes into the Ikhwan fold.

c) *North Hijaz*: along the Medina Line. Its general headquarters were located in Dakhna and Timah, and its chief was Ibn Nahit. Its responsibilities were to bring into line the tribes of Farhan al-Ayda, Chief of the Al-Faqir, and others of the Anayzah tribe around Mecca and Khaybar, such as the Wuld 'Ali, and Al-Ghadawarah and also the Hutaym, the Bani Salim, the Wuld Muhammad, and the Masruh elements of the Harb tribe.

d) *South Hijaz*: along the Mecca Line. Its headquarters was Al-Khurma, led by Khalid ibn Luwai. Its responsibilities were to bring into the Ikhwan fold the Hamran, Salim, Zubayd, and the Masruh element of the Harb tribe, and part of the Banu Salim and such groups connected with them that were located along the eastern road which connects Mecca and Medina.

e) *The Reserve Branch*: located in Al-Artawiyah, led by Faysal al-Dawish. Its responsibilities extended from the north provinces to the south Hijaz, and this branch went to the aid of those who needed its help. [31]

Al-Madani does not give any indication as to the source of his information on these headquarters, and this writer has not been able to

---

[31] Al-Madani, *Firqat*, pp. 43-45.

find any document or verbal source which substantiates the existence of such delegation of military authority or responsibility. To the contrary, the verbal sources among the Dushan and the Khathila families challenge the accuracy of Al-Madani's account, dismissing him as an outsider, who would not know such information, or have access to it. They state simply that the Ikhwan were a loosely organized group of warriors, coming under the immediate direction of their leaders, and that the general trend of the Ikhwan was set by the Mutayr of Al-Artawiyah and the 'Utaybah of Al-Ghat Ghat. One great omission which casts a shadow of doubt on Al-Madani's breakdown is his failure to mention Al-Ghat Ghat which took the lead in the conquest of the Hijaz by its thrusts at Turaba, Khurma and Ta'if. While his break-downs may be valid for a general distribution of strength, they should not be interpreted as meaning that these five outposts directed, administered, and organized Ikhwan activities as a highly co-ordinated network of headquarters.

Because of the dearth of records one can only estimate the actual Ikhwan membership, and then one must make a distinction between the total number of people living on the *hujar*, including the women and girls, and between the actual number of males who were either Ikhwan or would grow up to be such. 'Attar in *Saqr al-Jazira* provides the following estimates of the population of the *hujar*: Mutayr, 40,000; Dawasir, 7,000; 'Utaybah (Al-Ruwaqah, 14,000; 'Utaybah (Barqa), 8,000; Al-Ghat Ghat, 15,000; 'Ujman, 15,000; Harb, 30,000; 'Awazim, 15,000; Al-Murra, 10,000; Shammar, 15,000, for a total of 169,000. [32]

Majid bin Khathila said that the total strength of the Ikhwan at its height was 150,000 of which 75,000 were armed with rifles of some sort, and the rest armed with spears, swords, and other weapons. [33] He was talking about able bodied male warriors. Philby, Dickson and al-Rihani have left estimates but none of these extend farther than the year 1926; they are incomplete because *hujar* were still being established for new Ikhwan settlers after that date. In 1919 Philby estimated the total number of Ikhwan at 30,000 having arrived at this figure by taking 10% of the figure 300,000 which was quoted as Ikhwan strength by his bedouin sources. [34] Dickson writing in 1920

---

[32] 'Attar, Ahmad, *Saqr al-Jazirat* (Falcon of the Peninsula), pp. 200-201.

[33] Interview with Majid ibn Khathila on 19 April 1969 in Riyadh.

[34] Calling it "Doughty's rule," Philby was wont to take 10% of any figure provided by an Arab source as the correct figure.

reported that Ibn Sa'ud had estimated the number of Ikhwan at 300,000, [35] which represented the total number of men from the *hujar* which he could muster if there were total war. Since no accurate records were kept, it may be almost impossible to estimate accurately the military strength of Ikhwan during the peak of the movement's power. In any case, only a very small percentage of the Ikhwan actually were used in any given battle or combination of battles. Some British political reporters refer to groups of 20,000 in raiding parties, but they produce no evidence to back up these allegations. Philby estimates that the largest force that could be kept together in the field in view of the peculiar difficulties of the Arabian terrain is 5,000. In 1928 he gave the following strengths of seven Ikhwan contingents and Ibn Sa'ud's bodyguard at a preliminary concentration of troops at Tarafiya:

Hijra [36]	Strength in Men (With camels or on foot)	Strength in Horses
Artawiyah	1,000	100
Ghatghat	800	100
Dahina	700	80
Furaithan	700	75
Sajir	500	65
Mubaidh	500	58
Dhaba'a	300	50
Ibn Sa'ud's bodyguard	300	300
Total	4,800	828

A comparison of these figures with those of Dickson and al-Rihani's on the following pages show that they are in general agreement, insofar as they deal with the same *hujar*.

Majid ibn Khathila told this writer that the largest raiding party of Ikhwan did not exceed 4,000, [37] a figure which is not too far off from Philby's breakdown given above.

The following summary of activities of Ikhwan raiding parties

---

[35] Dickson, Memorandum to the Civil Commissioner, Foreign Office, 1920, MSS, Vol. 371-5062.

[36] Philby, *Arabia of the Wahhabis*, p. 296. Excluding Ibn Sa'ud's bodyguard, all of which was mounted, Philby's figure show a proportion of about one to ten of horses to camelmount and infantry. At the Ha'il operation, Philby reported a force of 6,000 warriors of whom 5,000 were Ikhwan. See Operations against Ha'il, 10 October 1918, MSS, Public Record Office, F. O. 371-3390, Document No. E. 17244.

[37] Interview in Riyadh.

during the period 15 December 1928 through 3 March 1929 is pre-served in the British Public Record Office, London: [38]

1. Mutayr raiding parties in Al-Jumaymah area:

Leader	Strength
Al Muraykhik	30 men on 16 camels
Jatli ibn Rashid	20 men on 15 camels
Ibn Ghunaim	8 camelmen
Ibn Rushdan	About 30 men
Manahi ibn 'Ashwan	150 camelmen
Lafi ibn Mu'allath	About 30 camelmen

2. 'Ujman and Mutayr raiding parties in Kuwait:

Dhidan ibn Hithlain	200-300 men
Ibn Hithlain (Ajman)	
Ibn Shuqair (Mutair)	
Ibn Al-Fughm (Mutair)	1000 men
Ibn Shuqair (Mutair)	200 men
Ibn Fughm (Mutair)	
Ibn Shuqair	
Ibn Fughm	600 men

3. 'Utaybah raiding parties in Hazul area:

Mohd. ibn Jabrin	800 men
Muhsin.	1000 men
Sultan ibn Humaid	1200 men

While not conclusive evidence that Ikhwan raids were very small, inasmuch as the above leaders represent the most active and famous of Ikhwan leaders the small size of their raiding parties is significant.

Al-Rihani's total figure for the Ikhwan is about 75,000 warriors. Even if this figure were doubled to account for the *hujar* that were established after he calculated these figures, the number of 150,000 fighters is not an exceedingly large number considering the results that they achieved. Giving full weight to the consideration that the conquest of the peninsula was not their doing alone, certainly the great prizes of the Hijaz were their contributions to Ibn Sa'ud's dominions. As Al-Madani put it: "The victories which the Ikhwan achieved during this

---

[38] Summary of Akhwan raiding parties, Public Record Office, London, MSS, F. O. 371-13714, Document No. E 1781 (1929).

very short period does not lend itself to an easy explanation, however, suffice it to say that the expansion and extending of the borders from the Asir Province to the ... border of Iraq and from Qatar and Kuwait to the border of Syria are the fruits of victory which were picked during the last three years, i.e., since the battle of Turabah." [39]

Not very much has been recorded on the description of the Ikhwan as soldier, although much is known about his fanaticism and dedication. For this reason, the description left by Captain C. C. Lewis is all the interesting, although he is speaking from hindsight, and even so, not very accurately:

> The Akhwan are the third important factor in Arabian politics. Mr. Philby numbers them about 50,000 fighting men, but Ameen Rihani puts the number at about 73,000. For years, throughout all Arabic-speaking countries the Akhwan have been a bogey with which to frighten not only the children but also the grown-ups, but I think myself they are little better than a myth. They are of poor physique. They are certainly fanatical, and brutal fighters, fanatical, perhaps in view of the comforting Wahabi tenet that if you are killed in battle you will enjoy a large number of houris in paradise. Whilst, if you survive you will share in the loot; brutal, as is shown by the fact that they put to death every man, woman, and child from Muwaila to the Transjordan frontier.... Nevertheless, a sound military appreciation of the Akhwan must lead one to the conclusion that untrained fighters, however brave they may be, have no possible chance against trained troops. I should very much doubt whether the Akhwan were better troops than the Shaban of Iraq. I would have backed any of my own companies of Shabana against double the number of Akhwan. [40]

Speaking as he was in 1933, several years after the Battle of Sabila where Ikhwan power was crushed, far away in London with no member of the Ikhwan to offer a rebuttal, Captain Lewis showed that he had a surprisingly short memory. He fails to explain why the trained regular troops of King Husayn were unable to defend Ta'if, Mecca and Medina, much less to protect Jidda from the "poor physiqued Ikhwan." Husayn even employed aircraft piloted by mercenaries against them. Nor does he explain why the well trained Iraqis, officered by the British, were unable to cope with the unruly Ikhwan, even after pitting aircraft, armored vehicles, and other motorized cars against them. Even the well

---

[39] Al-Madani, *Firqat*, p. 45.

[40] "Ibn Sa'ud and the Future of Arabia," Captain C. C. Lewis, Address given at Chatham House on 23 January, 1933, Professor H. A. R. Gibb in the Chair. Printed in *International Affairs*, 1933, p. 518.

trained forces in Jordan were unable to manage the Ikhwan, it taking concerted effort of Ibn Sa'ud and the British in Jordan and Iraq to subdue them. The Ikhwan may have been brutal, and one may justly indict them for this, but to write them off as Captain Lewis did as "little better than a myth" is unfair to the Ikhwan, and those Arab and British soldiers that had to face them on the battlefield. [41]

Lewis is on safer ground when he discusses loot. But even in this matter the Ikhwan were organized and disciplined. One British-Indian Muslim named Faziluddin recorded in his diary: "Loot collected by Akhwan $ 35,000 out of which 1/5 went to the Akhwan bait al mal. Rest of the money distributed among Akhwan troops.... The Akhwan are said to be very honest in the collection of their booty and deliver it faithfully to their Amir." [42] Al-Rihani confirms this:

> Not one of the Ikhwan ever dares to conceal anything, no matter how valuable or trivial. After the sacking of a town or the taking of a *gazu* party, they come with the booty—valuable things, money, live wealth —and lay it before the Sultan or one of his generals for common distribution; and every brother, *motawwa'*, beduin or other Arab receives his share of four fifths of it, the other one-fifth going to the Imam or the State.... No partiality, no favouritism is shown; no special advantage or privilege does anyone, not even the Imam, enjoy. [43]

Majid ibn Khathila told this writer that the Ikhwan collected all of the booty and sent it to Ibn Sa'ud, especially gold and silver which they did not use or wear. [44] Judging from the austere manner of their living, the Ikhwan even with their booty did not enjoy a comfortable life. For the most part, a fine sword or rifle was the greatest prize of war, and if there were fighting among them with regard to booty, more likely than not it was for possession of a better weapon.

The Ikhwan, then, were fanatical soldiers who neither feared death nor sought the material pleasures of life. If they brought terror into

---

[41] Lewis did not do much better in predicting the capability of the future King of Sau'di Arabia, Faysal ibn Abd-al-'Aziz, whom he described in 1933 as "quite useless"; he is titular Minister of Foreign Affairs, but he does not work in connection with it at all."

[42] Diary of Faziluddin, Public Record Office, MSS, Foreign Office, Vol. No. 371-5148, Document No. E 12528, 1920.

[43] Ameen Rihani, *Ibn Sa'oud of Arabia: His People and His Land.* London: Constable & Co. Ltd., 1928, p. 210.

[44] Interview in Al-Ghat Ghat, March 1968. Sheikh Majid said that Ibn Sa'ud was very kind, and would often, in appreciation for a considerable amount of valuable booty, present the donor with a lovely maiden.

the hearts of their enemies, they also brought peace and security to a troubled land, [45] a peace which Philby called *Pax Wahhabica*:

> Its achievements in war, however, seem to pale into insignificance compared with its record in peace. Throughout the length and breadth of Wahhabi Arabia, there is now an atmosphere of peace and security which is quite unprecedented in the history of the country. One may wonder about in any part of it now by motor car or by camel without risk of molestation; and in the Hijaz, once the most turbulent and unruly part of the whole land the pilgrims can go to and fro without the slightest anxiety as regards the security of their lives and property. Yet nowhere can one see any sign of the troops or police on which in any ordinary country such peace and security are based. The old guardposts on the roads of the Hijaz and the Hasa have fallen into ruins and are no longer used to accommodate the garrisons of former times. There are a few soldiers and police in uniform at Jidda and Mecca, but elsewhere in the desert and in the districts there is no outward and visible sign of any guardians of the peace. The shadow of the Wahhabi army, hidden away in the Ikhwan colonies scattered about the great desert, broods over all Arabia. Potential disturbers of the peace know it and have on occasion suffered severely from its sudden onslaughts—so they disturb the peace no more. And the army, like the old legions of Rome, cultivates its vegetables and dates and cereals in its cantonments peacefully until such time as it may be called for service by its King. [46]

Comparing the old bedouin now transformed into responsible Ikhwan, Wahbah wrote:

> The bedouin's only worry was plunder and loot which he considered among the greatest of bedouin traits. Alas for the weak person caught up amongst the bedouin... the commercial caravans were under their mercy and dared not pass through their territory without their permission.... But now the Ikhwan are the protectors of the road. They respect the traveller... for the Muslim's blood and property are sacred... where the bedouin once feared death now they rush to it seeking martyrdom and a meeting with God, and the Ikhwan mother, when she bids her son farewell on his way to battle sends him off with this greeting
> "May God unite us in Paradise." [47]

---

[45] H. St. J. Philby, "Arabia 1926-1929: Three Years of Wahhabi Rule," *Contemporary Review*, London, Vol. 137, January-June, 1929, p. 715.

[46] H. St. J. Philby, "Pax Wahhabica," *The English Review*, (March 1936), pp. 313-314.

[47] Wahbah, *Jazirat*, p. 295.

CHAPTER SEVEN

EARLY PROBLEMS WITH THE IKHWAN

Ibn Sa'ud began his reform movement among the bedouin against the advice of several advisors and close confidants, [1] most notably among whom was 'Abdullah ibn Jiluwi, the satrap of Al-Hasa. Ibn Sa'ud was told by Jiluwi that to tamper with the bedouin was to play with a hornet's nest; one could never fully predict how much trouble would ensue, although trouble there surely would be. History has shown both Ibn Sa'ud and his anti-Ikhwan advisors to have been correct. As Ibn Sa'ud had intended, the Ikhwan did provide the vanguard of his military force which unified the peninsula in his name, but only after a series of problems and a period of conflict during which it was not at all certain that his word and sword would prevail.

The swift successes of the first Ikhwan colonies caused a rush to the Ikhwan standards. Flushed with a zealousness that could not be contained, the Ikhwan began the task of bringing the non-conforming tribes to obedience (*ta'a*). From the early beginnings of the movement until the end of 1919 when forced conversion came under Ibn Sa'ud's official ban, Najd and the fringes of the western and northern provinces were the continuous battlegrounds of the Ikhwan pitted against the tribes. Some tribes resisted and fought back, the most stubborn being the 'Ujman of Al-Hasa and the Shammar, the backbone of Al Rashid's power at Ha'il. Yet, not satisfied with challenging the orthodoxy of the bedouins' faith, the Ikhwan, as their numbers swelled and their powers increased, zeroed in against the Wahabbis of the settled Najd communities, people who had remained steadfast in the Wahhabi faith while the bedouin had long ago lapsed into the practices of popular religion.

When not raiding their neighbors, the Ikhwan passed their days in the *hujar* praying in the mosque and doing only the most basic chores. Envisioning themselves as the chosen of God, the elite of the Muslims, they remained idle waiting for the Islamic millenium. They let Ibn Sa'ud arrange for the digging of wells, and lived on the early provisions which he had sent, seeds and other materials, as preliminary assistance

---

[1] Jacques Benoist-Mechin, *Arabian Destiny*, (London: The Garden City Press, 1957), pp. 119-120.

pending their achieving self-sufficiency. As bedouin, they considered this type of manual labor beneath them; as Ikhwan, they considered that the least pre-occupation with material things was not consonant with Islam as they understood it.

The question of Ikhwan fanaticism against the tribes which refused to settle in the *hujar*, and against the law abiding citizens of the towns and villages together with the problem of Ikhwan indolence on the *hujar* provided Ibn Sa'ud with the first taste of the bitter problems that he was to have with the Ikhwan until the decisive confrontation at Sabila. Even now the Ikhwan were muttering that Ibn Sa'ud was not fully practicing the faith; they were annoyed at him for his increasing contacts with the English, and especially because of his prescription against their raiding the tribes that remained steadfast in the Wahhabi faith but which refused to settle.

By 1919 a keen British observer, Captain Norman E. Bray, saw the beginning of the problem and wrote to the India Office:

> Bin Sa'ud is likewise uncertain of his own position and equally fearful as to what may result... he recreated the Ikhwan, originally to provide himself, with a means of self defense against aggression, but for the present the horse of religious ferment has exceeded his expectation in its power and the rider finds it harder to control than he had anticipated. [2]

A few years later Alois Musil, after making a trip through northern Najd described the problem more specifically:

> The Ehwan, like other mercenaries, are hated and feared. They hardly form a suitable basis for Eben Sa'ud's empire, since, with their commander, they would be the first to reject Eben Sa'ud should he fail to follow all of the prescriptions of their creed. They now accuse him of being too mild toward other Muslims and too obedient to the Europeans, and their disapproval of his attitude is increasing with his introduction of various reforms.... [3]

To resolve the problem of indolence, Ibn Sa'ud sent out an army of religious teachers and other missionaries. They told the Ikhwan that agriculture, trade, commerce and industry were not contrary to Islam; that a rich Muslim was preferable to a poor one. The accumulation of

---

[2] Letter from Captain Bray to the India Office, 28 July 1919, Public Record Office, MSS, Foreign Office, Vol. 4147, Document No. E 129678.

[3] Alois Musil, *Northern Negd (A Topographical Itinerary): American Geographical Society*, Oriental Explorations and Studies No. 5, edited by J. K. Wright, p. 303.

wealth and property through work was encouraged; ultimately the Ikhwan accepted this interpretation, and according to al-Rihani some Ikhwan settlements had outpaced the older, more experienced settled towns and villages in industry and agriculture. [4] To solve the touchy problem of the Ikhwan attitude toward the tribes and villagers, Ibn Sa'ud called a conference of '*ulema*' in 1919. Five fundamental problems [5] were presented to them in question form for their consideration:

1) May the term "unbeliever" be applied to those nonsettled bedouin who are in all respects followers of orthodox Islam?

2) Is there a legitimate difference between those that wear the '*immah* and those that wear the '*iqal*, even though the beliefs are the same?

3) Is there a difference between those Arabs who first lived the sedentary life and those who recently became settled, i.e. made the migration (*hijrah*). [6]

4) Is there a legitimate difference between the killing of bedouin who live in the realm of Islam and the killing of original sedentary people or the recent immigrants?

5) Do the immigrants have a right to attack those who do not migrate, or to discipline them, or to threaten them, or to force them to migrate without having the permission of the legal ruler?

That the first question should deal with the bedouin who did not settle, that is migrate to a *hijrah* is not strange, since the idea of migration was foremost in the minds of these simple Ikhwan who interpreted literally the preachings of the Wahhabi missionaries and the texts which these missionaries passed out among them. The principal manual which these missionaries used was the Wahhabi reformer, Muhammad ibn 'Abd-al-Wahhab's book, Al-Usul Al-Thalathah wa Adillatuha, (*The Three Fundamentals and Their Proofs*). Several editions of this book were reprinted in 1918 and 1920 [7] especially for distribution among the bedouin.

---

[4] Al-Rihani, *Najd*, p. 262.

[5] For the full texts of the '*ulema's fatwa*, (official rulings) which contain these questions, see al-Rihani, *Najd*, pp. 433-434.

[6] This is not a new question in Islam. See 'Abd-al-Mut'al al-Sa'idi, *Shabab Quraysh Fi Bad 'Al-Islam*, (Dar Al-Fikr Al-'Arabi, 1960, third edition), p. 174.

[7] E. E. Calverly, "The Doctrines of the 'Arabian Brethern,'" *The Muslim World*, Vol. XI, 1921, p. 364. Philby records that this book was reprinted in Bombay: see Philby, *Heart of Arabia*, Introduction, p. XVII.

Under the third principle which is "Knowledge of Your Prophet Muhammad," the Wahhabi reformer discussed the concept of migration as it related to the Prophet, and how it relates to the Muslims that follow after him. He cites Qur'anic verses as proof of the *hijrah* which he defines as the "move from the land of polytheism to the land of Islam." He states that "the *hijrah* is incumbent upon this nation ... and remains incumbent until the Hour comes." That the duty of *hijrah* is "not suspended until repentance and repentance is not suspended until the sun rises in the west." [8]

This manual was used together with the works of Ibn Hanbal, to whose school the Wahhabis belonged. Ibn Hanbal interpreted the *hijrah* as being incumbent on the Muslims until the "infidels are killed, their voices stifled, and their movement stopped." [9] To the Ikhwan, then, the bedouin who adopted the true fundamentals of religion but who did not settle did not in effect complete the requirements for becoming a true Muslim. To support their reasoning they cited the reformer Muhammad 'Abd-al-Wahhab and Ibn Hanbal, and to support their raids against those bedouin who did not "come to obedience," the dictum that the *hijrah* continues until the enemy's voice is stopped was cited. It was no wonder then, that Ibn Sa'ud was obliged to call a conference of *'ulema'* to answer these simple Ikhwan.

As for the wearing of the turban, the Ikhwan were on weaker grounds in assuming that all Muslims should wear it in keeping with the practice of the Prophet. Sulayman ibn Samhan had denied that the turban was an essential part of a Muslim's dress because the Prophet Muhammad both before and after receiving the revelation wore the regular Arab dress, and did not wear anything that distinguished him from them. Samhan continued, "the turban, the cloak, and the robe are matters which are neutral, one gaining neither grace if he wears them or sinning if he does not; therefore there is no place for the statement that he who eats such and such or wears such and such is perpetrating an innovation or committing a crime." [10]

At the end of the conference, the *'ulema'* issued a *fatwa*, an official ruling, the final paragraph of which stated:

---

[8] *Al-Usual Al-Thalathah*, p. 21. See footnote for Ibn Hanbal's interpretation of the *hijra*.

[9] *Ibid*.

[10] Munir al-'Ajlani, *Tarikh Al-Bilad Al-'Arabiyah Al-Sa'udiyah*, Al-Juz Al-Awwal, (Dar Al-Kitab Al-'Arabi, Beirut), no publication date given, p. 288.

Our Answer ... to those Muslims present is that all of these things are contrary to canonical law of Islam, and what the *shari'a* commands, and he who does these things must cease and desist. If he repents and confesses his guilt, he is forgiven. If he persists in this matter and is stubborn, he should be given public punishment among Muslims. He should not be hostile or friendly except to those that the legal ruler orders. He who contravenes this goes against the way of the Muslims. This is what we believe and call God's witness to. [11]

For the moment, the Ikhwan were satisfied; Ibn Sa'ud's efforts were successful, but the trouble was to reoccur, for he was never fully able to stamp out the problem at its roots without killing prematurely the movement which had not fully fulfilled its purpose.

Ibn Sa'ud's problems were not all of Ikhwan making, although they did involve the Ikhwan. His conquest of Al-Hasa had made him a riparian power, while his conquests in the western part of the peninsula had put him in direct confrontation with King Husayn. The outbreak of World War I found a number of British agents at Ibn Sa'ud's court to attempt to induce him to declare with the allies and to open a front against the Turks by attacking the Rashids. In return the British provided Ibn Sa'ud with five thousand pounds sterling monthly as a stipend in addition to a veritable arsenal of arms and ammunition. [12] While Ibn Sa'ud needed and appreciated the subsidy, he knew that it was only a fraction of the money which was pouring into King Husayn's coffers. On 2 August 1920, Bin Sa'ud wrote to the British authorities:

Firstly ... Turkish agents working through bona fide tools of Sharif, Faisal. Secondly all my efforts arrive at friendly settlement with Bin Rashid useless. Relations now broken off. Have absolutely trustworthy information that Sharif recently sent arms and money to Hail, more about to follow from Madina. Thirdly, Koweit is negotiating with me outwardly, secretly, he is planning my ruin. Fourthly, Hussein, Faisal, Bin Rashid, Sheikh of Koweit all pretend friendship with England, but are hard at work against her interests. Support me I guarantee to allow no anti English intrigues among Arabs. On the other hand, if you continue to place me on par with those who are playing you false then let me know. I will cease troubling you with further communications. *Fifthly, you give your traitor friends titles and rich lands. I your true friend remain poorer than I was before ... thus my revenue*

---

[11] Al-Rihani, *Najd*, p. 434 .

[12] Report on the Operations of the Najd Mission, Public Record Office, F. O. 371-4144.

all mortgaged. I beg you request H. M.'s Government increase my subsidy and help me more financially.

I cannot carry on. Answer let me know how I stand. [13] (italics mine).

He knew also that professional Arabists such as Lawrence had convinced Britain that Husayn was the man of the hour and that Ibn Sa'ud was a passing phenomenon. While it was conceded by them that Ibn Sa'ud personally was a great man, it was estimated that upon his demise the state that he had created would crumble. [14] Husayn in turn, impressed by British successes in Europe and by his own gains against the Turks in the Hijaz, assumed a greater arrogance toward Ibn Sa'ud, treating him like a vassal, and provoking him and the Ikhwan. He was confident, on the one hand, that he was powerful enough to defeat Ibn Sa'ud militarily, and on the other hand that the British were committed to defend him and guarantee his survival. Husayn's attack against the village of Khurma, a frontier town between the Hijaz and the Najd, sparked a confrontation that once again threatened to turn the Ikhwan against Ibn Sa'ud. The Ikhwan insisted upon coming to the defense of the town in response to the plea for help from its governor, Khalid ibn Luwai. Ibn Sa'ud, on the other hand, tried to persuade them that the time was not ripe to meet King Husayn's forces militarily and that it was more important to attack the Rashids at Ha'il. His advisors, and even his father, [15] whose advice he usually cherished, counseled him to attack Husayn's forces. They were convinced that Husayn, who was supported by the British, and who attacked their religious brothers, was the heretic and the enemy, not the Rashids who were Muslims allied with another Muslim power. Sensing the danger of the problem, Ibn Sa'ud once again had recourse to a public meeting and called all the Ikhwan leaders and other notables to meet with him at Shaqra, a town located somewhat halfway between Riyadh and Mecca. There, confronted with a large group of townsmen, bedouins, and Ikhwan, he made his stand. First he let the opposition speak. Led by Faysal al-Dawish, the Mutayr chief and spokesman for the Ikhwan, they demanded to be led against the English and Husayn "whom the English have armed and who threaten our Brethren in the Faith in Khurma, or to attack the 'Ujman who, protected by the

---

[13] Transmittal of Bin Saud Message, 17 August 1920, Public Record Office, MSS, Foreign Office, Vol. 5064, Document No. E 11890.

[14] Lewis, *op. cit.*, p. 524.

[15] Armstrong, *op. cit.*, p. 119. See also Report on the Operations of the Najd Mission, part 15 ,the Khurma episode.

English, are forever raiding into our land and escaping back with loot and without punishment. All we want is to attack the foe of the Faith." [16]

Ibn Sa'ud well knew that the time was too early to strike against Husayn, especially at Khurma. He still needed to convince the British, many of whom had begun to doubt his loyalty to the allied cause, and some of whom were actively working to destroy the existing links of confidence between Ibn Sa'ud and the British:

> What real proof had IBN SAUD given to show his entire loyalty to GREAT BRITAIN? On the contrary as stated in my dispatch No. 20 dated 24th November 1918 to Öour Excellency—he appears to have threatened to sever relations with us in certain eventualities.
> If IBN SAUD has been throughout thoroughly loyal and straightforward with us what is the origin of the information given against him throughout Arabia from Aden to Damascus and obtained from all kinds of independent sources?
> I submit that it is extremely likely that IBN SAUD has "sub rosa" been trying to "run with the hare and hunt with the hounds"; the only other explanation (and an extremely improbable one) is that there is a very highly organized system of propaganda working against him throughout Arabia. [17]

Even more important than British officials' suspicion of him, Ibn Sa'ud knew that the Najd and his other holdings would never be secure if he attacked the Hijaz without settling the problem of Ha'il. At one blow, namely by attacking Ha'il, he could prove his loyalty to the British while simultaneously reinforcing the security of his own domain. He rallied all his wisdom in handling men and set out to convince the assembly that only by attacking the Rashids at Ha'il could they serve their religion and country. Finally using all of the persuasive power that he could muster, he convinced them that the real threat was at Ha'il not at Al-Khurma. The assembly's attitude transformed from one of hostility to one of enthusiasm. A month later, as he had requested, they all met at Burayda, Ikhwan, and the unsettled bedouin, ready for the march on Ha'il. This first attempt to subdue the Rashids was foiled by elements of shepherd tribes which, loyal to the Rashids, had given the alarm, thereby allowing the Rashids to lock themselves safely within the town walls. Not wishing to undertake a long siege,

---

[16] *Ibid.*, p. 124.

[17] Colonel Wilson's dispatch, 4 December 1918, Public Record Office, MSS, Foreign Office, Vol. 4144, Document No. E 1181.

during which the Ikhwan and other forces would possibly lose their zeal, he contented himself with allowing them to plunder the shepherd tribes, confiscating whatever valuables they could collect, and then returned home.

Once again he had managed to ride out a storm with the Ikhwan. They had now become a power with which to be reckoned. They knew that they were his trump card, and they were not reluctant to press the advantage. For his part, Ibn Sa'ud decided to bear with their arrogance, to swallow their accusations that he was too permissive with the foreigners and infidels, while having to face the accusations of Ikhwan enemies that he was fostering their sinister plans against orthodox Islam. Ibn Sa'ud was not to be deterred from his overriding objective: the conquest of the Hijaz; until he had accomplished this he would do nothing to alienate the one single group which could realize this objective for him.

The time for this came sooner than he had planned.

KHURMA: GATEWAY TO THE HIJAZ

Until the military confrontation at Khurma the war between King Husayn and Ibn Sa'ud was largely a war of words, a war moderated by the British who had vested interests in keeping their two Arab allies from a physical clash. After the struggle at Khurma it was only a matter of time when Ibn Sa'ud would be sitting as ruler in Jidda, and it was King Husayn who gave Ibn Sa'ud the pretext that he had long needed to put his foot in the door of the Hijaz.

British policy in the peninsula was based on several considerations which changed as the international situation changed:

a) prior to World War I, British policy was to acknowledge Turkish control over the peninsula, and to do nothing which would detract from Turkish influence there.

b) during World War I, it was designed to foment a revolt of the Arabs in the Hijaz against Turkish rule there, and to induce Ibn Sa'ud in Central Najd to battle the Rashid supporters of the Turks.

c) after World War I, it was to retain a balance of power in the peninsula by keeping Husayn sovereign in the Hijaz, Ibn Sa'ud supreme in the Central Najd, and the Rashids, who, after the collapse of Turkey, no longer posed a danger, as a balance between Husayn and Ibn Sa'ud. Retaining them as a power in the north added a third element in peninsular tribal politics. The latter position was made unequivocally clear in a coded message sent by the Government of India to the Secretary of State on 7 January 1918: [1]

> Ibn Rashid is at present in no position to do us much harm and affords an occupation to Ibn Saud while his total elimination from Arab politics might be an embarrassment to us. His retention will assist in the maintenance of balance of power between Ibn Saud and Shereef. We therefore recommend Cox should keep Ibn Saud in play by presents of money but that assistance in arms and instructors should not be given except very sparingly. Otherwise we seem to risk establishment of two powers in Arabia mutually hostile but to both of whom we have given pledges of support.

---

[1] Cable to Sir R. Wingate from the Government of India, 7 January 1918, Public Record Office, MSS, Foreign Office, Vol. 3389, Document No. 4423.

> We realize fully our obligations to Ibn Saud and have no wish to play unfairly by him. But we wish to avoid possibility of our generosity putting him in a position to upset equilibrium of Arabia.

British policy in Arabia came to the crossroads at Khurma, a relatively small, intrinsically insignificant settlement located on the threshhold of the Hijaz. Once again the British position was further complicated by a fundamental dearth of information on the peninsula in general and Najd in particular. Of the area "experts" Philby and Colonel Wilson were identified as champions of Ibn Sa'ud while Sir Reginald Wingate and Colonel Lawrence were regarded as pro-Husayn. This was officially acknowledged in a secret report [2] on the Najd-Hijaz crisis which went on to say:

> ... it may be argued that the advice of local officers is so conflicting as to make it impossible for His Majesty's Government to form an equitable judgment on the merits of the case. Sir R. Wingate warns us that King Husain would probably abdicate sooner than accept even provisionally the assignment of Khurma to Bin Saud; and Feisal has made it quite plain to us that he will not tolerate Wahabi occupation of the district. On the other hand if Mr. Philby's reports are accurate, the inhabitants of Khurma have adopted Wahabi tenets and espoused Bin Sa'ud's cause of their own free will; and their forcible reconversion or expulsion would be unpleasantly suggestive of religious persecution. [3]

What was worse than the conflicting opinions of relatively skilled observers of the scene was the failure of Husayn to comprehend fully his own weakness, the Ikhwan strength, and the extent to which the Ikhwan were calling the signals and forcing Ibn Sa'ud to follow their lead. That the Ikhwan constituted the catalyst between Ibn Sa'ud and the Sharif was not always understood by their opponents. While the British authorities felt no special indebtedness to Ibn Sa'ud, there was a great reservoir of good will toward, and the feeling of a moral commitment to Husayn. Thus, when the storm over Khurma broke, the immediate reaction was to go his support. It was only the rare observer who would almost forlornly call for a review of the entire picture as one officer did:

> In our anxiety to support King Husain, other aspects of the question should not be overlooked.

---

[2] Arabia: The Nejd-Hijaz Feud, Public Record Office, 11 January 1919, MSS, Foreign Office, Vol. 4144, Document No. 5815.
[3] *Ibid.*

Recent events show him much in same light as that which he has long been regarded by important sections of Mohamedan thought, viz., as a puppet dependent on British for support and (? devoid of) real influence other than that bought with British gold.

Ibn Saud, on the other hand, owes his strong position alike to his race, his religion, his geographical situation, and his personality; he does not depend upon us and I submit we should be careful not to be driven prematurely into an attitude of hostility to him and his adherents; in this connection it may be considered desirable to depute Mr. Philby to proceed to his camp and to enter into direct negotiations with him. [4]

The question of Khurma from the international aspects of jurisdiction goes back far enough in peninsular history to get entangled in a web of Wahhabi, Turkish, Sharifian claims on precedence. Whatever the disagreements between the various parties, whatever their legal rights and claims, the uneducated fanatic Ikhwan knew only one thing: their brothers in Khurma were being attacked by Husayn's forces and they insisted on going to their aid. For Ibn Sa'ud who had to reckon with the British and with Husayn, the question was not so simple, and he was willing to put the matter of Khurma up for arbitration. As it turned out, Husayn's impetuousness and arrogance gave Ibn Sa'ud the opportunity to play the role of the moderate party while having overwhelming striking force on his side.

Khurma was an oasis town of about five thousand persons, two thirds of whom were freed slaves, and the other third members of the Subay' tribe. In addition there were about three hundred *ashraf* residents there. It was a trade center between the Hijaz and Najd and a commercial center for traders of the Najd provinces of Washm and Al-Qasim. The *amir* of the town was Khalid ibn Mansur ibn Luwai, a *sharif* himself and a member of King Husayn's branch of the family. Since the time of the first Wahhabi Empire the overwhelming majority of the townsmen had adopted the Wahhabi tenets of Islam, and since the rise of Ibn Sa'ud in the Central Najd, a large number of these had espoused the Ikhwan cause. Among these was Khalid ibn Luwai himself, who, having become angry with Husayn because of the latter's insults to him, decided to throw in his lot with Ibn Sa'ud. When the village *qadi* (judge) also began to preach the Ikhwan doctrine, Husayn brought both Khalid and the *qadi* to Mecca where he reprimanded them and sent them back to Khurma. When Husayn learned that the

---

[4] Telegram from Political, Baghdad to Secretary of State, 14 June 1919, Public Record Office, MSS, Foreign Office, Vol. 4146, Document No. 90222.

qadi continued to preach the Ikhwan doctrine, he sent another *qadi* to replace him, but Khalid refused to admit him. Husayn then sent a military force to implement his order of installing the new *qadi* but this effort was spoiled by Khalid and his Ikhwan's military victory over the Sharifian forces. This was the basic conflict. Husayn was acting lawfully in his attempt to replace the old *qadi* with a new one, since he was the legal ruler of Khurma, yet Ibn Sa'ud could not allow members of his religious sect to be punished by another leader without being rightly accused by the Ikhwan of Khurma and of Najd of failing in his duty as their *imam* to protect them. The simple matter of the change in religious loyalty had in effect signaled a change in temporal leadership and authority. [5]

The situation that prevailed in Khurma also existed in Turaba, a neighboring oasis. While the *ashraf* owned most of the land, the majority of the inhabitatnts were Wahhabis, and many of the latter were Ikhwan.

As early as 1917 Khalid ibn Luwai had warned Ibn Sa'ud that King Husayn had intended to recover Khurma and expel its Wahhabi leadership. The following year Husayn sent four expeditions, all of which failed to recover the oasis for him. As long as the Sharifian forces were occupied with the siege of Medina there was little that King Husayn could do to put a full army in the field against Khurma. Shortly after the fall of Medina, Sharif Abdullah, son of Hysayn, sent a message to Ibn Sa'ud advising him of the victory, and closing with an allusion to the fact that the pre-occupation with the Turks at Medina did not allow the Sharifian Government to keep its internal affairs in complete order, but that those who had tried to corrupt and ruin the tribes would be dealt with. [6] In response Ibn Sa'ud sent a short note re-assuring him that he wanted only peace and that he would like to come to an undersetanding on the tribal question, [7] to which 'Abdullah replied with an innocuous letter sending his "warmest regards to Ibn Sa'ud's father, his children and the Ikhwan." Enclosed with the letter was a less formal attachment which stated: "I am your sincere brother, and I am prepared to help you as you require. It is not necessary that the bedouin question which has no importance stand between you and my father. How is it possible that a difference could grow up between two great

---

[5] Stanley and Rodelle Weintraub, (ed.), *Evolution of a Revolt: Early Postwar Writings of T. E. Lawrence*, (The Pennsylvania State University Press, 1968), p. 67.

[6] Al-Rihani, *Najd*, p. 244, for text of the letter.

[7] *Ibid.*, p. 245, for text of the letter.

men over Turaba and Khurma and the bedouin. I am heading for Mecca; I urge you to send one of your men, preferably one of your sons, and I will guarantee the success in smoothing over the difference between you and my father." [8]

After receiving the letters, Ibn Sa'ud learned that 'Abdullah was heading for Turaba, and he wrote to the British Government's representative in Iraq who replied that the report was only a rumor. [9] Ibn Sa'upd wrote a second time confirming to the British that his in information was reliable, and that the purposes of his writing was not to complain or because he was afraid, but because he wanted to keep them advised of the danger of a possible confrontation. This letter and a third in the same vein went unanswered.

In response to 'Abdullah's advance on Turaba, Ibn Sa'ud ordered a contingent of Ikhwan, composed of 1,100 camel-borne troops, to proceed to Khurma and Turaba to protect the people. He ordered Ibn Bijad to undertake a defensive, not an offensive, plan. To supplement his Ikhwan, Ibn Sa'ud sent a group of spies to surveille Abdullah to ascertain whether he was going to Mecca or whether he was proceeding to Turaba. According to al-Rihani, 'Abdullah told him later that he did not want to go to Khurma and that he tried to persuade his father of this but that Husayn, as Chief of the Hashemite army, ordered 'Abdullah to obey his orders. [10]

As Abdullah approached Turaba picking up reinforcements on the way, Ibn Sa'ud received information on his movements which caused him to write the following to 'Abdullah: "I find a discrepancy between what you have previously told me, namely, that you are returning to Mecca, and what appears to be taking place, namely an attack on Turaba and Khurma. This is contrary to what you have indicated to the Islamic world in general and to the Arabs specifically. Rest assured that the people of Najd will not forsake their brothers and that life in the defense of them means nothing ... yes, it is better that you return

---

[8] *Ibid.*, for text of the letter.

[9] The British probably believed reports of 'Abdullah's march to Turaba were only rumors. See Note by Captain Garland on the Khurma Dispute, 11 June 1919, Public Record Office, MSS, Foreign Office, Vol. 4146, Document No. 91521: "It was feared by British Advisors on both sides (Iraq and Egypt) that 'Abdullah's ill advised move must inevitably result in a collision of the rival forces, and it is quite probable that had 'Abdullah remained in Medina the present crisis would not have arisen. Indeed, had we been aware of the Emir's actual warlike intentions, we should have no doubt strongly protested against the advance instead of merely suggesting the impropriety of it."

[10] Al-Rihani, *Najd*, p. 246.

to 'Ashira, and I will send to you one of my sons or brothers, to negotiate, and let the matter be settled in the best interests of both
parties." [11]

On 3 June 1919 Ibn Sa'ud sent a separate letter to Colonel Bassett,
the British representative in Jidda, which pointed out that he had agreed
to put the question of Khurma and Turaba under arbitration, and that
meanwhile he had been respecting all the terms of the treaty between
him and the British Government. He pointed out that "I shall not be
responsible if he [Husayn] commits an aggression; and awaited (sic)
a reply to my reference for one month, but have received none up to this
day and my tribesmen did not commit any trespass or transgression
until after he (sharif) [sic] had committed the same and his actions
with the inhabitants of Nejd were contrary to law and reason inasmuch
as bloodshed and plunder of property were committed in spite of my
writings to him to withdraw to his territories when I should do the
same in order to avoid any embroilment until the disputes are settled
and the boundaries are fixed by arbitration through His Majesty's
Government; but he never replied. On the other hand he says it was
not his intention in collecting these forces to advance on Turaba and
Khurma, but that he intended Al-Riadh and Al-Ahsa and the destruction of Al-Khawarij, meaning inhabitants of Nejd. The proof to
substantiate my statement is in the treaties and the letters under his
signature and those of my enemies which I hold in my possession." [12]

Ibn Sa'ud was referring to an oral message which 'Abdullah had
sent via one of the messengers after he had arrived in Turaba and had
set up camp there. Shortly after his arrival, he sent out letters to the various tribes and surrounding villages demanding that their leaders either
come to Turaba within six days or that 'Abdullah and his forces would
wreak havoc on them. To Ibn Sa'ud's messenger he gave the following
exhortation: "Tell the Khawarij [13] and those around them what has
happened here. Tell them ... that we did not come to Turaba for the

---

[11] *Ibid.*, p. 247.

[12] Translation of a letter from Shaikh Sir Abdul Aziz bin Abdur Rahman Al
Faisal as Saud to Colonel Bassett, 3 June 1919 Public Record Office, MSS, Foreign
Office, Vol. 4147. The person who translated this letter for the Foreign Office did
a clumsy translation which is not atypical of the translations found in the archives
for this period.

[13] Literally dissenters, rebels, foreigners, i.e. people who come from the outside.
In one letter, 'Abdullah wrote to Ibn Sa'ud, he remarked: "the 'Utaybah tribe are part
of us and we are part of them, oh 'Abd-al-'Aziz, long before you and your forefathers
came to Najd." (See al-Rihani, *Najd*, p. 248.

sake of Turaba and Khurma only ... we shall fast in Khurma, God Willing, and shall pass the Feast of the Sacrifice in Al-Ihsa'...." [14]

Upon receipt of the written letter and the verbal message from 'Abdullah, the Ikhwan, instead of reacting with the fear and docility that apparently had been expected, screamed their war cries: "The winds of paradise are blowing, Where are you, Who seek it!" "You Alone O God, do we adore, From You Alone Do We seek Help!"

One hour before the evening prayers the Ikhwan were already marching toward 'Abdullah's camp, accompanied by an additional four hundred fighters that joined the original contingent. 'Abdullah, as was his wont, [15] went to bed for the evening, and allowed his camp to do likewise, without taking the necessary precautions. Flushed by the prospect of an easy victory at Turaba, the Sharifian arrogance was further inflated to the extent that al-Rihani records that 'Abdullah ordered a bedouin, who brought a message that the Ikhwan were attacking, to be beheaded, or beaten to death, depending on the version of the story. [16] In any case the Ikhwan approached 'Abdullah's camp, then broke up into three different groups: a cavalry group, one group led by Khalid ibn Luwai, and another led by Ibn Bijad. They struck as one full surprise-blow bringing down terror and slaughter upon the unsuspecting Sharifian army. First, the regular brigade of the army met its fate; then they hit the brigade posted near the tent of 'Abdullah, killing all the troops; lastly, the Ikhwan raced without faltering to the barricades behind which the artillery were located, and began the slaughter of the officer who was chained to his artillery piece. [17] The cavalry cut the escape routes with the result that only 'Abdullah and some of his officers managed to escape, fleeing in their nightshirts. [18] Those troops that were not slaughtered during the battle and who managed to find refuge in the town citadel were killed the following day. An eyewitness to the slaughter at Turaba, a youth of fifteen, described the scene to al-Rihani in Jidda five years later: "I saw the blood at Turaba running like a river between the palms, and for the

---

14 The implication of this remark was that 'Abdullah and his forces could roll across Najd to the eastern province rapidly. Al-Rihani, *Najd*, p. 253.

15 Note by Captain Garland on the Khurma Dispute, 15 June 1919, Public Record Office, MSS, Foreign Office, Volume 4146, Document No. 95840.

16 Al-Rihani, *Najd*, p. 254.

17 Al-Rihani, *Najd*, p. 256.

18 Note by Captain Garland on the Khurma Dispute, Vol. 4146, Document No. 95840. "It is worthy of note that although they had previous warning of the night attack, the regular officers who got away did so in their night attire..."

next two years everytime I saw running water I thought it was red, by God! I saw the dead piled up in the citadel before I jumped out the window. But the strangest thing I saw, Sir, was the sight of the Ikhwan during the battle stopping long enough to enter mosque to pray, then returning to the fray!" [19]

The slaughter at Turaba was perpetrated by the Ikhwan, of that there can be no doubt. However, that the blame should be thrown only on the shoulders of the Ikhwan and Ibn Sa'ud is debatable. If Husayn himself did not realize to what holocaust he was sending his son and his forces, surely the British did. They knew of Ibn Sa'ud's desire to arbitrate the issue. They also knew that to the extent Ibn Sa'ud desired to remain leader of Najd to that extent he was under the control of the Ikhwan who were not totally without justification in their demands that they should be allowed to go to the aid of their brothers in religion. The whole case had been spelled out for the British government by their various officers from the historic, administrative, and religious aspects, in addition to valid estimates that the Ikhwan would not sit idly by while attempt after attempt was made by Sharifian forces to oust the Wahhabi leadership from Khurma. Finally the British knew in advance that 'Abdullah planned to attack Khurma as the following coded message, sent to the Foreign Ministry, shows:

Decypher. Sir R. Wingate (Cairo) January 15, 1919

My telegram of 14th.

As soon as Medina Garrison has been evacuated we may expect King Hussein to reinforce Shaker and to instruct him to attack Ikhwan and Khurma and occupy that place. If Bin Saud makes this action a casus belli and encourages Ikhwan reaction we shall see fighting on an extensive scale in Central Arabia. I think best chance of avoiding this is to make Bin Saud understand that we do not oppose (? Sheriffial) [sic] action at Khurma; and I submit formal injunction as suggested in my telegram quoted above should be sent him wtihout further delay. Information in my telegram 48 confirms probability that Bin Saud has been intriguing with Fakhri and now that former's hopes of getting assistance from latter are dispelled he may show himself compliant. [20]

In November 1918, Philby had written, as the conclusion to an extensive analysis of the Najd-Hijaz dispute, the following paragraph:

---

[19] Al-Rihani, *Najd*, p. 256.

[20] Telegram of Sir R. Wingate (Cairo) to Foreign Office, January 15, 1919, Public Record Office, MSS, Foreign Office, Vol. 4144, Document No. 9710.

... whatever the abstract merits of the dispute between the Sharif and Ibn Saud over their boundaries may be, the actions of the Sharif during the past year have so alienated the sympathies of the people of Khurma that they will not submit to his rule in any circumstances whatever, the delicacy of the task confronting H.M.'s Government in the near future can be readily imagined. On the other hand, if they decline the heavy responsibility of deciding and enforcing their decision of the dispute, they will find themselves on the other horn of the dilemma in determining the attitude to adopt in the event of the outbreak of hostilities between the Sharif and Ibn Saud which, to me, seems inevitable and to be fraught with far-reaching consequences. [21]

Despite the reports of Philby and other British officials, especially in the Political Office at Baghdad, it appeared that British policy was to allow Husayn to pursue his policy of the reconquest of Khurma and Turaba to which the British had decided he had legal title. The synthesis of British hopes and estimates from the two conflicting opinions given above appears to be found in the summary of the India Office's estimate of the situation as of January 1919:

It is difficult to believe that Bin Saud will not realise the necessity, in the present situation in Arabia, of keeping his hot-heads under control. It should be borne in mind that, even if we do not succeed in averting a conflict, the consequences may not be so formidable as is sometimes apprehended. Past experience of inter-Arab warfare tends to show that the results are not always very striking or decisive. The prolonged hostilities between Bin Saud and Bin Rashid are a case in point; the Hejaz operations around Khurma are another.... [22]

Khurma and Turaba showed just how far the British underestimated the Ikhwan by equating them and their play-for-keeps method of warfare with that of the old time bedouins. The failure, then, of the British Government to put sanctions on King Husayn to prevent him from embarking on a military solution to the problem before attempting a diplomatic settlement places some of the blame for the catastrophe on its shoulders. It was exploiting both Husayn and Ibn Sa'ud to achieve its war objectives in the peninsula, namely, the containment of Turkish power in the area, and the preoccupation of Turkish troops and officers on the Arabian front to avoid their being released for duty on the more strategic European and Fertile Crescent Fronts. Once this objective was achieved, once the Turks had been defeated, the

---

[21] Report on the Operations of the Najd Mission, part 15, page 35.
[22] Arabia: The Nejd-Hejaz Feud, p. 4, MSS, Foreign Office.

British Government decided to allow King Husayn and Ibn Sa'ud to be swept along by internal developments that resulted in the bloody Turaba confrontation, as the following definitive instruction sent to Sir R. Wingate shows:

> His Majesty's Government have had whole question under careful consideration in light of recent developments and particularly of surrender of Medina, news of which has just been received. Their conclusion is that in altered circumstances nothing is to be gained for the present by further intervention in dispute between King Hussein and Bin Saud. Instructions as to ultimatum to latter are accordingly cancelled and no action need be taken on my telegrams of December 13 and 24th. Should it appear at any time that Mecca or other districts of Hedjaz proper are seriously threatened by Bin Saud or his followers whole position will have to be reconsidered. His Majesty's Government would feel bound in that event to take such steps as might be practicable to secure maintenance of status quo. [23]

Various writers, including al-Rihani and 'Abd-al-Hamid al-Khatib in *Al-Imam Al-'Adil*, record that Ibn Sa'ud wept when he arrived at Turaba and viewed the terrible slaughter. To the Ikhwan cries of "on to Ta'if," he told them to be content with what they had already perpetrated and had gained. Instead, Ibn Sa'ud returned to Najd, heedless of his advisors who told him that the Ikhwan were not only ready to proceed to the Hijaz, but could conquer it with no problem. For him Turaba had happened too soon; it was brought about only by Husayn's intransigence and unwillingness to compromise. Now that it had happened, he wanted to reflect on this episode that had catipulated him and the Ikhwan into the international spotlight. Ibn Sa'ud's feelings were not all compassion. He had never forgotten his ultimate ambition and objective: to conquer the Hijaz. To do so now, however, would result only in the intervention of foreign troops to rescue Husayn. Ibn Sa'ud knew that if he waited long enough, he could count on him to make another mistake and provide once again the pretext which would enable the Ikhwan to be unleashed against him.

Turaba was the precursor of the conquest of Ta'if. Once the news of Turaba's slaughter reached Ta'if the population began to panic. Members of the royal family and notables and merchants that had moved to the summer resort of Ta'if were returning to Mecca. British officials who felt the moral obligation to Husayn urged military intervention;

---

[23] Cypher telegram to Sir R. Wingate (Cairo), January 17 1919, Public Record Office, MSS, Foreign Office, Vol. 4144, Document No. 2390.

foreign consuls demanded that the British impose military, economic, financial sanctions against Ibn Sa'ud, and the British Government itself was almost in a frenzy as to what was the proper course to follow, first making decisions to threaten Ibn Sa'ud, and then changing them, in an effort not to alienate their position with him.

However, the question now ceased to be Ibn Sa'ud and became the question of the Ikhwan. The fundamental issue was how much pressure could be put on Ibn Sa'ud to restrain the Ikhwan, and assuming that Ibn Sa'ud was willing to do this, to what extent would the Ikhwan respond to his counselling against further raiding. Apart from this, the British Government was obliged to review the whole situation, reassess the problem in terms of its commitments to both parties and to its own area interests. The first obvious result of the debacle at Turaba was that Husayn's army was totally demolished and that it was unlikely it could be resurrected in the foreseeable future, if at all. Captain Garland put it briefly but accurately when he wrote to Allenby in Cairo:

> It is a sad fact that, in every conflict with the Ikhwan the Sherifian forces have been badly defeated. Abdullah's regular army has failed the expectations of the British officers who served with it during the war. After two and a half years' experience of war service it has failed when put to its first crucial test, and although heavily equipped with guns and machine guns it apparently failed to put up any sort of a fight against an untrained enemy armed only with rifles. [24]

Equally important as the destruction of the Sharifian army was the loss of prestige which Husayn suffered among the bedouin of the Hijaz who hithertofore had inclined to Husayn's rule because it was less austere, because they could pressure him into paying higher subsidies, and because whatever restrictions he may have imposed on intertribal raiding could be ignored with impunity, while they still could exploit pilgrim caravans. Now, however, few tribes, if any, wanted to be caught on the wrong side of victory, and as the Ikhwan missionaries made their way through the tribal areas and into the small towns and oases on the fringe of the Hijaz, they found the bedouins more responsive and some down-right eager to become Ikhwan. While Ikhwan missionaries [25] had gone out from Khurma prior to Prince

---

[24] Captain Garland, Note on Khurma, Public Record Office, MSS, Foreign Office, Vol. 4146, Document No. 91521.

[25] Telegram from Wilson, 19 February 1919, Public Record Office, MSS, Foreign Office, Vol. 4144, Document No. 27283.

'Abdullah's defeat at Turaba and had made numerous converts among the bedouins, after the debacle Ikhwan propaganda and activity became bolder and more productive. By June 1919 'Abdullah had reported to Colonel Wilson in Jidda that Ikhwan propaganda had become so successful that he estimated no tribes would come to Husayn's assistance in the event of another attack in the Hijaz. 'Abdullah further estimated that Ibn Sa'ud would not advance further into the Hijaz until all of the tribes of the Southern Hijaz had joined the movement. [26]

Prior to the rout of the Sharifian army at Turaba, Husayn had sent a list of demands to Ibn Sa'ud, via the British, and stated that unless these demands were implemented, he would send his forces against the Ikhwan. Among the demands to Ibn Sa'ud were the withdrawal of all Ikhwan from Khurma, and the "dispersal within thirty-five days of various Ikhwan concentrations; particularly those at Ghut, Artawich [sic], (group undecypherable) [sic], Utny and Ferthian—and prevention of communications by Ateiba to those places." [27] From the British Government, he demanded that Ibn Sa'ud's monthly subsidies be stopped, [28] to back up these demands.

After his decisive defeat at Turaba, one would expect that King Husayn would have been more amenable to a negotiated settlement of his outstanding problems with Ibn Sa'ud, or to attempt to approach the difficulties with diplomatic efforts, or tact. Instead, he continued to rush headlong into more trouble with a series of demands that could only alienate the British. In a rambling memorandum [29] sent over the signature of his son, Faysal, in which he tied the Wahhabi movement

---

[26] Telegram from Wilson, 10 June 1919, Public Record Office, MSS, Foreign Office, Vol. 4146, Document No. 86986.

[27] Cable from Sir R. Wingate, Cairo, 6 December 1918, Public Record Office, MSS, Foreign Office, Vol. 3390, Document No. 202098.

[28] Philby, *Saudi Arabia*, p. 278. Records that Lord Curzon's Departmental Committee had agreed to the severance of the subsidy, and that a cable to this effect was sent to Sir Arnold Wilson, who seeing it "had the wit to consign the missive in his pocket and 'forget' about it." However, this appears to be inaccurate. Wilson, himself, recommended that the subsidy not be renewed. (See Cable from A. T. Wilson, 4 March 1919, Public Record Office, MSS, Foreign Office, Vol. 4144, Document No. 34661). Ibn Sa'ud apparently was informed of this, since he wrote on 27 June 1919 "...I do not deserve to suffer this ... but ... it would not affect my financial position..." (MSS, Foreign Office, Vol. 4147, 19 July 1919, Document No. 21809). In reply to Ibn Sa'ud's response, the Political Officer in Baghdad wrote: "HMG ... express satisfaction at action of Your Excellency in returning to Riyadh with your forces. They have directed me to continue payments to you which have been temporarily discontinued." (MSS, Vol. 4147, Document No. 21809).

[29] Translation of a Memorandum on the Wahabite Crisis from H.R.H. The Emir Feisal, Public Record Office, MSS, Foreign Office, Vol. 4146, Document No. 108194.

to Bolshevism, and to the seditious movements in Asia, in which he claimed not to be a fanatic, but "urged that the Wahabites should be killed, however successful other measures might prove," King Husayn demanded that the British implement the following steps. The memorandum reads more like an ultimatum from the victor than an appeal for help from the vanquished:

1. Immediate recruiting. I will take steps at once.
2. Occupation by Great Britain of the coasts of El-Hassa.
3. Great Britain to send at once a Moslem Military Force to the Hejaz in spite of all difficulties.

Great Britain has shown during the War that no obstacle can ever resist her wishes.

4. Aeroplanes should be sent to Kermah before other reinforcements, to prevent any further disasters.
5. I should like to be informed of the progress made in importing tanks. When are they expected in Egypt? Date of dispatch to Jedda. A state of the force manning them.
6. The collection of war materials in a special Dump so that no delay should take place in the expedition of the same. I consider it essential that provisions and reinforcements should be sent gradually and at short intervals.

As early as January 1918 he had two other simple solutions to the Najd-Hijaz dispute. "The question of Khurma is due to Ibn Sa'ud," he wrote, "and can be very easily solved thus. Great Britain should sever relations with him...." [30] He coupled this solution with a threat to abdicate if this "recommendation" was not implemented, and if Britain did not pressure Ibn Sa'ud to order his Ikhwan out of Khurma. A year later, not having had any luck persuading the break in relations between Ibn Sa'ud and Britain, he persisted in his threat to abdicate, which led a senior official in the British Foreign Office to pen the following note on the cover sheet of a message containing this new threat: "Meanwhile, Hussein's constant threats to abdicate become monotonous and it might perhaps have a healthy effect to pretend to take him at his word and ask whom he would wish to designate his successor." [31] Once again his own worse enemy, Husayn had planted

[30] Telegram from King Hussein for Emir Feisal, 18 January 1919, Public Record Office, MSS, Foreign Office, Vol. 4144, Document No. 10448.

[31] Cypher telegram to Wingate, MSS, Foreign Office, Vol. 4144, Document No. 2390.

the idea of abdication in the minds of the very people who were making some efforts to assist him. His threats to abdicate were seriously picked up by the Political Office in Baghdad which suggested that "the abdication of King Husayn would, in the long run, probably be the best thing that could happen; it would make it easy for Ibn Sa'ud to withdraw, and it would make an adjustment of difference(s) between Nejd and Hedjaz possible, for it is mainly assumption by Hussain of his title that has brought about the present situation." [32]

In spite of the eroding effect of Husayn's machinations on the few friends he had left, they were making positive steps to come to this aid. In very strong words, Ibn Sa'ud was advised by the British Government that unless he withdrew his Ikhwan from Hijaz territory, his continued occupation of those areas would be construed as his "having adopted attitude of definite hostility towards themselves." [33] The question of sending Muslim troops to defend the Holy Cities was being seriously considered, [34] and arrangements were being coordinated to have several aircraft sent to the Hijaz. However, it was soon realized by on-the-spot reporters that airplanes would not resolve the problem. Wilson felt "it imperative that aeroplanes should be sent in earnest of our readiness to help King Hussein, although I do not beleive a flight of aeroplanes would stop 20 or 30,000 highly fanatical Akhwan. Their arrival would also have effect on town people and may even induce wavering Arabs to rally to 'Abdullah." [35] The decision to send planes was made over the objections of the India Office, largely on the

---

[32] Political Office, Baghdad, 14 June 1919, Public Record Office, MSS, Foreign Office, Vol. 4146, Document No. 90222.

[33] From Secretary of State to Civil Commissioner, Baghdad, 30 May 1919, Public Record Office, MSS, Foreign Office, Vol. 4146 Document No. 83242.

[34] As early as January 1919, the British War Office was considering the possibility of sending Muslim troops, but according to a secret summary of the Nejd-Hejaz Feud dated 11 January 1919 Public Record Office, MSS, Foreign Office, Vol. 4144, Document No. 5815 this idea "seems clearly undesirable and is understood to have been dropped." By 11 June 1919, however, the matter was still under consideration (Document No. 86085 Vol. 4146, 11 June, 1919, since the Eastern Committee supported the idea while the India Office opposed it: "We have backed Hussein, for better or worse, and must support him now. If the I. O. persist in their objections... we must let the French go..." In a discussion with Wilson, the Italian Representative in Jidda, Cavaliere Bernabei expressed the opinion that the Ikhwan movement must be contained and gave the impression that a pretext was being sought to send Italian troops (Dispatch on Conversations with Cavaliere Bernabei, 8 January 1919, Public Record Office, MSS, Vol. 4144, Document No. 12831.

[35] Telegram from General Allenby to Foreign Office, 10 June 1919, Public Record Office, MSS, Foreign Office, Vol. 4146, Document No. 86805.

strength of Wilson's aforementioned plea. However, the India Office was given assurances that the pilots selected to accompany the planes would have experience enough to avoid unnecessary risks which come from the "inevitable uncertainty of aeroplane bombing." [36] Nevertheless, the India Office still opposed the idea of sending Muslim troops, either as an escort for the aeroplanes or for combat.

While these elaborate arrangements were being made, Ibn Sa'ud had already taken the steam out of the problem by returning to Najd; once again his own vision had guided him to the correct decision. An assault on the Hijaz could only bring down the wrath of Britain on him and his Ikhwan, and justify Husayn's accusations that they were a menace to peace in the peninsula. By withdrawing, Ibn Sa'ud left the initiative in the hands of the British and Husayn; if they wanted war he was ready, but he would not seek it. He correctly estimated what the British attitude would be, namely one of relief that Ibn Sa'ud did not press the advantage. Thus the year that began with Sharifian threats to remove the Ikhwan from Khurma in two days, saw the Sharifian army demolished by the summer. When winter came the British were counselling negotiations once again. Their efforts were directed to persuading Husayn that unless a negotiated settlement was reached with Ibn Sa'ud, another attempt to call for the Ikhwan withdrawal would only lead to a new conflagration in which Husayn's forces would once again be overcome. As for the Sharifian suggestions that the British would intervene, "no one knows better than His Majesty that British troops could not come to his assistance. He would be the last to invite or expect them to do so. In these circumstances, it would seem the height of unwisdom to provoke a further advance which His Majesty has not the means to resist.... The interest of both Governments are in fact the same, viz., to avoid any such calamity and, by an agreement, between the two powerful potentates principally concerned, to bring about a condition of peace and unity in the Arabian peninsula." [37]

Thus it was that Ibn Sa'ud's son, Faysal, was invited to visit London to discuss among other things the Najd-Hijaz question, to represent his father who had to decline the invitation because of the press of business at home. Fourteen year old Faysal's visit to London in the

---

[36] Telegram from India Office, Whitehall, 13 June 1919, Public Record Office, MSS, Foreign Office, Vol. 4146, Document No. 88374.

[37] Cable from Foreign Office to Colonel Wilson, 1 December 1919, Public Record Office, MSS, Foreign Office, Vol. 4147, Document No. 156742.

fall of 1919 was at an end when instructions were sent to Colonel Wilson to meet Husayn in Jidda for discussions. For the moment the Hijaz question was cooled off. Ibn Sa'ud was well isolated in Central Najd, but his Ikhwan stood guard at the gates of the Hijaz more powerful than ever.

PART THREE

THE DECLINE OF THE MOVEMENT

CHAPTER NINE

THE IKHWAN IN THE INTERNATIONAL ARENA

The events leading to the Khurma incidents and the subsequent military confrontation at Turaba propelled the Ikhwan movement into the international arena. Up until this time, the Ikhwan threat, its growing power, and its reputation for fanaticism concerned only that small cadre of professional British political and intelligence agents, and the rare group of non-British westerners who were somehow brought in contact with Arabia, i.e., diplomats, travellers. For the most part Ikhwan developments were discussed only at high level private talks between Husayn and his British patrons. As long as Ikhwan military activity was contained within the isolated hinterland of Najd, its potential for danger was largely an academic question. Ikhwan contingents bringing tribal elements into "obedience," missionary activity of intrepid Wahhabi preachers among the bedouin, the seemingly unending construction of new *hujar*, all of these were developments remote from the awareness of all but those very few professional observers of the Arabian scene. Early in its development, the Ikhwan movement was dismissed by the high British officials as an internal, religious phenomenon which did not threaten the well-being of the international community ,or British interests, regardless of how distasteful its reputation may have been. [1]

Turaba changed all this! Positioned at the threshhold of the Hijaz, the Ikhwan almost overnight became a stark reality to the outside world. The British were stunned by the magnitude of the debacle, while Muslim pilgrims and foreign traders in the Holy Cities and the port towns learned of Ikhwan ferocity first hand from the remnants of Husayn's defeated army. Foreign consuls at Jidda, Muslim and Christian alike, could feel the menace by sheer geographical proximity, and Muslim Governments, such as India, viewed the developments in the Islamic Holy Land with grave concern.

Alarmed at the implications of the Ikhwan victory the Italian representative at Jidda, Cavaliere Bernabei, as earlier noted, suggested to Colonel Wilson that the Ikhwan movement should be destroyed through a joint Anglo-French-Italian expedition against Najd, emanating from

---

[1] Letter from Sir Reginald Wingate, 3 October 1918, Public Record Office, MSS, Foreign Office, Vol. 3390, Document No. 177596. See cover sheet for notation.

Basra and Jidda simultaneously. [2] In Mecca, Husayn was describing the Ikhwan spectre as a Bolshevik motivated menace, a theme which was coincidentally, if not deliberately echoed in the partisan reporting of some British political officers.

As early as 1918, the German vice-consul expressed concern over an intra-bedouin feud involving Ibn Bijad [3] and other elements within the 'Utaybah tribe that had not converted to the Ikhwan life, and by 1922 French intelligence reports had traced Ikhwan missionary activity as far as Syria. [4] Yet it was the British who really felt the brunt of Ikhwan power, for it was they who had to hold the Ikhwan at bay for the rest of the international community. The British, then, were quite pleased that Ibn Sa'ud did not press the advantage and embark upon a military campaign against the Hijaz, but they did not remain idle. Instead, they began a new policy of intrigue: wooing Ibn Rashid back into an alliance with Husayn in order to form a strong counter-balance to Ibn Sa'ud. They were even prepared to provide their former enemy a subsidy. [5]

Ibn Sa'ud was not to be outdone. He had returned contentedly to Najd after the Turaba victory because he knew that to move on the Hijaz would be to force the British to oppose him militarily, thereby postponing indefinitely, if not destroying forever, his dream of con-quering the Hijaz. Further, Ibn Sa'ud had outstanding problems with Kuwait, and the Rashids at Ha'il were still a thorn in his side. To counterbalance British collusion with the Rashids, he made contact with the French in Damascus. [6] He was delighted with French opposi-tion to the rule of Husayn's son, Faysal, in Damascus; by 1922 British intelligence agents had collected a report of a secret treaty between him and the French whereby the French would pay him a substantial sub-sidy, and provide him with a considerable amount of arms in exchange for continued attacks against the Hijaz tribes loyal to the Sharifian ruler there, and against the Arabs in Transjordan under his brother, 'Abdullah. [7] Although nothing in detail is later heard of a Saudi-

---

[2] Colonel C. E. Wilson's conversation with Cavaliere Bernabei, *op. cit.*

[3] Decypher of telegram from Sir R. Wingate (Cairo), 8 January 1918, Public Record Office, MSS, Foreign Office, Vol. 3389, Document No. 4067.

[4] Appreciation of the Wahabi Movement by the French Army, 31 August 1922, Public Record Office, MSS, Foreign Office, Vol. 7715, E 11187/248/91.

[5] Decypher of Allenby telegram from Cairo, 9 June 1919, Public Record Office, MSS, Foreign Office, Vol. 4146, Document No. 85980.

[6] Armstrong, *op. cit.*, p. 140 .

[7] Neutral View on Alleged French Treaty With Ibn Saud, 20 September 1922, British Public Record Office, MSS, Foreign Office, Vol. 7714, Document No. E 9565.

French entente, the British were not slow to realize that such a pact could materially change the balance of power in the Arab East. With the British Government already undertaking an agonizing reappraisal of its pro-Sharifian policy, the possibility of a French supported Saudi state may well have expedited its ultimate decision to remain neutral between the ruler of the Hijaz and the Sultan of Najd: after Turaba, British policy finally evolved into a position of non-interference in the dispute as long as it remained an internal matter between the two rulers, both of whom were friends of the British Crown.

While Ibn Sa'ud was keeping his political and military options open, the Ikhwan were busy acting as catalysts in bringing latent problems to the foreground. One festering problem was the increasingly hostile posture adopted by Sheikh Salim, the ruler of Kuwait. After the death of Sheikh Mubarak, Ibn Sa'ud's original Kuwaiti patron, and the death of Mubarak's son, Jabir, who succeeded him, Salim, Jabir's brother, the new ruler, aggravated the natural differences that were sure to exist between Ibn Sa'ud, as ruler of bordering Najd, and any Kuwait ruler, however friendly they may desire to be. No Kuwait government could be pleased with the prospect of a single powerful ruler controlling the peninsula, be he a Rashid, a Sa'ud, or a Sharif. A city of merchants and traders, Kuwait depended on a free flow of goods and tradesmen into the city. A large part of its economy also depended on smuggling. Economic and political differences caused the Kuwait Government to prohibit Najdi traders from the town, [8] while, in turn, Ikhwan leaders prohibited all "true Muslims" from purchasing any products which came from or via Kuwait, or to visit that "sin city" of the Gulf until it had forsaken its laxity in matters of religion and morals and returned to the correct Islamic path. The Ikhwan declared Kuwait a den of iniquity and even transient travellers from the city had to be quarantined before they could enter Al-Artawiyah in order to insure that they had not been contaminated ideologically by their fleeting contact with the citizens of Kuwait. Further aggravating the already abrasive relationship between Najd and Kuwait was Salim's support for the 'Ujman tribe, the notorious, implacable enemy of the Al Sa'ud, and for whom Ibn Sa'ud had an insatiable distrust. The 'Ujman had twice pretended to be his loyal subjects, and twice they had betrayed him. [9] He vowed to punish them severely. Salim's support for the 'Ujman, seriously eroded

---

[8] Arabia Series, Part X, Memo from Officiating Civil Commissioner, Baghdad, 10 May 1919, British Public Record Office, MSS, Foreign Office, Vol. No. 4147.

[9] Philby, Najd Mission, page 12.

whatever hope there was for a reconcilation between these two men.

The crisis erupted when Salim sent a force of his men to compel Ikhwan settlers of the Mutayr tribe at a site called Qarya to abandon the settlement on the grounds that it was Kuwaiti territory. Several battles ensued, the most notable being at Al-Jahra on 10 October 1920 with the Ikhwan under the leadership of Faysal al-Dawish emerging victorious. The rout of the Kuwaitis and the possible onslaught of the Ikhwan against the city itself caused the British to send gunboats to Kuwaiti waters and to place aircraft on alert, a powerful reminder that they were committed to the defense and protection of their protege. [10] These Ikhwan military operations, however, cleared out forever Kuwaiti shepherds and flocks from the area, and resulted in these lands becoming an integral and internationally recognized part of Najd based on the Najd-Kuwait Border Agreement signed at 'Uqayr on 7 December 1922. [11] This agreement constituted the first territorial limit that Ibn Sa'ud agreed to impose on himself.

With the Kuwait matter settled, Ibn Sa'ud then led his armies against the Rashid capital at Ha'il. Unlike the battle at Turaba in the west and Al-Jahra in the east, both of which were undertaken only by the Ikhwan, the army which attacked Ha'il had non-Ikhwan units. However, the Ikhwan forces, under the command, once again of Faysal al-Dawish, provided that zenophobic leaven which turned the battle into a religious crusade, as well as a political-military contest. Further, the Shammar tribe had long been a target of Ikhwan proselytizing; this, together with the tragic Rashid family disputes which resulted in fraternal killings, further increased their vulnerability even before the unified military force of Ibn Sa'ud pounded on the gates of the walled city. After a fifty-five day siege the city fell, having suffered the woes of a city in the state of war for more than one year. On 20 November 1921 Ibn Sa'ud accepted the surrender of the city. The Ikhwan were not allowed to rampage through the town, or to loot it. Ibn Sa'ud appointed a local resident of Ha'il as its governor, so as to reduce the sting of conquest. He left the city to move once again into its old routine and adjust itself to becoming part of his domain.

The fall of Ha'il opened the Jawf, Wadi Al-Sirhan, and the Sakaka

---

[10] Al-Rihani, *Najd*, p. 274.

[11] *Majmu'at Al-Mu'ahadat min 'Am 1341-1350 Hijriyah Al-Muwafiq 1922-1931 Miladiyah*, Al-Tab'a Al-Ula 'Am 1350, (Collection of Treaties, 1929-1931, Saudi Arabian Ministry of Foreign Affairs), pp. 6-7. Matba's Umm Al-Qurah bi Makkah Al-Mukarimah, Wizarat Al-Kharijiyah, Makkah Al-Mukarimah.

areas—the tribal grounds of the Al-Ruwalah—to the attacks of the Ikhwan. Earlier the Ikhwan missionaries had planted their faith there also, and with the fall of Ha'il elements of the population revolted against their chief, Nuri Sha'lan, and Ibn Sa'ud sent a camel corps of one hundred men to assist them. Other Sha'lan leaders were forced to leave, and the area fell almost bloodlessly to the Ikhwan. [12] Now at the northern fringes of the peninsula, in full control of the Wadi Al-Sirhan, which was a natural highway leading into the heart of Transjordan, the Ikhwan shadow fell on Palestine and Syria.

Sir Herbert Samuel, the British High Commissioner for Palestine, while not optimistic about the chances of an armed recovery of this territory on behalf of 'Abdullah of Transjordan, raised the fear that Wahhabi propaganda already appearing in Transjordan had created a clear danger to Palestine. [13] Philby too felt that the fall of the Jawf was a *fait accompli* which must be accepted, but urged the government to avoid a "policy of drift which would inevitably expose the Transjordan area to Wahhabi infiltration and involve it in chaos." [14] He warned that:

> the definite occupation of Jauf by Ibn Saud must spell the breakdown of the Sharifian policy, on which His Majesty's Government have set their official imprimatur. The proximity of the oasis to Azraq via the Wadi Sirhan, to Ma'an and to Tabuk, the last two being stations on the Hijaz Railway line, would place Ibn Saud in a position to paralyse the administration both of the Hijaz and of Trans Jordan, which as His Majesty's Government are well aware, are based on the slenderest of foundations... [15]

The Ikhwan did not leave the Transjordan border tranquil for long. Shortly after the conquest of Ha'il, a force of 1,500 Ikhwan made a record breaking march from mid Najd [16] to the heart of Jordan wreaking havoc with the towns near Amman and ruthlessly killing male children as well as adults. The British gave chase with planes, vehicles, and armored cars, and decimated the Ikhwan. Of the 1,500

---

[12] Telegram from the High Commissioner for Palestine, 28 July 1922, Public Record Office, MSS, Foreign Office, Vol. 7714, Document No. 8278.

[13] *Ibid.*

[14] Disptach from Mr. Philby on the Wahhabi Movement, 3 August 1922, Public Record Office, MSS, Foreign Office, Vol. 7714, Document No. 40733.

[15] *Ibid.*

[16] Armstrong, *op. cit.*, p. 148 identifies the Ikhwan as Harb bedouin from Shaqra; Nasr, *op. cit.*, page 167, gives them as 'Utaybah Ikhwan from Sajir.

that made the improbable march, only eight returned and were abruptly punished by Ibn Sa'ud for conducting an unauthorized raid.

Once again the Ikhwan confronted the English! It seemed to them that those 'Christian devils' were everywhere: they protected the Kuwaiti Amir, Salim, and saved him from receiving his just punishment at their hands; they had intimidated their Imam, Ibn Sa'ud, who feared British power and the loss of the 60,000 pounds sterling annual subsidy. Now at the threshold of Transjordan, the Ikhwan saw the British as military protectors of Amir 'Abdullah, whom they had only yesterday defeated at Turaba.

Nevertheless the Ikhwan advance continued, following a usual pattern, Wahhabi missionaries preceeding the arrival of the military contingents. By July 1922 these missionaries were reported actively proselytizing in Damascus. [17] In August of that year reports that the Ikhwan were operating in Sinai caused Winston Churchill, then Secretary of State for the Colonies, to ask the Foreign Office to query the Governor of Sinai about the spread of the Ikhwan movement in that region. Allenby replied on 12 September that a force of 1,500 Wahhabis were reported to be near Al-'Aqabah advancing northward, and noted that he had authorized the use of British and Egyptian troops to intervene if it became necessary. [18]

These Ikhwan attacks against the northern neighbors resulted in an Anglo-Najdi agreement on the borders formalized at the 'Uqayr meeting in general terms, and then officially agreed upon at the Hada Coonference on 2 November 1925.

Ibn Sa'ud had consolidated his east and north flanks, although at the expense of his popularity with the Ikhwan. An astute politician, he knew only too well that the British presence in Kuwait, Iraq and Jordan were based on valuable vested interests which they would not relinquish easily. The Ikhwan could not comprehend this, hence could not appreciate the limitations which British power placed on Ibn Sa'ud. They considered his agreements with the British, on border delineations, as examples of his catering to the Christians. However annoyed they may have been, as long as the real prize—the Hijaz—was still to be claimed, the Ikhwan could be diverted from the border developments. Ibn Sa'ud, now that the Kuwait and Jordan matters were settled,

---

[17] Disptach from Consul Palmer in Damascus, 3 July 1922, Public Record Office, MSS, Foreign Office, Vol. 7714, Document No. E 7361.

[18] Telegram from the High Commissioner on Palestine, Public Record Office, MSS, Foreign Office, Vol. 7714, Document No. 8278, 1922.

was disposed to move against the Hijaz. His policy of patience had
paid off, not only in resolving the problems of Ha'il and Jawf too,
but because in the interim Husayn had made himself even more un-
popular and had all but completely lost the sympathy and support of
the British. From a pro-Husayn policy, British interests had developed
into a stance of neutrality in an internal quarrel between two Kings,
both of whom were friends of the Crown. Even Husayn's sons, Abdullah, now Amir of Trans Jordan and Faysal, now King of Iraq were
disenchanted with the idealistic, but totally impractical policy of their
father.

That Ibn Sa'ud, from the advent of his power in Riyadh in 1901
intended to reclaim the Hijaz as his rightful inheritance, his ancestral
birthright, cannot be doubted. He had made this clear in many private
and public statements. Now the road to the Hijaz was open to him,
and all that he needed was a *casus belli*. True to form, Husayn provided
several, not the least of which was his assuming the title of *khalifah*
(calif), after the califate was abolished by Ataturk in Turkey; his
giving himself the title of King of the Arabs, and finally his prohibiting
the Ikhwan to make the pilgrimage on the grounds that they constituted
a physical threat to the safety of the foreign pilgrims. As Husayn
added to the list of provocations, which annoyed not only Ibn Sa'ud
personally, but enraged the Ikhwan *en masse*, the Ikhwan continued
to exert pressure on their Imam until he could no any longer resist
their demands. By this time, however, he was not inclined to resist
them.

On 5 June 1924, [19] 'Abd-al-Rahman, Ibn Sa'ud's father, presided
over a conference of Najdi *'ulema'*, tribal chiefs, Ikhwan, and tribal
notables. After noting that he had received a large number of letters
from the Ikhwan expressing their desire to make the pilgrimage to
Mecca and complaining that Husayn had prohibited their exercise of
this inalienable right, 'Abd-al-Rahman, pointing to his son, opened the
floor to a discussion of their complaints. Ibn Bijad, the fanatical 'Utaybah leader, also known as Sultan al-Din (the sultan of religion),
spoke for the Ikhwan. He noted that after three and one half years,
their patience had been exhausted. They were prepared to go to Mecca
to make the pilgrimage, either peacefully or by force if necessary.
Other Ikhwan spoke up, also, supporting Ibn Bijad and recounting
all of the provocations which Husayn had flung at them during the

---

[19] 'Attar, *op. cit.*, p. 281.

past years. They demanded that Ibn Sa'ud lead them against Husayn.
After acquiring an opinion from the *'ulema'* on the validity of making
war in order to guarantee the right to perform the pilgrimage, Ibn
Sa'ud announced to the assembly that the previous policy of patience
and negotiation had failed, but that their rights would not be surrendered, nor their interests abandoned. [20] Amid cries of "to the Hijaz,
to the Hijaz," the assembly broke up to prepare for the oncoming
battle. [21]

At the conclusion of the conference, a statement was issued to the
Arab-Islamic world over the signature of Ibn Sa'ud's second oldest
living son, Prince Faysal, in which Husayn's failure to listen to the
complaints of the people denied the right of pilgrimage was noted as
well as Husayn's provocative self-appointment as calif. The statement
reassured the Arab world that Najd had no territorial ambitions, and
would act as the agent of the rest of the Arab world to clear out the
Hijaz of the incompetent rulers. The statement gained much support
from India's large Muslim population which was annoyed at Husayn's
disregard for tradition by unilaterally assuming the title of calif, as well
as his inability to bring stability to the Holy Land where pilgrims were
exploited both by the urban merchants and tribal bandits. Reports of
Husayn's personal business monopolies connected with the pilgrimage,
i.e., the cost of beasts of burden to carry the pilgrims, and the prices
of water, were allowed to circulate, perhaps in somewhat exaggerated
form in order to denigrate him further among world Muslim public
opinion, and to justify Ibn Sa'ud's campaign to rid the Holy Land
from the incompetent sharifian rule.

The Riyadh Conference having decided to invade the Hijaz, Ibn
Sa'ud mobilized his forces, sending some to probe the borders of Iraq
and Transjordan, thereby feinting possible attacks on those countries,
which would prevent the rulers from going to the aid of their father,
while other forces were sent straight in the direction of the Hijaz.
Ikhwan forces were already located at Turaba and Khurma, and their
leaders, Khalid ibn Luwai and Sultan ibn Bijad were ordered to move
in the direction of Ta'if. The overall command of these Ikhwan forces
was given to Khalid ibn Luwai; it was composed of sixteen brigades
(*liwa*) as follows:

---

[20] Al-Rihani, Najd, pp. 236-237.
[21] Salah al-Din al-Mukhtar, *Tarikh Al-Mamlakah Al-'Arabiyah Al-Sa'udiyah* (History of the Kingdom of Saudi Arabia) (Beirut: Dar Maktaba Al-Hayat, 1958, two
volumes), pp. 289-290, vol. 2.

Brigade Commander	Name of the Hijra
"Khalid ibn Luwai Campaign Commander	Khurma and Taraba
Sultan ibn Bijad	Al Ghat-Ghat
'Aqab ibn Yahya	Sajir
Jahiah ibn Humayd	'Arwa
Nafil ibn Tuwayq	'Usayla
Qad'an ibn Darwish	Al-Artawiyyah
'Abd al-Muhsin ibn Husayn	Al-'Ammar
Fayhan ibn Samil	Ranya
'Abdullah ibn Sa'mar	Al-Radaniyah
Tha'ar ibn Al-Zami'a	'Arja
Hizam ibn 'Umar	Al-Rayn Al-Ulya
Hathal ibn Suaydan	Al-Rayn Al-Sifla
Mu'ayd ibn 'Abud	Al-Nasf
Hizam al-Mumaydani	Sabha
Majid ibn Humayd	Halban
Hathal ibn Fahd	Al-Rawdha" [22]

The forces were allowed to move once the pilgrimage, which was at its peak when the Riyadh Conference decided to invade the Hijaz, was completed, and the pilgrims had left the Holy Land. By September of 1924, all but a few pilgrim stragglers were left in Mecca and Medina. That same month the united Ikhwan force under Khalid ibn Luwai attacked small settlements around Ta'if and occupied Kalakh Castle, and Al-Ukhaydhir. By the time various local tribes joined his standard, he could count about three thousand warriors under his command. When Ta'if itself was attacked, the Hashemite forces, superior in number, training, and equipment were routed, and the commanders of the military units, the leading personalities in town, some employees and their families fled Ta'if at night, under the cover of artillery, abandoning the inhabitants of the town to their fate. From here, accounts of the conquest of Ta'if vary.

Some writers claim that the gates of the city were opened up by the citizens, that the Ikhwan marched in peacefully, but were then set upon, thereby incurring their wrath and causing the ensuing slaughter; [23] some sources lay the tragedy at the foot of the Hijazi tribes which joined the Ikhwan forces; [24] others blame Khalid ibn Luwai,

---

[22] 'Attar, op. cit., p. 284.

[23] Armstrong, op. cit., p. 167. He is sympathetic to the Ikhwan.

[24] London Times Clippings (Arabia), July 1920-April 1926, Pilgrims' Account of the Taif Massacre, October 1924.

and Sultan ibn Bijad, [25] since they were in command of the Ikhwan. In any case, what is not disputed is the bloody massacre of the town's male population, child and adult, and some casualties among the women. That houses were looted, offices and businesses plundered, and other buildings deliberately destroyed is also not disputed. News of the slaughter was brought down by terrified escapees who recounted the tale of horror at the hands of the Ikhwan and the bedouin that joined in the melee.

When Ibn Bijad entered the city finally at the height of the massacre, he ordered all of the civilians, mostly women and female children, into the gardens of the Turkish built Shubra palace, where he provided them with food and water pending their evacuation. Majid ibn Khathala told this writer [26] that he was the person responsible for rounding up the women and children and protecting them at Shubra. While admitting that the Ikhwan showed little mercy toward the military combatants, he insisted that innocent persons were not deliberately killed or injured.

The news of the Ta'if massacre reached Ibn Sa'ud who was still in Riyadh. Almost all writers report him to be deeply saddened by the news, and as having expressed regret that this victory should have come to him at such a price. He immediately sent an order to the Ikhwan commanders that they should cease and desist from such savage behavior, but given the time and distance for such a message to reach Ta'if, it arrived too late, and could serve only as a notice of his extreme displeasure. Later, deeply annoyed by the adverse publicity which the Ikhwan conquest of Ta'if had created, [27] and feeling morally responsible for the loss of life and property, he sent a letter to his advisor and confidant, Sheikh Hafiz Wahba, once again assuring non-combatants of complete safety for their persons and their property, [28] and promising to make compensation for those that unjustly suffered in the Ta'if battle. If the axiom 'nothing succeeds like success' is true, it can be unequivocally said that the struggle for the Hijaz was won at Ta'if, and that when Ta'if fell, so did Mecca, Medina and Jidda; if the Ikhwan committed atrocities in Ta'if, they also presented Ibn

---

[25] 'Attar, *op. cit.*, p. 288. He treats Ibn Luwai and Ibn Bujad harshly.

[26] Interview with Sheikh Majid ibn Khathila in Al-Ghat Ghat, March, 1968.

[27] Wahbah, *Khamsun*, p. 243 for the complete text of Ibn Sa'ud's letter. He was particularly annoyed by the accusations printed in the Syrian, Egyptian, and Iranian papers that his Ikhwan killed women and children. He sent a cable of denial to these papers over the signature of his son, Faysal.

[28] Wahbah, *Khamsun*, p. 245 for the complete text of the letter.

Sa'ud with the Hijaz, for slightly more than a month later, Mecca fell to the Ikhwan without a shot, Husayn having abdicated in favor of his son, 'Ali. While Ibn Sa'ud in Riyadh was discussing the best way to conquer Mecca without violating the rule that arms may not be carried into the Holy City, [29] Khalid ibn Luwai had sent four of his Ikhwan dressed as pilgrims in white linen loincloths (*ihram*) to reconnoiter the town. They found a city tightly shuttered, waiting for the Ikhwan tempest to strike. The next day about four thousand Ikhwan, all dressed as pilgrims, but this time carrying arms, descended upon the town. They were not allowed to loot or plunder; since there was no resistance, there was no need to shoot or kill. The Ikhwan did undertake, however, a systematic destruction of domes over mosques, pictures, and other "anti-Islamic" innovations. The fall of Ta'if and Mecca sealed the fate of the Hijaz and ended the Sharifian family's rule there.

It was the Ikhwan that occupied these two towns; not a huge modern army, but rather a relatively small contingent of troops armed with the most basic rifles, and perhaps a few odd pieces of artillery which they captured in battle, and barely knew how to use. The London *Times* correspondent writing from Alexandria on 16 September 1924 reported that the number of Ikhwan which conquered Ta'if did not exceed 2,000. [30]

Ibn Sa'ud and his forces were not yet half way to Mecca from Riyadh when the Ikhwan consolidated their hold on the city. Long before Ibn Sa'ud's dramatic arrival, Ibn Bijad and Khalid ibn Luwai had met delegations of the principal persons of the town to discuss peace and how best to avoid a Ta'if type of tragedy. These two leaders then sent a letter to the foreign consuls located at Jidda inquiring on their official stand on the Najd-Hijaz War. An answer, signed by the representatives of Britain, Italy, France, Holland, and Iran clearly stated that: "our governments are maintaining a completely neutral stand in the present war between Najd and the Hijaz, and we will not intervene in any way whatsoever in this dispute, aware as we are of your statements guaranteeing the well being of our citizens." [31] The Ikhwan were well in command of the situation; these unsophisticated bedouin were already treating with the elite of the Hijaz and representatives of the Great Powers before their leader arrived.

---

[29] 'Attar, *op. cit.*, pp. 289-307.

[30] London Times Clippings (Arabia) July 1920-April 1926, *The Wahabis At Taif*, 16 September 1924.

[31] 'Attar, *op. cit.*, pp. 306-307.

Ibn Sa'ud entered Mecca on 18 October 1924 dressed as a pilgrim to claim a prize that was already won. He had marched across the entire peninsula, accompanied by two of his brothers, Muhammad and 'Abdullah and a group of *'ulema'*, some contingents from the towns of Burayda and 'Unayza, and from various *hujar*. As he entered Mecca, he must have thought about his first efforts in creating the Ikhwan; how he was correct in bearing with their arrogance, their impatience, and their fanaticism, for there now waiting for him as he made the descent into the town were his Ikhwan, once again happy to see their Imam, once again eager as children to pass on to him the prize. All the advice, sought and unsought, on how to discipline the Ikhwan, that they should be disbanded, that they were a menace to him and to his ambitions, all must have paled before his triumphant entry, as he repeated the great conquests previously made by his forefathers. It was the Ikhwan who made this possible, but they received little credit, if any. And yet, had they failed, it would have been easy for Ibn Sa'ud, still in Riyadh, to claim that they moved against Ta'if and Mecca without his permission and without his knowledge, and that because they did, God did not grant them victory. This would have been a plausible excuse to his British friends too. The Ikhwan later felt that Ibn Sa'ud never fully publicly acknowledged the role that they played in reducing the Hijaz; they were irked by the claims put forth that Ibn Sa'ud and his family together with sedentary, non-Ikhwan bedouin had conquered the Hijaz. Yet, Majid ibn Khathila, who was among the Ikhwan at Ta'if and in Mecca, unequivocally stated that not a single sedentary villager participated in either battle, and the written record sustains his statement. [32] This does not lessen the role of Ibn Sa'ud who must be credited as the chief architect of the Ikhwan scheme. Certainly without his guidance, organization, his inspiration and personality, the Ikhwan would not have been the viable force that they actually were—this was proven later most decisively at Sabila. Nevertheless, it was the self-sacrificing Ikhwan, with defeat farthest from their mind—for death in battle was the key to paradise, the ultimate victory—and victory as certain as the existence of the God they worshipped who dared attempt the impossible, fought, and won.

It is beyond the scope of this study to examine the question whether or not Ibn Sa'ud ever had any real intention of allowing independent

---

[32] 'Attar's, *Saqr*, a sympathetic account of Ibn Sa'ud, brings out this point indirectly but nevertheless effectively.

or autonomous rule for the Hijaz, but his ingenuity and statesmanship in waving this possibility before the faces of the Muslims, as he prepared to advance on Medina and Jidda must be a hallmark of one-upmanship. Claiming to go to Medina only to purge the rest of the Holy Land from the vile rule of the Sharifian family, and to restore the dignity and respect to the sacred places, Ibn Sa'ud sent letters to the Imam of Yemen, and other Islamic leaders asking them to send representatives to a conference in Mecca to resolve the issue. [33] With the Ikhwan already at Ta'if and in Mecca, flushed with victory but not yet satiated, their reputation for terror and massacre still fresh in the minds of the world Muslims, there were few takers of this proposal—until Ibn Sa'ud had the situation well in hand, at which time it was too late.

Medina and Jidda surrendered after a year's siege only on condition that the Ikhwan would not be allowed into the town. Ironically, even in adopting a negative role, the Ikhwan were having a positive effect in bringing the Prophet's City, and the pilgrim's port into Ibn Sa'ud's domain. Having reached the sea, the saga of the Ikhwan really ends here—the climax is reached and their *raison d'être* no longer exists. It only remained for them to play themselves out on the stage of history. Now they constituted an embarassment to Ibn Sa'ud, no longer providing a counterbalancing benefit. The fact is that Ibn Sa'ud's vision and plans were much larger than what they could ever imagine. He was a genius, and they were just one aspect of his genius. They were spent of their usefulness. His job had just begun! He made them into that indomitable, fanaticial, uncompromising force precisely because that was the type of military-religious force he needed at that time. Now that he had achieved his dream, he most certainly would have prefered to send them back to Najd, in gratitude, with suitable rewards of stipends, land, rifles and ammunition—all the spoils of war—spoils which they did not want. What they wanted ,he could no longer allow; the continuation of the religious march, a march to no where because they had already reached the limits of their allowable expansion. Their Imam had affixed his signature to border limitations which he would either obey, or be forced to obey by the military might of the British Crown itself.

The Ikhwan soon learned that they were not welcome in the Hijaz. Denied the last fruits of victory—entry into Medina and Jidda—the

---

[33] Al-Rihani, *Najd*, p. 359.

Ikhwan found themselves replaced by the Wahhabi *'ulema'* of Najd, as Ibn Sa'ud's right hand, and except for the occasional Ikhwan who acted as a mutawwi', there was no place for them in the sophisticated society of the Hijaz. Their constant vigilance and insistence on the application of the most petty beliefs of Wahabism, almost put Ibn Sa'ud at war with Egypt. The ascetic Ikhwan, objecting to the use of bugles by the Egyptian army which was escorting the annual *mahmal* [34] to Mecca because it violated the injunction against musical instruments, rushed into the camp and were fired upon by the Egyptians. The incident was put under control by Prince Faysal, but the bad blood between Egypt and Ibn Sa'ud continued for ten years, symbolized by the break in diplomatic relations for that length of time.

And so the Ikhwan were sent back to Najd. They had literally worked themselves out of a job. They had been too successful. Back to Najd they went, nursing their grievances against Ibn Sa'ud, against the omnipresent English, against the infidel Muslims of the Hijaz, whom Ibn Sa'ud was treating so carefully, they thought, against the infidels of Iraq and Jordan whom they were never allowed to discipline properly. It is no surprise then that this dynamic force, sent back to Najd at the peak of its power and success exploded into rebellion. The borders with Jordan had been settled and were guarded by the British; the borders with Iraq and Kuwait had been delineated, and the British were there also. Prohibited from raiding outright, barred from raiding within the country ,with no more lands to conquer, the cream of Ikhwan leadership plotted rebellion.

Even with the Ikhwan gone, Ibn Sa'ud discovered that the Hijaz was not so easily integrated into his kingdom as were Najd and the other more remote areas. Control of the Holy Cities of Mecca and Medina made him responsible for the physical security of thousands of foreign Muslims who made the annual pilgrimage there. Administration of the pilgrimage with its gigantic logistical, housing, health, food, and security problems was no simple task. The responsibility of dealing with foreign diplomatic representatives, no longer as a regional Arab chieftain, but as head of an independent sprawling kingdom, placed new and serious burdens on him also. Finally, the matter of governing the more sophisticated liberal-minded people of the Hijaz, as contrasted with the simple, conservatives of the hinterland, occupied much of his time and effort. While populated by many tribes, the

---

[34] The *mahmal* is the camel borne frame which carries the elaborately woven *kiswah*, donated annually by the people of Egypt as the covering for the Ka'bah at Mecca.

the Hijaz was fundamentally urban—Ta'if, Mecca, Medina, Wejh and Yenbo setting the pace of the province—and its religious enthusiasm while no less profound than that of other Muslims in the peninsula was reflected in far less ascetic values and attitudes.

The Hijazis correctly anticipated that the Wahhabi grip would be tightest in the realm of religion. The memories of their forefathers' experience under Wahhabi rule were still vivid. Ibn Sa'ud did not disappoint them. Although one of his first official acts was to reassure them that he intended to govern justly, making no unfair distinctions [35] between them as citizens and the people of his ancestral Najd —as part of the surrender terms, he had committed himself to retaining the cities' employees and religious teachers and imams—he soon began enforcing a Wahhabi imprint on the religious administration. Conscious of the role which Wahhabism had played in his rise to prominence, in the form of the Ikhwan movement, as well as that of his forefathers, and under pressure from the Ikhwan [36] who were determined to purge the Hijaz from its nonconformist religious leadership and traditions, Ibn Sa'ud replaced a large number of the regular *imams* of the mosques with Wahhabi *imams*, instead of allowing each of the four *Sunni* schools to retain its own. There were now Wahhabi *imams*, qadis, preachers, and *mutawi'in*. More drastic than this was the launching of the Committee for the Doing of Good and the Avoiding of Evil [37] whose most zealous members usually consisted of illiterate, fanatical, bedouin who were only too eager to enforce the literal prescriptions of prayer, and the closing of shops during prayer time, in addition to enforcing the prohibition of smoking and other "immoral" habits. Ihsanullah, the Vice Consul for the Government of India described the Committee's activities colorfully, accurately, albeit with deep emotion:

> It has been given summary powers and it has brought a large number of Nejdi soldiers employed in its service. There are 20 Nejdi soldiers on behalf of the Religious Committee in each Hara, [38] thus their total

---

35 Ibn Sa'ud in one instance favored the Hijazis. He allowed their merchants to sell out their stock of cigarettes and tabacco, to save them financial loss. No new imports were allowed. In other provinces the sale and use of tobacco were punished by public flogging for the first offense.

36 Bond to Henderson, 20 July 1929, Public Record Office, MSS, Foreign Office, Vol. No. 13740, Document No. 3947.

37 Known in Arabic as *Ha'at Al-Amr bil Ma'ruf wa Nahy 'An Al-Munkir*. The committee is still active in Saudi Arabia, especially in Riyadh.

38 A small neighborhood.

number with the municipal jurisdiction of Mecca is 260, which is even greater than the military force kept at the Jedda garrison ... the presence of such a large number of the inhuman and unsympathetic element in each Hara of Mecca has naturally created a terror in the hearts of the public. These brutes being let loose are perpetrating all sorts of cruelties ... there is no law to restrain them. Especially on the occasion of the five times a day prayer, these incarnations of the devil wildly run through the public thoroughfares and enter the lanes in pursuit of the defaulters who might have taken shelter there, and on discovery fall upon them with all their might and beat them mercilessly. There is no distinction between good or bad, rich or poor, young or old, and even school boys of minor age are not spared. They lay (them) down on the public road and flog them indiscriminately. [39]

The people of the Hijaz could do little to resist these changes, and British officers resident in the Hijaz could do even less except to report these developments to Whitehall with the greatest disapproval. However, what the Hijaz lost of its freedom in technical religious matters, and of its less ascetic living patterns, it gained in an overall streamlining of rule, and in an increase of stability, and in public order. To this end Ibn Sa'ud remained there, having appointed his oldest living son, Sa'ud, Viceroy of Najd. Yet Ibn Sa'ud's long absence from Najd almost proved irrevocably disastrous. He hurried back to Riyadh in 1927 just in time to dampen the rising tempers of the Ikhwan, but this only postponed the inevitable military clash that loomed on the horizon.

---

[39] Report by Indian Vice Consul on Committee of Virtue, 14 August 1931, MSS, Public Record Office, Vol. 15298, Document No. E 4957.

CHAPTER TEN

THE IKHWAN AT THE RIYADH CONFERENCES

The Ikhwan returned to Najd with wounded feelings. Led by Faysal al-Dawish and Ibn Bijad, they felt that they were responsible for the great military victories which brought Ibn Sa'ud to his present position of power and they sincerely believed that without them he could not retain his control over the peninsula. They were the pillars on which his Kingdom rested, they thought, and yet Ibn Sa'ud had sent them back to Najd under a cloud. Once in Najd, the old deep rooted ambitions of al-Dawish again rose to the surface nurtured by the great power and influence which he wielded over the Mutayr tribe, [1] the prominence of Al-Artawiyah among the Ikhwan, and the significant position which he had occupied as the right hand of Ibn Sa'ud. Without doubt al-Dawish had become a legend among the Ikhwan, the nomadic tribes and the sedentary. Ibn Bijad of the 'Utaybah too returned as a hero. His Ikhwan of Al-Ghat Ghat had wrested much of the Hijaz from Husayn and were still feared throughout the country. Unlike al-Dawish however, who was always considered to be an opportunist, Ibn Bijad enjoyed the reputation of being a devout, sincere Wahhabi Muslim who was bent on spreading the Word of God, and was not out for personal glory or material gain. Dhidan ibn Hithlain of the turbulent 'Ujman soon became restless under the prodding of al-Dawish and Ibn Bijad, and not much encouragement was needed. Hithlain never successfully concealed his dislike for the Al Sa'ud and Ibn Sa'ud in particular, and he sought the opportunity to seek revenge against the latter's suppression of the tribe in the Al-Hasa. Each of them, in varying degrees of conviction opposed Ibn Sa'ud because of his introduction of modern inventions and innovations into the country, and because of the prohibition against internal and external raiding. All three leaders in due time raised the standard of rebellion.

Early in 1925 Faysal al-Dawish, accompanied by a group of his Ikhwan at the first celebration of the end of Ramadan in Mecca, had

---

[1] Faysal al-Dawish's extraordinary power over the Mutayr stemmed from his right to put a member of the tribe to death without a tribal conference, and on his orders alone, a privilege unique among the bedouin of Arabia.

sent down the lines which they had expected Ibn Sa'ud to follow; at
the meeting was Khalid ibn Luwai and other prominent Ikhwan:

> We thank God, on Khalid, and oh Ikhwan, for we have entered the
> Holy Land and have thrown out the Sharif from this place. We are
> soldiers of God and servants of his religion. We only want God's
> word to prevail and his religion to be victorious, and to lift the oppres-
> sion, remove innovations, and evil. [2]

By 1926, having returned to Najd, the Ikhwan became more specific
in their grievances against Ibn Sa'ud. At a conference of the Ikhwan
in Al-Artawiyah attended by chiefs of the Mutayr, 'Utaybah, and
'Ujman ,they lashed out against him for:

a) Sending his son, Sa'ud, to Egypt which was occupied by the
Christian English and inhabited by infidel Muslims.

b) Sending his son, Faysal, to London, the land of polytheism.

c) Using automobiles, telegraph, wireless, and telephones, all of
which were Christian innovations, and inventions of the devil.

d) Taxing the tribes in the Hijaz and Najd.

e) Allowing the infidel Muslim tribes of Iraq and East Jordan to
graze their flocks in the land of the Muslims (Arabia).

f) Prohibiting trade with Kuwait because if this was meant as
punishment because the Kuwaitis are infidels then the Ikhwan should
be allowed to raid them, and if they are true Muslims then why boycott
them?

g) Failing to force the shiites of the Al-Hasa to adhere to Wahhabi
Islam. [3]

In response to these grievances of the Ikhwan, Ibn Sa'ud returned
to Najd from the Hijaz to convoke a meeting of Ikhwan leaders and
chiefs; about 3,000 persons attended. [4] At the meeting held in Riyadh
in January 1927, Ibn Sa'ud once again reaffirmed his dedication to the
shari'a and re-iterated that his earlier promises to them about this had
not been altered. The meeting ended with the issuance of a *fatwa* by the
'ulema' in which all of the above mentioned Ikhwan objections were
answered, and which even covered problems not raised by the Ikhwan.

---

[2] Wahbah, *Jazirat*, p. 289.

[3] *Ibid.*

[4] Umm Al-Qura, No. 126, 10 May 1927. It was attended by Faysal al-Dawish, Ibn
Bijad, and all sheikhs of the Mutayr, 'Utaybah, Qahtan, Shammar, Harb, 'Ujman,
Murra, 'Anazah of Najd, Dawasir, Subay', Suhul, Bani Hajir, Bani Khalid, and
'Awazim.

Containing no decision on the telegraph since there was no precedent either in the *shari'a* or among the learned men, the *fatwa* ordered Ibn Sa'ud to prohibit the *mahmal* from entering the Holy Places, to refuse admittance to Egyptian troops carrying arms; it ordered the destruction of the mosque of Hamza because of its overtones of saint worship, demanded that the shiites of the Al-Hasa be obliged to accept Wahhabi Islam, make a profession of faith, abandon all forms of innovation in their faith and in their public assemblies, and conform to the rule of prayer five times daily in the mosque. They were also to study the Three Principles of the Wahhabi tenets and those that objected to this would be exiled. The Shiites of Iraq were to be prohibited from entering Najd. As for the villages and cities which came recently under Ibn Sa'ud's control, they were to be provided with Wahhabi teachers to teach the people the true Islam; the amirs of these villages were to be ordered to assist these teachers in carrying out their work. As for the taxes, the *'ulema'* decreed that they were illegal, but that the Muslims did not have the right to disobey the *imam* (Ibn Sa'ud) if he persisted in levying them. With regard to *jihad*, they deferred the matter to Ibn Sa'ud as *imam* saying that he had to make the decision, always keeping in mind the best interests of Islam and the Muslims. [5]

Acting on the recommendation of the *'ulema'* as set forth in the *fatwa*, Ibn Sa'ud acted immediately to implement them even to the extent of prohibiting the use of the radio and telegraph in certain parts of the kingdom, even though the *'ulema'* had not specifically prohibited their use. By so doing, he hoped to please the Ikhwan and remove the causes of their grievances, or at least to postpone the day of insurrection which appeared to be inevitable. When the meeting broke up the Ikhwan leadership and individuals once more pledged their allegiance showing their loyalty by shaking his hand, and in Najdi bedouin fashion by kissing him on both cheeks and on the tip of the nose, saying "we pledge loyalty to you in word and deed." Yet none of these positive actions satisfied the Ikhwan. Hardly had the conference broken up when they resumed their raiding against the tribes at the Iraq border, confident that Ibn Sa'ud who had returned to the Hijaz would find it difficult to stop them; yet it was these raids which acted as the catalyst in the long dispute between him and the Ikhwan.

After the conquest of Ha'il, a large number of Najdi Shammar tribesmen had fled to Iraq, but sometimes crossed the border back

---

5 Wahbah, *Jazirat*, pp. 300-301.

into Najd to graze their flocks and sometimes to raid other tribes, after which they would return to the sanctuary of Iraq. The Shammar tribesmen were later joined by groups of Najdi Ikhwan who had joined them in raiding, and then fearing Ibn Sa'ud's swift retribution remained in Iraq. These Ikhwan came to be known as Ikhwan refugees, and together with the Najdi Shammar in Iraq were a thorn in Ibn Sa'ud's side by their constant raiding. Efforts by Ibn Sa'ud and lesser attempts by the British to halt these raids were not very successful. By 1926, however, these raids had been largely halted. By this time, however, the Ikhwan returned from the Hijaz; as long as they had been preoccupied with other fields to conquer, they were content to let these Shammar-Ikhwan refugee raids go unnoticed. Now that they had no such preoccupations, they looked to Iraq as the closest legitimate targets of raidings because the Iraqi tribes were infidels, and the Ikhwan refugees were traitors. What began first as border incursions, soon grew into bold forays well within Iraq, and among the victims were the defenseless tribes known as shepherd tribes which lived and grazed their flocks in the border areas. They were not known for military prowess and for the most part were unarmed. Soon the shepherd tribes fled to Iraq causing an additional influx of refugees which could no longer be ignored by the British. Long used to grazing their flocks where the rains caused patches of green, the tribes in general, and the shepherd tribes specifically considered the border an arbitrary line. They could not survive only on the Iraq side since their traditional pasture lay on the Najdi side also, and now both sides of the border were unsafe due to the Ikhwan raids.

Captain John Bagot Glubb, a young, British officer, newly assigned to the area, through dint of hard work and dedication, generated interest in Baghdad—which was generally more concerned with the problems of inner urban, agricultural Iraq than with peripheral tribal affairs—to look after and protect not only the tribes, but the sovereignty of Iraq from Ikhwan raids. Under his direction, the British attempted to pacify the area first through the use of airplanes for reconnaissance purposes, and then by air strikes against Ikhwan raiding parties. In response to this British military activity, Ibn Sa'ud ordered his newspaper, *Umm al-Qura* to protest editorially British attacks on Ikhwan raiders, and to imply that it was all part of an imperialist plot against his Government. However, Ibn Sa'ud well knew that the Ikhwan were at fault and that sooner or later, he would have to resolve the problem with them, and not with the British.

The savagery of Ikhwan raids, their method of killing all males, infants and the aged alike, and sometimes even women and female children—something completely alien to traditional Arab warfare and raiding—exacerbated the problem, and was a key element, but not the immediate cause of the Iraq Government's decision to construct a police post at the Busaiya wells, based on the recommendations of Captain Glubb. The purpose of the posts was to discourage raiding on either side of the border through the vigilance of armed patrols. Oddly enough, the decision to build the posts was made after a large raiding party of Iraqi Shammar looted a large number of camels belonging to Kuwaiti tribes. In September 1927 twelve workmen went to Busaiya to construct a police post there. This provoked an immediate protest from Ibn Sa'ud who claimed that this constituted a violation of the 'Uqayr protocols which read in part:

> Both Governments agree that each will not use the waters and the wells located in the region of the border for any military purposes such as constructing forts there, and not to post its soldiers in the region... 6

As Glubb put it:

> Ibn Sa'ud's protests were plausible. The Iraqi case was based on the fact that Busaiya was eighty miles from the Nejed border and not in its vicinity. It was, moreover, not a military fort but a police post, to be manned by ten policemen. Yet other considerations made these arguments appear to Ibn Saud less valid than Europeans might consider them. For example, in Nejed, there was no difference between soldiers and police, so that a point which appeared of basic importance to the Iraqis and the British meant nothing to the king... Another essential factor was that the Nejed Government in those days made no use of maps. Thus the exact distance of Busaiya from the border, a point quite obvious in Baghdad and in Whitehall was less vivid in Riyadh. 7

The Ikhwan did not wait long to react to the British provocation at Busaiya, something which gave them an excellent excuse for an attack. By striking at these forts they could accuse the British of violating the treaty and pose as champions before the Muslims fighting an infidel military threat. On about 5 September fifty Mutayr tribesmen descended upon the workmen and killed them all, except one whom they left

---

6 *Majmu'at, op. cit.,* p. 6.

7 John Bagot Glubb, *War in the Desert,* (London: Hodder and Stoughton, 1960), pp. 193-195. This work gives an excellent and detailed account of the Ikhwan raids against Iraq.

for dead. Nevertheless the British decided to continue the construction of the post, a decision re-inforced by the renewed Ikhwan attacks on the Shepherd tribes which after two years of relative calm had prematurely planned to return to their grazing grounds in Najd. Continued Ikhwan raids into Iraq brought British retaliation against them in the form of better planned and executed air raids. However, when the British Government gave its Royal Air Force permission to pursue the Ikhwan raiders into Najd, the issue ceased to be a local problem with the Ikhwan but developed into an international question involving the violating of Najd's sovereignty. Ibn Sa'ud's weekly paper, *Umm al-Qura* denounced these raids as British provocations and violations of the 'Uqayr treaty and while the editorials denounced the British air attacks against primitive horsemen armed only with rifles, they never mentioned the heavy casualties inflicted by the Ikhwan on the defenseless shepherd tribes. [8]

The British Government's permission to pursue the raiders across the border into Najd was prompted by the failure of their protests to Ibn Sa'ud to produce any peace on the border by stopping the raids. Ibn Sa'ud's response to these protests had been strange and inconsistent. While on the one hand rejecting the protests with a counter protest that the Ikhwan were being provoked, he would, on the other, send a private message to the Ikhwan castigating them for carrying out unauthorized raids. Other times he would accept the protests, promise to discipline the Ikhwan, while secretly expressing to them his pleasure with their raiding activity. Ibn Sa'ud's motivation for such equivocal behavior was in large measure determined by his desire to avoid an outright confrontation with the British, while at the same time putting maximum pressure on the Husayn-influenced government in Iraq. Yet he wanted to avoid an insurrection among the Ikhwan without allowing them absolute free rein. This was a tense tightrope balancing act which succeeded... for a while.

Ever since his creation of the Ikhwan, various advisors had warned him that they would cause him great trouble. British reporters had consistently reported that the Ikhwan were getting out of control, and the Public Record Office contains many examples of this reporting. Alois Musil [9] accurately noted after a trip through Najd that "the inviolability of the frontier will have to be enforced. No longer will the opportunity

---

[8] *Umm Al-Qura* for the years 1927-1928, front page articles.
[9] Alois Musil, *op. cit.*, p. 303.

of gaining booty attract the levies, and the Ehwan whom he has used against his friendly neighbors will become a source of internal trouble." British reporters had predicted the insurgency; Musil pinpointed the cause.

Glubb, who was never reluctant to express his intense dislike for the Ikhwan was quite sympathetic to Ibn Sa'ud. He attempted to analyse Ibn Sa'ud's equivocal reaction to the Ikhwan raids, first describing the problem:

> In past years one of the principal controlling factors ... was Ibn Sa'ud's fear of the Akhwan his own subjects, and the need under which he lay, or the policy which he favoured, of deliberately bowing to fanaticism. It is difficult to say exactly to what extent this policy was forced upon Ibn Sa'ud by public opinion in Najd, and to what extent it was used by Ibn Sa'ud as an excuse to oppose to British protests, or even, as he feared, encroachments. [10]

Glubb then summed up Ibn Sa'ud's motives toward Ikhwan raids under four categories:

1) Genuine fear of rebellion by his own subjects, if he opposed the raids.

2) Personal ambition, which was constantly served by the Ikhwan attacks, even though perhaps not authorized by him.

3) Distrust of the British Government.

4) A genuine sense of pride at the exploits of his unruly subjects. [11]

Yet Ibn Sa'ud was too sharp a statesman not to realize that an accommodation with the British was essential if he was to retain control over his hard fought and newly won kingdom. Accordingly, he agreed to hold negotiations with British and Iraqi officials in Jidda which was mutually acceptable as the venue. The Anglo-Iraqi delegation was led by Sir Gilbert Clayton, and Captain John B. Glubb attended as desert advisor. The Saudi side was represented by Ibn Sa'ud's non-Saudi Arab advisors, foremost among whom was Hafiz Wahbah, an Egyptian. The first meeting was held on 7 May 1928. After more than ten days of negotiations, the conference broke up with no tangible results, and no agreement on the salient points. The Sa'udis insisted on the dismantling of the fort at Busaiya, while the Anglo-Iraqi delegation vainly attempted to argue that the post was actually beneficial to Sa'udi

---

[10] John Bagot Glubb, Relations with Najd, 1931, Public Record Office, MSS, Foreign Office, Vol. 13736, Document No. E 3273.

[11] *Ibid.*

security. The post was not the only obstacle to agreement. The Sa'udis wanted an extradition treaty that would also include political offenders, while the Anglo-Iraqi delegation was determined to exclude political offenders, although it expressed a willingness to give a separate pledge that it would not give asylum to Faysal Al-Dawish if Ibn Sa'ud decided to punish him.

The British and Iraqi delegations returned to Iraq at the end of May 1928. Captain Glubb set himself to bracing the border area for the intensification of the raids which were predictable not only because the conference was a failure, but because the Ikhwan themselves were becoming more openly hostile toward Ibn Sa'ud. Whereas they originally were focusing on the infidels, the Ikhwan were unabashedly accusing Ibn Sa'ud of selling himself to the English Christians, and of being in league with them, at the expense of his earlier commitment to spread Islam, and fight the infidels.

Ibn Sa'ud had agreed to meet with the three Ikhwan chiefs in the town of Burayda, but when the time came to meet both the Ikhwan and Ibn Sa'ud feared to meet with each other; each side mistrusting the other; each side was not certain yet that it could defeat the other. It was then agreed that the meeting would be postponed to allow Ibn Sa'ud to attempt to negotiate their differences with the British. Negotiations in Jidda having failed, the Ikhwan threat to Ibn Sa'ud, and the open break that loomed ominously on the horizon sharpened. Ibn Sa'ud was now convinced that the three Ikhwan leaders were motivated less by religious zeal than by personal desires for power. He believed that they had already agreed upon the spoils once he was overthrown: Faysal al-Dawish was to become ruler of Najd; Sultan ibn Bijad ibn Humayd would govern the Hijaz, and Dhidan ibn Hithlain would be sovereign of Al-Hasa. Such a division was logical from the standpoint of tribal distribution and the influence of the various sheikhs in the corresponding region. Yet despite the worsening situation in Najd, Ibn Sa'ud did not return there from the Hijaz until November 1928. By this time the Ikhwan were all but in open rebellion. They were raiding at will, and had thereby made Ibn Sa'ud almost powerless to act. He could hardly admit that they were raiding against his will, since this would be open admission of his lack of control over them; yet he could not condone what was blatantly cruel and inhuman attacks on defenseless tribes, and flagrant violations of agreements which he had made with the British Government. When he decided to act, it was almost too late.

Ibn Sa'ud had now reached the limits of his patience with the Ikhwan represented by Faysal and Ibn Bijad. Out of deference to them he had prohibited the use of the radio, wireless, vehicles and other modern inventions in Riyadh. He had outlawed the Egyptian *mahmal*, and had sent various preachers among the shiites of the Al-Hasa to oblige them to conform to Wahhabi Islam. Apparently none of these measures appeased them. Yet Ibn Sa'ud realized that the Ikhwan enjoyed popularity among many of his subjects, since Al-Dawish and Ibn Bijad had succeeded in their whispering campaign among the tribes that they represented the legitimate interests of Islam, and that they were defending the cause of religion, while Ibn Sa'ud, having won the Hijaz through their prowess had now sold himself to the English and the Christians. There is no doubt that Ibn Sa'ud realized that a confrontation with the Ikhwan was unavoidable. However, when it came, he wanted to have the backing of as many of his subjects as possible, and to make his case clearly before them. Ibn Sa'ud replied to the Ikhwan demands that he lead them in battle against the infidels in Iraq and Jordan by convening an assembly of the representatives of all elements of the Najd population. [12] Called *Al-Jam'iyah Al-'Umumiyah* i.e. the General Assembly, it is also referred to as the Riyadh Conference of Notables. The Conference began on 5 November 1928 [13] in Riyadh amid an atmosphere of uncertainty, and concluded several days later with Ibn Sa'ud's hand considerably strengthened.

In response to Ibn Sa'ud's call to meet, thousands of villagers, townsmen, *'ulema'*, tribal chiefs, village chiefs, and Ikhwan from the *hujar* descended upon Riyadh. According to a report written by Captain Glubb between 12,000 to 16,000 [14] visitors arrived. According to this report the bedouin were accommodated in tents outside the town, while visiting townsmen from places such as Burayda and Unayza were housed within the city itself, and issued rifles and ammunition in order to guard the walls. The gates were closed at dusk and the town contingents guarded the walls until dawn, shooting off rounds of

---

[12] *Umm al-Qura*, number 208, 18 December 1928.

[13] Hafiz Wahbah in *Jazirat*, gives the date as 19 October 1928, based on 10 Jumada Al-Ula 1347; however the correct date is 22 Jumada Al-Ula. Other authors including Benoit-Mechin, *Arabian Destiny*, also give incorrect dates. Kenneth Williams, *Ibn Sa'ud* correctly gives 5 Novemebr as the date, and Glubb in his secret report on the meeting also provides an early November 1928 date.

[14] Glubb Report from Busaiyah, 1929, Public Record Office, MSS, Vol. 13713, Document No. E. 114. *Umm al-Qura* reported that 25,000 persons had received the hospitality of the King during this period. Number 208 (18 December 1928).

ammunition from time to time to demonstrate that they were awake and alert at their posts. The principal sheikhs and heads of the Ikhwan colonies were detained in Riyadh until Ibn Sa'ud's correspondence with Faysal al-Dawish and Ibn Humayd was concluded. [15]

The above description is quite plausible. The bedouin being traditionally less reliable, more fickle than the townsmen, and at this particular time their loyalty being rather questionable in view of al-Dawish's and Ibn Bijad's propaganda among them, it is logical that Ibn Sa'ud would want them kept outside the wall. Conversely, the townsmen, longtime supporters of the Sa'ud family would be welcome within the town. The townsmen had much to lose by a resurgence of unguided bedouin power: they not only feared their intolerant religious zeal, but the instability which their undisciplined conduct caused public order. Finally, to keep the Ikhwan chiefs as hostages, under the guise of hospitality, was in keeping with tribal tradition. As a practical matter it kept the Ikhwan chiefs from conspiring with al-Dawish and Ibn Humayd and from coordinating their activities with them. In effect the picture resembled once again the situation that prevailed pre-1912 before the creation of the Ikhwan: the bedouin, untamed, self-seeking, and having no permanent loyalties except to their tribe; the townsmen seeking, and needing a strong ruler who could provide some form of central government and keep the bedouin in check.

At the very moment when some representatives of the Mutayr, the 'Ujman, and the 'Utaybah were pledging loyalty to Ibn Sa'ud at the Public Assembly, others were already secretly committed to fight under the banners of their rebellious Ikhwan chiefs, and when the time came, did not hesitate to do so.

Although hundreds of delegates arrived, many sincere supporters of Ibn Sa'ud, undoubtedly the larger number came uncommitted, waiting to see just how strong Ibn Sa'ud was, and to assess his chances of winning against the rebels. Perhaps nowhere is the finger on the pulse of power so sensitive as it is among the bedouin. In a land where the deprivation of water through the prohibition of the use of wells is tantamount to genocide for a tribe, political flexibility is the order of the day. It can be convincingly argued that bedouin are fickle because their environment and mode of life require flexibility for survival. Ibn Sa'ud was well aware of this; not to be undone, he provided a flair of showmanship worthy of a more modern age.

---

[15] Glubb, *Ibid.*

Because of the large number of arrivals in Riyadh, not all could speak or attend the Conference. A list of eight hundred or so delegates was composed and presented to Ibn Sa'ud for his approval. Judging from the description of the preparations for the conference, and the proceedings of the meeting provided by *Umm al-Qura*, Ibn Sa'ud had spent considerable time in its planning. A large balcony of his huge palace was selected as the meeting site. Having approved the list, he ordered them invited individually, the date and time of the meeting being set for two o'clock in the morning [16] on 5 November 1928. Special waiting rooms were prepared for each separate group, with townsmen placed in one room, religious leaders in another, and the Ikhwan in another. One half hour before the proceedings began, Ibn Sa'ud took his place surrounded by members of his family. He then called in the delegates by estate: first the *'ulema'* took their place occupying the front row to the right and to the left. [17] When they had taken their place, he called in the townsmen and villagers, some of whom sat behind the *'ulema'*, and others around the back and two sides of the balcony. Then he called in the Ikhwan and tribesmen. They came in by *Hijrah* and by tribe, and sat row by row facing the King. The routine of seating took approximately fifteen minutes.

Connecting rooms of the huge balcony were fitted with rugs and armrests, as was the main assembly site, to be used by persons who could listen to the proceedings. A similar room above on the next level was also fitted out for those who would neither listen nor speak at the proceedings.

After the serving of ceremonial coffee, Ibn Sa'ud rose and spoke. Having related how God had given him victory with the help of only forty close friends, and how he had found them disunited, and killing one another, and how he had joined them into brothers and brought glory to them and to their tribe, he offered to abdicate his position. He made it very clear that he was doing this not out of fear for any one of them as individuals, or as a group, but because he did not want to rule a people who did not want him as their ruler, and because more than anything else he did not want to sucumb to the sin of arrogance. He was content to resign himself to a life of contemplation of God. Pointing to members of the royal family there assembled, he asked the Assembly to choose one of them to rule, and he would accept their decision. Ibn Sa'ud well knew that he was speaking to a group of

---

[16] According to sun time. This would be two hours after the crack of dawn.

[17] *Umm al-Qura*, number 208.

people who distrusted each other more than anyone distrusted him. With the possible exception of the representatives of al-Dawish and Ibn Bijad, neither of whom attended the Conference, he knew that no group or individual would accept his offer. They had too much to lose; each faction would expose itself to the jealousies and rivalries of the other with no power shield as Ibn Sa'ud to separate them. With shouts of "we'll have no one else than you to rule us," the delegates rejected the offer outright. Quickly then, in what most certainly was a planned performance, he demanded that each person speak freely. He promised that no one would ever be punished for what he may have said at the Conference.

Although the Conference was ostensibly called to discuss the dangers represented by the British violations of the 'Uqayr protocols, and their violation of Najd sovereignty through air raids on the tribes, everyone knew at the Conference that the issue was Ibn Sa'ud himself. Could he vindicate his attitudes toward the Ikhwan and toward the British, which were mutually irreconcilable?

First representatives of the *'ulema'* spoke. They vowed that they had never found Ibn Sa'ud lacking in his zeal toward religion, or in his sincere dedication toward the advancement of Islam. If he had made some mistakes, they said, this was natural because only Muhammad the Prophet was infallible. What mistakes Ibn Sa'ud may have made were not sufficient for his people to turn their backs on him, or he to turn his back on them. They concluded that they were speaking not out of fear of him, because as *'ulema'* it was their duty to guide him. Their decision was honest and correct.

Then members of the Ikhwan spoke, the principal spokesmen being representatives of al-Dawish for the Mutayr tribe, al-Bahimah and al-Firm and al-Tuwaybi and Ibn Bakhit for the Harb chiefs, and Ibn Rubay'an of the 'Utaybah and Ibn 'Ummar and Ibn Khasr of the Qahtan. They acknowledged Ibn Sa'ud's help, his leadership, his respect for their weak and their aged, how he had given them a share in the national wealth (*bayt al-mal*) and how he had built mosques for them on the *hujar* and sent missionaries to teach them the true religion. All this they were not disputing. But he too should remember that they had abandoned their nomadic ways, their tribes, and sometimes their wealth to follow his call to the true religion, and to fight *fi sabil allah*, for God and country, and that their swords and blood had brought him victory.

He brought them this far down the road, now they wanted some points clarified before continuing to follow him unquestioningly, for they feared the wrath of God more than they feared him. Some questions which they had previously asked were answered; the answers had satisfied some Ikhwan, but not others. They now wanted to put the following questions to him, Ibn Sa'ud, and to the *'ulema'* assembled, and they vowed to follow the rulings:

1) The question of the telegraph (*al-atiyal*). As far as they could see, this was sorcery, and Islam prohibits sorcery. Can true Muslims use it without contravening their religion?

2) The question of following the Qur'anic injunction of doing Good and avoiding Evil. Was he sending religious teachers to conquered areas to teach those people who claimed to be Muslims, the true religion? They feared that Ibn Sa'ud was lax in this endeavor.

3) The question of the forts which the British had erected in the Najd-Iraq border areas. This was a matter with which their patience was now exhausted. Did Ibn Sa'ud consider that his religion had given him the right to delineate borders in lands which had belonged to them and their forefathers for generations? Having undertaken to make such borders with the Christians, how could he allow them to violate the very treaty which he made governing the construction of forts at the wells? Even the women in their cloistered quarters were demanding an answer to this question, they told him. The question of the forts could not longer be put aside. They were willing to accept his judgement on this matter only under the following conditions:

a) That they get a ruling based on the *shari'a* from the *'ulema'* that if they remain quiet on this subject, and harm comes to the Islamic religion, or to Muslims, then they are absolved before God from any blame.

b) That Ibn Sa'ud personally guarantee that he will neither allow any harm to come to them as the result of these forts, nor to their religion or to the country. If he cannot do this they said, then "by God we will not allow them to stand as long as there is a pulse which beats, or there is a breath of life in any one of us, for we prefer to die and be killed all together than to see danger to our religion and to our country and remain silent." [18]

4) The question of stopping the people from holy war, *jihad*. Why has he done this and stopped God's word from being spread? [19]

---

[18] *Umm al-Qura*, number 208.

[19] In Glubb's report, Vol. 13713, Document No. E 114, he indicates that the speakers had objected to the payment by the tribes of the *zakat* tax; *Umm al-Qura* does not list this as a grievance of the Assembly.

At the conclusion of the speeches, Ibn Sa'ud called for more; there was no reply, he asked a second and a third time, and the speakers said that they had cleared their chests of all their problems. Then Ibn Sa'ud set out to answer them. With regard to the question of the telegraph and the other modern inventions, he asked the *'ulema'* to speak. They then read from a *fatwa* previously prepared which expressed their decision that inasmuch as they could find no precedent, either in the Qur'an, or in the sayings of the prophet, or the writings of any of Islam's learned men on the subject, they had absolved themselves of this problem. However, until any one who objected to the use of this could provide an Islamic precedent, they had no right to object to its use. As for teaching lapsed Muslims the true religion, he reminded them that he had sent preachers to every town, and just recently to a tribe in the North Hijaz called the Bani Malik. If the sheikhs are not doing their duty in this respect, he told them, then they should let him know and he will carry out their recommendations. As for the question of the forts, Ibn Sa'ud told them that these forts were erected because of the Ikhwan's aggression. The British were accusing al-Dawish and his followers of killing policemen. "I, Ibn Sa'ud, did not do this, and they say that it is from fear of you that they have built the forts."

In reply the Ikhwan said, "yes, we disassociate ourselves from the activities of al-Dawish and we are willing to fight him on two conditions:

a) that you destroy the newly constructed forts whose existence we regard as a matter of life and death.

b) that the British promise not to come between ourselves and those that they want to punish, such as Yusif Sa'adun, the Iraqi leader."

The forts, the Ikhwan said, are being strengthened every day, and "we tell you frankly that our religion and life are in danger and that they (the British) began the evil not us."

At this point the *'ulema'* gave their decision on the matter of the forts. In effect siding with the Ikhwan, they told Ibn Sa'ud that the forts constituted a danger to the Arabs, to the Muslims, and specifically to the people of Najd, and that he must do everything in his power to remove them, and that the effort to remove the fort is not *jihad* but defense of religion.

Obviously pleased with the *'ulema'*'s answer, the Ikhwan shouted: have you heard what they have said. We ask you, by God, what do you say about these forts? The king replied, I say that what the *'ulema'* have said is correct, and I vow to resolve the matter. As for the question of *jihad*, I want to speak about it elsewhere, privately. He then told them to select fifty persons from the group to represent them, and to meet with him. At that time he will tell them what he thinks of the matter, and they can come to some decisions to resolve the question. In conclusion, Ibn Sa'ud told the Assembly, "I say to all of you, whether your station in life be large or small that I see no full life for us except in peace which guarantees our full rights to defend our rights and to achieve them. We must either be victorious or die defending our sanctuaries and our nation; to this do I pledge myself before God." [20]

The conference ended with Sa'ud, his oldest surviving son, introducing the guests to him, as each one pledged allegiance once again. After the evening meal, fifty persons met with the King from two in the evening until six. [21] The proceedings of this meeting and subsequent ones on the same subject of *jihad* were not revealed, except to say that the group and the King had reached unanimous decisions on how to handle the matter.

The Conference ended with Ibn Sa'ud having at least the backing of the *'ulema'* and the Ikhwan against al-Dawish and Ibn Bijad; however, his mandate against them was mitigated by the conditions which he accepted, namely to rid the borders of the forts, presumably by successful negotiation or through military force, and to satisfy their demands for *jihad*.

---

[20] *Umm al-Qura*, number 208.

[21] According to sun time this would have begun two hours after sunset.

CHAPTER ELEVEN

THE IKHWAN REBELLION

Even after the conclusion of the Riyadh General Assembly the majority of the Ikhwan, the *'ulema'*, and other religiously oriented groups maintained a posture of cautious neutrality in the dispute between the three senior Ikhwan leaders, which now verged on the brink of open rebellion. While loyalty to Ibn Sa'ud remained fundamentally intact among these parties, they seriously questioned the wisdom of his activities. They were keenly aware of the many material blessings which accrued to them since his rise to power, yet they were genuinely convinced that the rebels had legitimate grievances which Ibn Sa'ud had not adequately resolved; these grievances had made the rounds of the Ikhwan *hujar* where they were openly discussed. The non-Ikhwan elements of Najd also were aware of them, and they formed the subject of whispered conversations among some of Ibn Sa'ud's most loyal partisans. At the base of the problem was the inability of these unsophisticated folk to understand the pressures which Ibn Sa'ud faced, and to visualize the larger world into which he had led not only them but the entire kingdom. Ibn Sa'ud had not, on the other hand, provided a sufficient solution to the dilemma which faced the Ikhwan, the dilemma which Faysal al-Dawish so succinctly presented in a letter which he sent to Ibn Sa'ud's son, Sa'ud:

> ... You have also prevented me from raiding the Bedouins. So we are neither Moslems fighting the unbelievers nor are we Arabs and Bedouins raiding each other and living on what we get from each other. You have kept us away from both our religions and our worldly worldly concerns. It is true that you have not failed to do what you can for me and my people but where are the rest of my tribes to go? They will perish and how can we be contented with this? In the past you used to forgive any of us who committed a sin, but now you treat us with the sword and pass over the Christians, their religion and the forts built for your immediate destruction, Saud. [1]

Ibn Sa'ud's repeated efforts to resolve his differences with the rebel chiefs, especially Ibn Bijad and al-Dawish, were unsuccessful. This was

---

[1] English translation of a letter from Feisal bin Sultan Ed Doweisch to Amir Saud, Public Record Office, MSS, FO 371-13736, Document No. E 3457.

due in no small part to the fact that each of the three senior rebel chiefs were motivated fundamentally by different grivances, and united only in their opposition to Ibn Sa'ud. Undoubtedly, Ibn Bijad was a sincere, devoted Muslim profoundly concerned with the trend toward modernization of the country, and the tendency to work closely with the Christians. [2] Faysal al-Dawish definitely had political and power ambitions, his claims to be concerned with the fate of the true Muslims to the contrary. [3] Dhidan ibn Hithlain and his 'Ujman never were fully reconciled to Ibn Sa'ud, and marched under Ibn Sa'ud's banner only after being severely beaten in two major battles, and because all the other tribes had submitted to Ibn Sa'ud. They could not but do the same, unless they wanted the full retribution of the King to fall on them.

A series of messages exchanged between the leaders and several attempts to arrange face to face meetings never bore fruit. Meanwhile Ikhwan raiding not only continued but accelerated. While Ibn Sa'ud most certainly would have preferred a negotiated settlement—least costly in money, tribal relations and risk of power struggle—he saw the chances slipping away, and then finally disappearing altogether when the Ikhwan raided in December of 1928 the defenseless Najdi camel traders at Al-Jumaymah, as well as sections of the Najd Shammar, all of which were Ibn Sa'ud's own subjects. The camel traders were massacred. No longer could the Ikhwan claim that they were only attacking infidels; similarly, Ibn Sa'ud could no longer stand idly by while his leadership and power was challenged in the form of unpunished attacks upon his own subjects.

By January 1929 Ibn Bijad had declared his intention of embarking upon a holy war against Iraq—a blatant challenge to Ibn Sa'ud and to those who supported him at the Riyadh Conference. He moved with his supporters in the direction of Iraq where he joined up with elements of al-Dawish's Mutayr Ikhwan, and Hithlain's 'Ujman who were engaged in sporadic raiding [4] against the Muntafiq shepherd tribes.

The situation continued to deteriorate, and Ibn Sa'ud's inactivity was

---

[2] This is the opinion expressed by some Ikhwan, like Majid ibn Khathila, and some members of the Sa'udi Royal Family, such as 'Abd-al-Rahman ibn 'Abdullah. Interviews, Riyadh, 1969.

[3] His threat to flee to Iraq is proof of this, not to say his actual attempts to seek political asylum in the very countries which he described as enemies of Islam.

[4] Mr. Henry Bilkert, an American missionary in Basra who was riding in a car with Mr. Charles R. Crane, was killed when part of the 'Ujman raiding party shot at the car in which they were riding. See Dickson, *Kuwait*, p. 300.

interpreted by many cautious bedouin and fence sitting Najdis as proof of his weakness. [5] In part to counteract this gossip and in part to prepare himself to meet an open military challenge, Ibn Sa'ud moved into the Qasim area where he recruited levies of townfolk and oases dwellers, many of whom were especially anxious to fight the Ikhwan, not only to take revenge for their fellow townsmen who had suffered by Ikhwan raids, but to ensure the safety and security of their own future. These levies formed the nucleus of Ibn Sa'ud's army and were, as Glubb described them, "to the wilder mounted bedouin somewhat like the London trained bands in the English civil war, in relation to the dashing individuals of the undisciplined cavalries." [6] These warriors were joined by loyal elements of the Mutayr, groups from the Hutaym, most of the Harb, almost all of the Najdi Shammar and some Al-Zafir and 'Anay-zah tribesmen. In the meantime, Ibn Sa'ud had won the support of the 'Utaybah led by Sheikh Rubay'an, a decisive victory which weighed the scales in his favor. If Ibn Rubay'an had joined his fellow 'Utaybah Sheikh ibn Bijad, the final results of Sabila most certainly would have been different. Even during the rallying of his army, Ibn Sa'ud and the three rebel chiefs exchanged messages, with the hope of bringing about some type of negotiated settlement; these efforts lasted up until the last night before the battle at Sabila.

Having made recruitment levies in the Qasim area, Ibn Sa'ud moved east toward the Ikhwan forces of Ibn Bijad and al-Dawish which had moved toward the general area of Al-Artawiyah. Dhidan ibn Hithlain and his 'Ujman remained in the Al-Hasa, ostensibly in rebellion but making no effort to participate in an open military confrontation. The Ikhwan forces and the loyalist forces camped several miles from each other in a flat area, interrupted only by slight rises in the terrain. Called Sabila, it was located between the Ikhwan capital at Al-Arta-wiyah and the old sedentary town of Zilfi. The two opposing groups busily set to work settling into their camps. Even now there was no irrevocable declaration of hostilities, and it seems that they gravitated toward open warfare more by default than calculation. It was a drift toward war that both sides tried to forestall. First Ibn Sa'ud sent a venerable sheikh, 'Abdullah al-'Anqari, a prominent Najdi 'alim to the Ikhwan camp to try to convince the Ikhwan to submit to arbitration based on the shari'a. This attempt failed. Then Ibn Bijad sent his chief

---

[5] Glubb Report from Busaiyah.
[6] Glubb, War in the Desert, p. 285 .

aide, sheikh Majid ibn Khathila with a letter to Ibn Sa'ud. This attempt also led to a dead end, with the added drawback of an unexpected backlash. According to some written accounts, Majid entered Ibn Sa'ud's tent and, in keeping with the Ikhwan practice of not saying *Salam 'Alaykum* to those whom they considered not to be true Muslims, did not answer Ibn Sa'ud's similar greeting. 7 Irked by this disrespect and angered by its implications, Ibn Sa'ud angrily told him to tell Ibn Bijad that he and his followers had only two alternatives: either to surrender unconditionally and submit themselves to the judgment of the *shari'a* or to fight on the battle field the next day. The visit of al-Anqari and Khathila both being abortive, Faysal al-Dawish went with the intention of asking Ibn Sa'ud to allow him to sleep in his tent thereby setting the stage for the accusation that he had been detained. Glubb 8 claims that al-Dawish actually slept in Ibn Sa'ud's tent, and that Ibn Bijad tried unsuccessfully to convince al-Dawish's son, 'Abd-al-'Aziz that his father was a prisoner and that the Ikhwan should make a surprise attack. Other accounts claim that Faysal al-Dawish promised Ibn Sa'ud that he would send the Ikhwan rebels' reply to his demands that same night but that no reply was forthcoming. 9 While still others record that al-Dawish not only swore loyalty to Ibn Sa'ud but promised to try to persuade Ibn Bijad to renounce rebellion, and that if he did not succeed, he himself would return peacefully to Al-Artawiyah. 10 Glubb's account that al-Dawish remained in the Saudi camp is almost certainly incorrect. The battle at Sabila took place early the next morning, at sunrise, and when it opened al-Dawish was in the rebel camp. Wahbah is probably correct when he says that Ibn Sa'ud told al-Dawish "to disassociate himself from the others, and that if he did not then the full force of punishment would fall on him." 11 None of this writer's Ikhwan sources claim that al-Dawish remained overnight in Ibn Sa'ud's camp. Al-Dawish almost certainly returned to the camp that night and met with Ibn Bijad and the other leaders. Wahbah records that al-Dawish told the Ikhwan that he had seen, in Ibn Sa'ud's

---

7 When I asked Majid ibn Khathila about this matter, at first he was equivocal; when I pressed for an answer, he stated that he did give the Islamic greeting to Ibn Sa'ud when he entered the tent.

8 Glubb, *War in the Desert*, p. 286.

9 *Umm al-Qura*, number 224, 12 April 1929.

10 Glubb, *War*, p. 286.

11 Wahbah and Saqr both report this, and add that Ibn Sa'ud told al-Dawish to return to his own camp and spend the night there, because he had expected al-Dawish's attempt to set a trap. Wahbah, *Jazirat*, p. 304; 'Attar, *Saqr*, p. 421.

camp, an army of cooks and soft men used to sleeping on mattresses. While Glubb also records that this story had been making the rounds, he is quite correct when he says probably we shall never know exactly what al-Dawish told the Ikhwan. What is certain is that upon his return the Ikhwan decided against submission and for war.

On the morning of 30 March the two armies faced each other, [12] the Ikhwan hopelessly outnumbered in men at least three to one. [13] Although in the past the Ikhwan had won brilliant victories when severely outnumbered, their enemy had been Hijazi tribesmen and Sharifian troops, not their wiry cousins from Najd. Umm al-Qura described the battle:

> "... the King ordered his charger to be brought, mounted, took his rifle and put on his belt and rode forward surrounded by a mounted retinue. The battle was a strange sight. The troops were drawn up in one line three or more miles in length with their banners flying. His Majesty took the command of the centre, placed his brother Amir Muhammad in command of the cavalry on the left and his eldest son Amir Saud in command of the cavalry on the right. He then ordered a general advance. The opponents had thrown up fortifications to protect themselves. When the two parties approached each other and the battle began between the infantry, His Majesty's sons, nephews and cousins rode in front of the cavalry and fought most bravely until they routed the opposing cavalry and broke down the infantry resistance. After only half an hour the guilty ones fled pursued by the King's forces. Those who threw down their arms were spared and after one hour the evildoers were defeated and routed. When the battle was over His Majesty returned on his horse thanking God for His help, afterwards inspecting the state of the troops and demobilizing them. [14]

The critical part of the battle lasted about one half hour, after which it was clear that the Ikhwan could not win. Some of the rebels surrendered. An hour later the battle was entirely over with Ibn Bijad and Faysal al-Dawish who was seriously wounded fleeing the battlefield. The next morning they sent a delegation asking for pardon and for-

---

[12] Dickson, *Kuwait*, p. 303 claims that Ibn Sa'ud made a morning surprise attack while the Ikhwan were still under the impression that negotiations were going on. None of the Ikhwan whom this writer interviewed made this accusation; they described it, instead ,much as was reported in Umm al-Qura, number 24, 12 April 1929.

[13] 'Attar, *Saqr*, estimates that Ibn Sa'ud's army numbered 28,000, including 8,000 townsmen and 20,000 Ikhwan and bedouin. The Ikhwan's estimate vary, but all agree that they were significantly outnumbered.

[14] *Umm al-Qura*, number 224, 12 April 1929.

giveness. [15] Ibn Sa'ud promised that their lives would be spared, but that they would have to submit to the judgement of the *shari'a*. Because al-Dawish was thought to be seriously wounded, Ibn Sa'ud allowed him to return to Al-Artawiyah on condition that he surrender himself in Riyadh if and when he recovered. However, few, if anyone, expected him to recover. As for Ibn Bijad, he was not allowed to enter Ibn Sa'ud's camp because the troops were too angry with him, and the King feared for his life; instead he was ordered to surrender either in Riyadh or Shaqra. [16]

Dhidan ibn Hithlain did not actively participate in the rebellion and kept his forces in Al-Hasa, hence he avoided an open clash with Ibn Sa'ud.

After the battle, Ibn Sa'ud met with the *'ulema'* who were with him, including sheikh 'Abdullah al-'Anqari, sheikh 'Abdullah ibn Zahim, sheikh Abu Habib Shutri, plus the important commanders and cheiftains, a total of 2,000 men. In a speech he told them that:

a) The Qur'an and the sunna must form the bases on which decisions regarding religion are made, not personal interpretation.
b) They should obey the monarch in accordance with the *shari'a*.
c) They should not allow their people to hold meetings either to discuss religion or worldly questions without permission from the monarch.
d) They must respect the Muslims and those under the protection of the Muslims. [17]

The Ikhwan had violated these principles, and Ibn Sa'ud was making it unmistakably clear to those assembled that they could expect the same treatment from him as he had meted out to the Ikhwan rebels if they disregarded these precepts.

The battle of Sabila over, Ibn Sa'ud decided not to pursue the rebels [18] in the hope that they would mend their ways while he returned to the

---

[15] Faysal al-Dawish's delegation consisted of women among whom was the mother of 'Abd-al-Rahman al-Dawish, one of this writer's sources in Al-Artawiyah. (She was the sister of Faysal and her name was Walha). The custom of sending veiled women is called *mughatiyah*. Umm al-Qura, number 224 described the arrival of the women: "...when His Majesty saw the women coming to ask for pardon he wept, and all those present wept too on account of such a pitiful sight. His Majesty's heart and the hearts of all the troops were touched and so he agreed to the entreaty of the women..."

[16] *Umm al-Qura*, number 224.

[17] *Ibid.*

[18] *Umm al-Qura*, number 239, 31 July 1929.

Hijaz for the *hajj,* and that during this time they would reflect on, and realize their errors. However, the failure to follow up his victory and remove the rebel problem at its source forced him to return posthaste to put down a second rebellion. This time he put his entire efforts and military capabilities into the fray, all the time coordinating his overall plans and operations with the British.

While Ibn Sa'ud was away in the Hijaz an incident involving the 'Ujman tribe inflamed the entire eastern province and united bedouin and Ikhwan elements against Ibn Sa'ud, many of whom had no prior intention of involving themselves in another rebellion. Not that a second rebellion would not have occurred anyway. What happened to the 'Ujman, however, provided the catalyst for the new revolt and broadened the scope and the number of participants.

As noted earlier, Dhidan ibn Hithlain had not participated in the battle at Sabila. He was in a state of passive rebellion and there is good reason to believe that after the Ikhwan debacle at Sabila he had no plans to confront Ibn Sa'ud militarily. Further Ibn Sa'ud had succeeded in dividing the 'Ujman much as he did the 'Utaybah by supporting rival chiefs. His support of Na'if ibn Hithlain against Dhidan seriously weakened the fighting strength of the tribe. At this time 'Abdullah ibn Jiluwi, the amir of Al-Hasa sent his son, Fahd, accompanied by Na'if and their troops to capture Dhidan who was then settled in at his *hijrah* of Al-Sarrar. Fahd's troops consisted mostly of townsmen from Hufuf, while Na'if's of course were 'Ujman. Before arriving at the *hijrah* Fahd sent a note to Dhidan saying that he wanted to speak with him concerning the possibility of raiding some rebels in the area; Dhidan invited Fahd into the *hijrah* but Fahd refused, asking Dhidan instead to meet him at his camp. Against the advice of his advisors, Dhidan went to Fahd's camp where, after drinking the traditional Arab coffee, he was put in chains; when he did not return that evening for supper, his 'Ujman moved against Fahd and Na'if. The ensuing battle saw Fahd and his troops losing the battle, and in an act of bad judgement, he ordered one of his men to kill Dhidan who was then put to death. Seeing one of his own family and tribesmen cut down ruthlessly, in violation of strict Arab rules governing hostages, Na'if turned against Fahd and joined the 'Ujman once again, assuming the leadership left vacant by the fallen Dhidan. Fahd was then slain by one of the 'Ujman who captured all the supplies and horses of Fahd's troops, most of whom were killed. The united

'Ujman then headed north to join Faysal al-Dawish's Mutayr Ikhwan. [19]

When Ibn Sa'ud in the Hijaz learned of Dhidan's death and the manner in which he had died, he knew that rebellion would follow. He had already had reports of al-Dawish's recovery, of his increased belligerency, and raiding, and had decided to put an end completely to the insurgency of the Ikhwan using all the military power, diplomatic support, and mechanical and modern means at his disposal. No moves against the Ikhwan could be completely successful unless he had the cooperation of the British. Therefore even before leaving the Hijaz he had, through negotiations, acquired British promises that they would not allow any of the three countries which they governed, Kuwait, Jordan, and Iraq, to give aid or assistance or refuge to the Ikhwan, and if the Ikhwan were allowed to cross the border and remain in any of the countries as sanctuary, that he would have the right of hot pursuit. The British made only one stipulation, namely that the lives of any Ikhwan rebels returned by them to him would be spared. Ibn Sa'ud accepted this condition, but noted that apart from their lives which he would spare, he would insist that they be tried by the *shari'a*.

It was well within British interests to support Ibn Sa'ud's fight against the Ikhwan, once His Majesty's Government had made the decision not to support the Ikhwan clandestinely against Ibn Sa'ud in an effort to create a weak Arabia which it could dominate, and which would threaten its Hashemite charges in Jordan and Iraq, and the Al-Sabah ruling family in Kuwait. Hashemite circles in Jordan and Iraq, as well as the Al-Sabahs of Kuwait were all for supporting the Ikhwan, possibly with the hope of establishing Faysal al-Dawish as *amir* of a petty amirate dominating the triangular area which joined their countries at a common border. Certainly some of al-Dawish's arms and equipment as well as money and supplies came from these sympathizers, but without continued British support and concurrence such a plan was not viable, if indeed there were such a plan. [20]

In accordance with Najdi tradition, Ibn Sa'ud had disbanded all of his troops after the battle at Sabila, and only isolated detachments

---

[19] Muhammad ibn 'Abdullah Al 'Abd al-Qadir al-Ansari al-Ahsa'i, *Tarikh al-Ahsa*, Riyadh Publishing Company ,1960, p. 230-231. See also Dickson, *Kuwait*, who gives a slightly different version of the incident. pp. 304-5.

[20] Muhammad Asad, *Road to Mecca*, pp. 259-261, advances the theory based on his clandestine activities, allegedly on behalf of Ibn Sa'ud, that a 'Great European Power' was behind the rebellion, and strongly implies Great Britain. His information provides convincing evidence that Kuwait supported the rebellion.

under his brother Musa'id and 'Abdullah al-Jiluwi were not dispersed
since levies were collected to do a job and then disbanded upon com-
pletion. The militant Ikhwan of Al-Artawiyah and Al-Ghat Ghat
were no longer available since they were now the enemy. Ibn Sa'ud
had to return to Najd, recruit an army, seek arms and money. He turned
to the British for weapons, asking for at least 3,000 Lee-Enfield rifles
and 1,000 boxes of ammunition. In addition he requested that a troop-
ship transport 1,000 men from Jidda to 'Uqayr. [21]

Having taken these precautions, Ibn Sa'ud set out for Riyadh,
sending ahead messengers to the chiefs of the loyal 'Utaybah tribe
asking them to come with other tribal notables to the town of Al-
Dawadimi for a meeting. The dissident 'Utaybah had been in rebellion
at Sabila. Some of them still were unsubdued, and others while not in
a state of active insurgency had not yet reconciled themselves to defeat;
still others were outlaws inasmuch as they had escaped from Ibn Sa'ud
after the battle, but had not been pardoned. Ibn Sa'ud arrived at
Dawadimi on 9 July 1929. There, in a huge tent pitched for the
occasion he met with about 2,000 'Utaybah tribesmen led by their
chiefs: 'Umar ibn 'Abd-al-Rahman ibn Rubay'an, Sheikh of the Al-
Ruwaqah; Jihjah Bijad ibn Humayd, brother of Sultan ibn Bijad who
was in jail after his defeat at Sabila. He headed the Al-Maqatah;
Manahi al-Haydhal who used to be head of the Barqa but now was
chief of the Da'ajin; Sultan Aba Al-'Ala head of the Al-Asmah;
Khalid ibn Jami', head of the Al-Rusan. [22] At the meeting Ibn Sa'ud
disclosed his plans to move against the 'Ujman and sought their support, if not active, at least passive; the 'Utaybah tribesmen were distributed among the most sensitive territory of Ibn Sa'ud's realm, i.e.
between the extreme eastern part of the Hijaz, and the western part of
Najd. 'Utaybah hostility to Ibn Sa'ud while he was subduing the
'Ujman in the Al-Hasa would threaten his control over the Hijaz and
the land between Riyadh and the west. Anxious to mend his fences,
Ibn Sa'ud asked for their support. In his talk, he told them that there
were three groups among them, one sincere to their religion, and loyal
to him. The other was opportunistic. The third, which he described
as the smallest, is the nucleus of the rebels. He then explained to them
that after the battle of Sabila he was in a quandary: either he would

---

[21] Military Aid to Ibn Sa'ud, Public Record Office, 1929, MSS, Vol. 13736,
Document No. E 2380, 8 May 1929.
[22] *Umm al-Qura*, number 239, 31 July 1929.

miss the *hajj*, (and as *Imam* this would be injudicious) in order to remain in Najd and try to discipline the rebels, or he would return to the Hijaz. Yet he felt that it was too difficult a matter to distinguish between those rebels who were maliciously inclined, and those who were just misled, hence he decided to make the pilgrimage. In any case, the 'Ujman had now raised the standard of revolt and he planned to "march against them when the crescent of Rabi'a al-Awwal (7 August) is first seen. I will not accept that anyone who attended the battle at Sabila and fought with the rebels there should remain behind. He who fights with us belongs to us, and he who remains behind without a legitimate cause will either be killed, or his weapons and horse will be taken away." [23] The King then pardoned those dissident 'Utaybah who were present, and in response to their pleas extended this pardon to include those who were absent, on the following conditions:

a) that if there was anyone among them who was a criminal, in thought or in deed then efforts would be made to rehabilitate him; if he refused, he would then be tried and judged by the *shari'a*.
b) the State has the right to punish bandits who plunder and harass travellers, and cut the roads.
c) anyone who remains behind when a *jihad* is called without a legitimate reason must be dealt with by the Muslims before the enemy is taken care of. [24]

Ibn Sa'ud continued on to Riyadh, after the conclusion of the conference at Dawadimi convinced that he had finally won the 'Utaybah over to him. But he was wrong. Once again they rebelled forcing him to subdue them with an intensity and effectiveness that precluded them from creating further trouble. As a result of the 'Utaybah's second betrayal Ibn Sa'ud called another conference, this time at Sha'ara, a town between Mecca and Riyadh, and there he met on 6 September with the heads of other tribes, as well as those sections of the 'Utaybah that had remained loyal. Ibn Sa'ud recounted how he had forgiven the 'Utaybah several times and that how each time, after pledging loyalty to him, they rose in rebellion. He expressed his views on what had to be done, and then asked the representatives to leave, to think about what he said, consult with their own people, and to return on the next

---

23 *Ibid.*
24 *Ibid.* See the text of Ibn Sa'ud's speech in 'Abd-al-Hamid al-Khatib, *Al-Imam Al-Adil* (The Just Imam), (Cairo: Matba' Mustafa al-Banna, no date of publication given, pp. 174-177.

day with their decision. The morning of the second day saw a four hour discussion at which the following decisions were taken: [25]

1) All of the (dissident) 'Utaybah and the Bani 'Abdullah branch of the Mutayr must be vanquished, so that not one of them will have the power to engage in anything illegal.
2) All of those who participated in the rebellion and who are still alive will be deprived of their weapons and equipment of war and they will be judged by the *shari'a*.
3) Those who are accused of supporting the corrupt ones (rebels) and not fighting with the Muslims will be deprived of their riding camels, horses and rifles.
4) The Imam allows the warriors to keep what they have taken from the rebels so that they can strengthen themselves.
5) That an amir accompanied by forces be sent to Shaqra (which contains the corrupt people) to review the matter of corruption in relation to the *shari'a* and the public good.
6) Every *hijrah* which succumbed to corruption will be evacuated: Its inhabitants will be distributed among the tribes, and none of whom will be allowed to meet in one place.
7) A brigade will be sent to execute these decisions during the time that the King is in Sha'ara, but within ten days.
8) All of the platoons after carrying out these decrees, will meet in the area of the border where the rebel 'Ujman and al-Dawish have congregated.

Prior to going to Sha'ara, Ibn Sa'ud had ordered all the soldiers from the towns and *hujar* to assemble at a designated place, and to wait his return from Sha'ara, at which time he would advise them when to move. He estimated that the move would be no later than the middle of the month of 4 November 1929.

On 25 November, the special car of Ibn Sa'ud stopped in front of his palace, followed by more than thirty other automobiles. He entered his vehicle followed by his brothers, some of his children, princes of the Rashid family, employees of the Royal Diwan and a group of guards and servants. The convoy moved north stopping at a place called Al-Khafs, [26] about 115 kilometers from Riyadh. There his oldest brother, Muhammad had been waiting for him; the King and his party camped there overnight and then went on to Al-Shawki, a distance of 80 kilometers from Al-Khafs. It was to this place that Faysal al-Dawish sensing that he faced an unbeatable army, sent a delegation headed by

---

[25] Al-Khatib, *Al-Imam*, pp. 174-177. See also *Umm al-Qura* number 252, 18 October 1929.

[26] Now a favorite hunting spot of the Sa'udi Royal Family.

Al-Humaydi ibn Miflah asking for forgiveness and safety. Al-Dawish, in the letter which he sent with Miflah put the blame for his predicament on his son 'Abd-al-'Aziz who was just recently killed by Ibn Musa'id, Amir of Ha'il, at the Battle of 'Um Urdama. [27] Ibn Sa'ud received the delegation, and after one day's consideration sent the following reply in which he told al-Dawish that his motives were one or all of the following:

a) seeking pardon from me after all roads have been blocked in your face once again; I see your weakness and I loathe it; you have no more tricks left other than to come running to me now.

b) you're crafty. You will tell the people after this that you do what you want, and then ride over to Ibn Sa'ud and get what you want from him.

c) you want to win over those from whom you have asked assistance, but who have not given it, by telling them that you will make a reconciliation with me.

d) you want by your life to infuriate the Muslims who killed each other because of you, and want their pardon.

e) it would have been better if your letter and your delegation had not reached me, but inasmuch as it has, I give you a guarantee that you and yours are under my protection, and that I spare your blood. [28]

When al-Dawish received this reply, he wrote to Ibn Sa'ud saying, "I thank you for your reply, however, I want you to know that the roads are not blocked in my face as you think, for certain governments have written to me offering the opportunity to become their subject, and I can accept this invitation, except that my religion does not dispose me to have refuge in a country that is under the rule of infidels; going back to you, the Imam of the Muslims is better than others, in any case." [29] Al-Dawish promised that he would go shortly to Ibn Sa'ud to profess his obedience and sincerity. Ibn Sa'ud never answered the letter inasmuch as he was waiting for al-Dawish to come, but the latter never showed up. Other letters passed between Ibn Sa'ud and al-Dawish but they came to naught. No type of compromise appeared possible.

The situation in the Al-Hasa continued to worsen. Ikhwan raids disrupted the peace, and the movement of different Ikhwan parties with their camels and flocks gave the region an air of great activity

---

[27] *Umm al-Qura*, number 293, 18 July 1930.
[28] Al-Khatib, *Al-Imam*, p. 180.
[29] *Ibid.*, p. 181.

and excitement. The most serious of the raids was the joint 'Ujman-Farhan Ibn Mashhur attack against the 'Awazim, but as news was received in the rebel Ikhwan camps that Ibn Sa'ud's army was moving into Al-Hasa, Ikhwan preoccupations were less with raiding than with seeking agreement on how to cope with the impending attack. Efforts by the Ikhwan to send their women and children to Kuwait for refuge were repelled by the British who obliged the Amir of Kuwait to make good his promise not to support the rebels. Efforts by Faysal al-Dawish, himself, to meet and talk with the Amir were brushed off. After the defeat of the 'Utaybah in western Najd, and the British rejection of al-Dawish's request to provide protection for rebel women and children in Kuwait, while he and his Ikhwan were off attacking Najd, or to protect them from being bombed by the British, it became all too clear that the rebellion would be quelled. British air craft were chasing the Ikhwan out of Kuwait as fast as they entered seeking protection, while Ibn Sa'ud's forces were pressing every day closer to the triangle near the Kuwait border into which the Ikhwan had cornered themselves. After the British refusal to assist the Ikhwan in any way, even passively, al-Dawish allowed those of the Ikhwan rebels who wanted to seek pardon from the King to leave and each go his own way. Many of them took this opportunity, sought and received forgiveness. Faysal al-Dawish knew that it was too late for him. He could only either fight or flee!

By early November 1929 the remnants of the Ikhwan which had fled to Kuwait had left on orders from the British. Every day more Ikhwan rebels deserted to Ibn Sa'ud's camp seeking his pardon, while others streamed out of Kuwait in an almost leaderless conglomeration of confused people. Short on food and water supplies for themselves, the Ikhwan could hardly provide for their camels and cattle, hundreds of which died of thirst. As Ibn Sa'ud's army came closer, the British had sent their planes and armored cars to reconnoiter the Ikhwan keeping them under constant observation to obstruct any attempt to flee into Iraq or Jordan both areas under British administration. In January 1930 Na'if ibn al-Hithlain, convinced that there was no possible escape or hope in combat, surrendered to an armored column of the RAF. Then on 10 January Faysal al-Dawish and Sahud ibn Lami, the other two prominent Ikhwan leaders surrendered. For lack of even nominal leadership the Ikhwan rebellion just ceased to exist. It now became a British problem to reorganize the Ikhwan groups, to round up the chief leaders, to take an inventory of the loot which the Ikhwan still had and which had to be turned over to the rightful owners, and then finally to turn over these leaders to Ibn Sa'ud.

Earlier the British had promised Ibn Sa'ud that they would turn over the Ikhwan rebels on condition that he spare their lives and treat them humanely. Now that they actually had these rebels in custody, they tried to renege. On 17 January 1930, the Foreign Office instructed Colonel Biscoe, [30] Resident in the Persian Gulf to take Dickson and Burnett to meet and discuss with Ibn Sa'ud on the fate of the rebels now in British hands. Biscoe was given the following guidelines:

a) The lives of the Ikhwan rebel leaders and their relatives should be spared.
b) Punishment will not be excessive, or outrage Arab sentiment or run counter to British traditions.
c) Effective measures will be taken to eliminate the possibility of Iraq or Kuwait suffering further from Ikhwan raids.

Before putting forth these conditions, Biscoe was instructed to try to persuade Ibn Sa'ud to agree to exile the Ikhwan leaders either to Cyprus or to some other colony. Al-Dawish, al-Hithlain and Ibn Lami were flown to Basra and there transferred on a British warship, H. M. S. Lupin which was anchored in the Shatt al-Arab. The rest of the 'Ujman and Mutayr rebels were instructed to congregate about fifteen miles south of the Kuwait frontier at Safwan where they were guarded by RAF armored cars until they could be handed over to Ibn Sa'ud. [31] Once the three Ikhwan leaders were safely aboard the craft, Biscoe flew by RAF aircraft from Kuwait to Ibn Sa'ud's camp where, after some discussion, he agreed to turn over the rebels on the basis of the three conditions cited above. He justified his not pushing for the exiling of the rebels as follows:

a) Britain had provided Ibn Sa'ud with arms, ammunition, and even planes and personnel to help subdue the rebels.
b) Britain had taken drastic measures to ensure that no facilities should be accorded to the rebel tribes.
c) Britain's attitude had been one of readiness to assist in the struggle against the rebels.
d) While refusal to turn over the rebels would not constitute a technical breach of faith, Ibn Sa'ud would have returned to Najd angry,

---

[30] Cable from Colonel Biscoe, 17 January 1930, Public Record Office, MSS, Foreign Office, Vol. 14449, Doc. No. E 275.

[31] Dickson, *Kuwait*, p. 320.

and would be supplied with a good reason to overlook the resumption of border raiding on the part of the tribes there once new leaders arose to lead them. [32]

Ibn Sa'ud provided the British with the following written guarantees for the lives of the rebels:

"1) That in spite of the punishment which the three leaders, Faisal-ad-Dawish, Naif-bin-Hithlain and Jasir-bin-Lami, and their followers deserve for their offences against neighbouring Governments and their rebellion against us, we will spare their lives and those of their tribes in compliance with the wish of the British Government.

2) We regard it as our prerogative to inflict upon these people such punishment as will restrain them in future, and restrain others whose souls may lead them to do evil; these punishments, however, will be saturated with the spirit of justice and mercy for which we are known, but we reserve the right to take from them any property that they may have taken from others.

3) As regards the raids, we promise to prevent any raids against the neighbouring Governments, Iraq and Koweit, whether by Mutair, Ajman or any other Nejd tribe; should anything of the kind take place in future, we shall be prepared to apply without delay the Bahra Agreement in the case of Iraq, and to restore immediately whatever may be plundered from Koweit and Nejd. If the ruler of Koweit desires to enter into an agreement in regards to raids, similar to the Bahra Agreement, we are prepared to enter into such an agreement with him.

4) As regards property that has been carried off from Iraq nationals in the past, we are prepared to apply the procedure prescribed in the Bahra Agreement and, in the case of Koweit, to effect a settlement of claims in accordance with the procedure at present in force, provided that none of the rebellious Mutair and Ajman and their followers who are in the hands of the British authorities or their property remain in Iraq or Koweit territory." [33]

On 28 January the rebels were flown to a landing strip near Khabari Wadhha in an English warplane. They were accompanied by Colonel Dickson and met by Hafiz Wahbah, and taken by car to the King's tent. Dickson records that the meeting between "rebels and master was pathetic. With tears streaming down his face Ibn Sa'ud allowed each of the prisoners to kiss him on the nose, Badawin fashion." [34] Hafiz

---

[32] Consul General Biscoe to Lord Passfield, February 26, 1930, Public Record Office, MSS, Foreign Office, Vol. 14451, Document No. E 1981.

[33] Enclosure No. 1 to Volume 14451, Document No. E 1081.

[34] Dickson, *Kuwait*, p. 324.

Wahbah was more impressed with how this poignant meeting contrasted with earlier ones when the King and al-Dawish met as friends. In the past, noted Wahbah, al-Dawish was accompanied by about 150 armed men and always arrived at the *majlis* as a great man of high rank and station who sat near the King. When he left to return to Al-Artawiyah, it was always with a large amount of arms, ammunition, food and material from Ibn Sa'ud. Now, disgraced and appearing before the King as a traitor, Faysal al-Dawish heard Bin Sa'ud ask:

> ...did you want to be King? But each of you were kings in the areas over which you were stationed. Which of you is better than me? Superiority belongs to God alone! Which one of you have I not taken with my sword. There is not one of you whose father or brother I have not killed, and did not subdue except by God's help and then by the sword. I granted your every wish. I became wretched because of you, working day and night for all of your comfort and happiness. Did you not fear God when you wrote to Glubb that you wanted to move to Iraq, and that you wanted to belong to him. Did you think that you would have a higher station in life there than you had with me? 35

According to Wahbah, Faysal replied:

> God knows, oh 'Abd-al-'Aziz, that you were not cheap with us, and that you did everything to show yourself a great man; we returned the good with evil, and we fled from your face to infidelity, and they brought us back to you on one of their own airplanes. It is sufficient how small I feel before the brothers after you were generous with us; may God kill the devil who led us to this stage where we are now. 36

Immensely pleased with the final submission of the Ikhwan, Ibn Sa'ud summed up his feelings saying "From today, we shall all live a new life." 37 He wasted no time in bringing the country together by the telephone and wireless, and the telegraph, with the Ikhwan powerless to do anything about it.

Ibn Bijad, Faysal al-Dawish, ibn Hithlain, the three chief rebels were now all in prison in Riyadh. Ibn Sa'ud spared their lives as he promised, much to the astonishment of some British observers who thought that he would renege. While it is almost certain that they were not abused, beaten, or otherwise harrassed in prison, it is equally true

---

35 Wahbah, *Jazirat*, p. 308.
36 *Ibid.*
37 *Ibid.*, p. 309.

that the conditions in which they lived out their last days were far from ideal. [38]

In retrospect, one must consider the state of social development in Arabia at the time of their imprisonment and the immense suffering and killing that these Ikhwan leaders had caused, not only among warriors, but among unarmed tribesmen, women and children. Considering these, and the need to establish precedent for potential insurgents who may contemplate similar activity, Ibn Sa'ud's treatment may have been relatively lenient.

In addition to obliging Ibn Sa'ud by turning over the three senior rebels, the British also assisted him in rounding up most of the eighteen whom he had put on a wanted list: [39]

Surrendered voluntarily to Ibn Sa'ud:
1) Mutlaq al-Sur
2) Mahar ibn 'Asam

Escaped to Iraq, refugee with Al-Zafir
3) Abu Hoqtah al-Motalaqim
4) Muhammad ibn Juwaiyid
5) Madhkar ibn Hadhran
6) 'Abdullah al-Dhamir
7) Muhammad ibn Hadhran
8) Shu'aifan Abu Shaqrah
9) Khalid al-Muhammad
10) 'Abdullah ibn Mikhial

Found by a British search party and sent to Ibn Sa'ud
11) Nasir ibn Juma'ah and sons of Ibn Tuflan

As punishment for their rebellious activities, the followers of the three rebel leaders were obliged to pay the following:

a) Faysal al-Dawish: All of his camels including the famous *shurf,* the black herd, and all of his horses.
b) The Dushan Clan of the Mutayr tribe: Half of their camels including all "riding" camels and all their horses.
c) Rank and File Mutayr: Two thirds of their camels including all "riding" camels and horses.

---

[38] Dickson to Political Agent, Kuwait, 27 October 1930, Public Record Office, MSS, Foreign Office, Vol. 14452, Document No. E 5776.

[39] Attachment to report on number and type of loot found in Ikhwan tents, 16 April 1930, Public Record Office, MSS, Foreign Office, Vol. F. O. 14451, Document No. E 1991.

d) 'Ujman: no exact details, but treatment was probably more severe than the Mutayr. [40]

Glubb has recorded that of the *shurf* camels which numbered 120, Ibn Sa'ud confiscated one hundred which he gave to his son, Muhammad, while leaving 20 with the Dushan. [41] That the Dushan kept some *shurf* camels was confirmed to this writer by Muhammad ibn Jab'a al-Dawish who said that one of Faysal al-Dawish's sons still have some on a farm not far from Al-Artawiyah.

All of Ibn Sa'ud's problems did not come to an end with the suppression of the Ikhwan rebellion. The Ikhwan who were never called upon to participate in either the rebellion or the suppression by either of the interested parties were still on their *hijrdah*, and while they may not have condoned insurrection, many of them felt that Ibn Sa'ud had betrayed them and their religion, certainly that he had used them as a tool to achieve personal, ambitious objectives. Dickson concluded that the Ikhwan nurtured resentment for Ibn Sa'ud because they believed that:

a) Ibn Sa'ud had not stood by the Ikhwan; it was he who had made them what they were, and they too were good Muslims.
b) He called the infidel British to aid him, and with their help was able to crush Muslim subjects.
c) He had treated Faysal al-Dawish, Na'if ibn Hithlain and Sultan ibn Bijad, three of the greatest chieftains in Arabia, with cruel and uncalled for severity, when more chivalrous methods would have sufficed. [42]

As for (a), this was presumably the crux of the whole rebellion, hence it is not reasonable to expect that the very Ikhwan who were not convinced of Ibn Sa'ud's position prior to the rebellion would be persuaded by the force of arms. As for (b) there is no doubt that this must have rankled with the Ikhwan, not only because their defeat would have been impossible without it, but because their own Imam had enlisted the aid of the very people whom he taught were their mutual enemies. (c) Ibn Sa'ud's treatment of these people has not been fully documented, and therefore not available for analysis. One must keep in mind however what the Ikhwan treatment of their prisoners

---

[40] *Ibid.* separate, unnumbered, unlettered attachment.
[41] Extract from Glubb Report, 20 May 1930, Public Record Office, MSS, F. O. Vol. 14451, Document No. E 2578.
[42] *Dickson*, Kuwait, 329.

might have been if they were victorious. The Ikhwan had no right to expect better treatment than they were prepared to give to their victims.

Aside from the Ikhwan proper, rebellions existed in the north-western part of the peninsula against Ibn Sa'ud led by a tribal chief, Ibn Rafida. These were definitely supported by and/or fomented by the Hashemite rules of Iraq and Jordan, most notably 'Abdullah. While never serious threats to the control of Ibn Sa'ud over the rest of the peninsula, they did preoccupy him with military matters at least up until the end of 1932, and almost forced him into a military confrontation with the British once again over Jordan, not because of his own Ikhwan who were itching to be released against the Hashemites, but because of attacks coming from the other side of the border, a reverse situation to what existed less than a decade earlier. [43]

With the rebellions over, Ibn Sa'ud turned toward the economic development and administrative renewal of his now united kingdom. He had pardoned many of his enemies, not a few of whom were given responsible positions and re-instated in his good graces. Faysal al-Shiblan, a Mutayr Ikhwan chieftain, who surrendered to Ibn Sa'ud, was forgiven and ultimately rose to high favor and given responsibility for all of the King's camels. [44] Majid ibn Khathila, the man who had delivered the fateful letter of Ibn Bijad to Ibn Sa'ud at Sabila, was later given a responsible government position and subsequently authorized to form remnants of the Ikhwan into what is now the present day National Guard. His punishment was the shaving of his beard and mustache and "exiling" himself for several weeks near Dhurma." [45] Members of the al-Dawish family still governed the Al-Artawiyah, while the Sha'alans of the Al-Ruwalah maintained their positions of power in the Jawf despite the fact that some senior Sha'alans had joined the rebellion. Ibn Sa'ud's ability to consolidate his hold over the country, after rebellion, was due in no small measure to his ability to rise above small and petty rivalries and sometimes over major clashes, to forgive his enemies and to give them a share and vested interest in the regime. Even if his purposes were pragmatic rather than altruistic, this in itself required a man of vision and foresight. There

---

[43] The Ibn Rafida rebellion, in itself, constitutes a separate story. Relative documents are Sir F. Humphrey's report, 15 August 1932, Public Record Office, MSS, F. O. 16016, Document No. 4101, and F. O., 16017, Document No. 6943, 31 December 1932, paraphrase of telegrams from Secretary of State for the Colonies.

[44] Dickson, *Kuwait*, p. 325.

[45] Personal interview in Al-Ghat Ghat, March 1968.

was little in Ibn Sa'ud's character, despite his capability to be quite ruthless with enemies if this were the only solution, to show that he was a man who preferred or enjoyed violence, or to wield power for its own sake. From his youth he had felt that he had a role to play, namely to recoup his family's losses; it is difficult to know when he saw that vision encompass something far bigger, namely, a modern, independent, viable country rising on the territory of what is now the Kingdom, but he must have seen this vision somewhere. Those who have lived in the extensive wastes of Saudi Arabia can appreciate how powerful that vision must have been; the desire to create a modern kingdom in such a forlorn, divided country could only have been motivated by a profoundly felt inspiration.

CHAPTER TWELVE

EPILOGUE

The Ikhwan Movement was the unique instrument which Ibn Sa'ud used to unify the peninsula. His personality, genius and moving drive excepted ,the Ikhwan were certainly the most important single factor in the unification of the greater part of the Arabian peninsula into one independent country. Despite the Movement's short chronological existence, its gigantic contributions to the cause of unity are out of all proportion to the size of its ranks, and its costs in human and material resources. Despite its demise, the force of its impact on the character of the country which it helped to create was felt long after it ceased to exist as a viable Movement, and in many instances its force is still felt throughout the country to the present day.

Ikhwan contributions to unity are many and easily isolated for review, the most significant being:

a) All of the strategic, important areas fell to Ikhwan units, including Khurma, Turaba, Ta'if, Mecca and Medina, with Ikhwan contingents participating notably in the conquests of Ha'il and the Jawf. It was fear of Ikhwan reprisals that kept many of these subdued areas free from insurgency or open rebellion, especially the Ha'il area.

b) The Ikhwan thwarted Hashemite attempts to weaken and destroy the resurrected Sa'udi dynasty, taking the offensive themselves by raiding Jordan, Kuwait, and Iraq border areas.

c) They injected into daily life a new asceticism, a spartan temperament sharpened by religion, as well as a fierce national pride and loyalty that never before existed among tribal elements in the peninsula. While this national pride and loyalty never fully percolated into the Hijaz levels of society, its effects were measurably felt there nevertheless.

While it would be rash to say that Ibn Sa'ud's unification of the peninsula would have been impossible without the Ikhwan, certainly the cost in human and material resources, and the length of time required to effect unity would be substantially higher with a corresponding lower chance of success.

The extraordinary military feats of the Ikhwan are all the more outstanding when one considers that while they were statistically numerous only a small number of them actually participated in battles and raids. The faction of the 'Utaybah tribe led by Ibn Bijad centered at Al Ghat Ghat, and the elements of the Mutayr tribe under al Dawish at Al-Artawiyah complemented by such independent leaders as Khalid ibn Luwai of Khurma bore the brunt of Ikhwan martial responsibilities. The rest of the Ikhwan were located on small *hujar* in the hinterland and contributed their share in less active ways, i.e., by acting as sentinels on the fringes of settled areas, by becoming obedient citizens who required no firm hand to police them, and finally by constituting an ever ready reserve force to re-inforce the Ikhwan activists, if the need arose. Ironically, the largest single levy of Ikhwan, certainly the most representative of all tribes and *hujar*, was imposed not to subdue the infidels or to fight in the Hijaz, but to suppress their rebellious comrades at Sabila and later at the confrontations near the Kuwait border.

As for costs, the Ikhwan must be reckoned among the cheapest military force ever mobilized to conquer large stretches of territory. For the most part, armed only with vintage rifles, or locally made crude spears, provisioned with only a handful or two of dates, and a cup of flour, these warriors embarked on military expeditions at a trifling cost to the Public Treasury, and little in logistical or arms support; the little public money that may have been expended on them was more than repaid by the booty in livestock, silver, gold and other valuables which they brought to the Public Treasury after their victories. Yet these warriors received no individual salaries and collected no pensions, either for themselves in life, or for their families in the event of their death. Their only form of payment was the extent to which they shared the benefits of life on the government subsidized *hujar*.

In terms of human costs, both to themselves and to their victims, the price was higher. Hundreds of Ikhwan fell in battle due in part to their religious fanaticism which inclined them to seek death on the battlefield, due in part to their inadequate military training and lack of better equipment, and due in part to the new military strategy which they, themselves, introduced, namely, a fight to the death with no retreat. These same attitudes cost their victims equally severe casualties. Generally speaking, infidels were shown little or no mercy, prisoners were seldom, if ever, taken, and their worldly goods were forfeited. To be sure, the Ikhwan were often ruthless and their excesses unprecedented in peninsula history, yet without defending what they did, it is important to understand why they did it; their excesses cannot be fairly compared with those perpetrated by combattants of other societies which enjoy a more advanced level of civilization. Their excesses were neither the extremes of educated, disciplined troops fighting for expansionist nationalist objectives, nor atrocities motivated by greed, avarice and other material gain, such as that of colonialists who subjugated then exploited weaker peoples in the quest for territorial gain and material wealth. The Ikhwan indeed added territories; booty was garnered, but these were incidental to, and not the primary objective of, their own endeavors which was to restore Wahhabi Islam among people whom they regarded as lapsed Muslims. In short, the Ikhwan personally lived no better materially after their conquests than they had before, and they did not exploit the resources of the conquered territories for their own use.

Ikhwan atrocities while serious and regretable were distinguished more by the intenseness with which they were perpetrated and by the break with traditional nomadic traditions of combat than by the number of victims involved or the frequency of their recurrence. Considering the extensive territory of Arabia, and the tribal and racial differences that therein prevailed, the wonder is that not more atrocities were committed. As for booty, sheep, goats, camels, and other cattle exchanged hands, or may have been destroyed, but this was not new to Arabia. Yet no areas were economically ruined, or crops maliciously or otherwise destroyed, and no cities or towns burned or devastated. With the exception of the unfortunate incidents at Ta'if—not all of which can be laid at the door of the Ikhwan—cities, towns, villages and other settlements were left unscathed. The Ikhwan swept through Arabia much like a surgeon's knife, deftly cutting out the "malignancy" and leaving the healthy parts intact.

Yet with all due respect to the Ikhwan, without the guiding hand of Ibn Sa'ud, the Movement would have run rampant, wreaking havoc not only along the frontiers, but internally as well, wrecking thereby much, if not all, of the gains which they had achieved. Cleverly, but not without serious difficulties, Ibn Sa'ud, through foresight and statesmanship, never allowed the Ikhwan to commit him to a course of action which he calculated could lead only to disaster. He successfully fought their attempts to discriminate between the new converts who lived on the *hujar*, and the non-*hujar* residents, a distinction that would have weakened the internal unity of the country; he saw the adverse implications of continued raiding of the non-conformist Muslims in Iraq,

Kuwait, and Jordan, territories which the British administered. He knew when to set territorial limits to conquests, refusing to annex territory which he knew could not be easily integrated into his Kingdom, northern Yemen and Kuwait both being examples of territories which he could easily have overrun. If the Ikhwan had their way, they, blinded by unlimited religious faith, would have sallied forth, oblivious to the political ramifications of their actions, and conquered these territories, but at the same time providing the pretext for unfavorable military action against Ibn Sa'ud by his enemies.

Few countries have built their unity on less internal disruption and destruction than that which occurred in Sa'udi Arabia. Aside from a few changes in religious administration, and the compulsory implementation of Islamic obligations (public prayer, attendance at the mosque, etc.), the new government did not alter the way of life of the people in the conquered areas in any detrimental way. In exchange for these fundamentalist changes, however, the new rulers instituted a more efficient system of administration, provided a degree of public security heretofore unknown in the area, and encouraged economic freedoms conducive to growth and expansion. The pilgrim centers of Mecca and Medina prospered; the pilgrims themselves were not molested or exploited, hence more Muslims made the pilgrimage, thereby benifiting the local merchants and other persons engaged in the pilgrimage trade. Not only the Hijaz people benefited; the conquered aristocratic familes of Najd were not forgotten either. Some of the Al Rashid children were adopted by Ibn Sa'ud and were raised with his own children, after the conquest of Ha'il and the death of parents or parent. He married some Rashid women while some of his lieutenants married others, not only as a method of binding the wounds of battle and making political alliances, but also in deference to Arab bedouin tradition that the killer of the bread winner assumes the responsibilities to the surviving wife and children. Some womenfolk of the Dushan clan of the Mutayr were given monthly pensions, despite the fact that their men folk had twice before borne arms in serious rebellion against Ibn Sa'ud. Al-Artawi-ah, itself, was left to be governed by members of the clan. Majid ibn Khathila who had personally delivered Ibn Bijad's provocative letter to Ibn Sa'ud on the eve of the battle at Sabila was pardoned by Ibn Sa'ud himself and ultimately became Minister of Animal Husbandry and one of Ibn Sa'ud's most trusted advisors, accompanying him to Egypt to meet with President Franklin D. Roosevelt on an American warship anchored in Egyptian waters during World War II.

After the shock of the Ikhwan rebellions wore off and Ibn Sa'ud emerged as the unchallenged leader, the Ikhwan once more came into their own. Although the Movement as a meaningful separate entity ended in 1930, after the capture of Faysal al-Dawish and other Ikhwan principals, Ikhwan contingents continued to raid into Jordan which was fostering the Ibn Rafida revolt in northwestern Arabia. Husayn's son 'Abdullah, ruler of Jordan, was attempting to foment revolution in Sa'udi Arabia in order to topple the regime there, hoping thereby to restore Hashemite rule in the peninsula.

Ikhwan participation in the suppression of the Ibn Rafidah revolt is less proper to the study of the origins and development of the Ikhwan movement than to the study of what the Ikhwan ultimately became, because 1) these Ikhwan units were herein used for the first time to preserve and defend Sa'udi territorial integrity, not to acquire new territory; 2) they were performing under the direct command of Ibn Sa'ud as the head of an independent, internationally recognized state. They were, in effect, the vanguard of what is known as the White Army, or the National Guard, and constituted its irregular units, called *liwas*. The Ikhwan *"liwas"* are still located in their *hujar*, come under the immediate command of the local amir, and are organized into tribal units and answer emergency calls only, bringing with them, as of old, their own rifle, ammunition, and other provisions.

Finally, even after the demise of the Movement the Ikhwan remained a significant political-religious factor in the country. Instead of reverting to nomadism, most remained sedentary and attached to the *hujar*. They were poor but proud, and retained their religious dedication and commitment to the *shari'a*. Although they were no less fanatic, their fanaticism was felt less. Once they ceased to be a military-political threat to the regime, they gradually worked their way into the confidence of the government. In addition to bearing arms, and forming the backbone of a home militia (the irregular units of the White Army), they and their children were given positions of trust and responsibility in the ever expanding government, since they were regarded as the most stalwart citizens, firmly committed to Islam as an ideology and to the patriarchal-king system of government as the appropriate form of rule. In return for service and allegiance to the King, they demanded, and received, unhampered access to him and his court. And this tradition persists until the present day.

In recognition of their contributions to the creation of the Sa'udi state, old surviving Ikhwan receive monthly pensions from the government, individual payments ranging from several hundred to several thousand dollars annually. These benefits extend to a lesser degree to the children of the old time Ikhwan, a constant reminder to them that their fathers and grandfathers marched bravely with banners unfurled along with Ibn Sa'ud when he was a poverty stricken youth, with no political base of power, armed with old rifles, and filled with the determination to win back the estate of his ancestors.

APPENDIX

The following pages provide several lists of *hujar* identified by tribe, based on Philby, Ibn Nasir, Dickson, Umm al-Qura, other written sources, and on verbal sources which this writer interviewed. To facilitate the identification of these *hujar* as they appear in these various works their names have been left as they originally appear; however, it is not too difficult to compare them with the *hujar* of the same names on the other lists. Variations in bedouin dialects, regional pronunciations, as well as different Arabic spellings have resulted in several renditions of the same name by different writers. Generally the bedouin use the diminutive of a word (*tasghir*) when they pronounce a name, although when the name is written it is quite easy to read it, and subsequently spell it, differently, i.e. Usila/Usayla, or Al-Hufirah/Al-Hufayrah. The only completely accurate method of getting the correct pronunciation would be to have a native of each *hijrah* pronounce the name aloud, quite a formidable task.

Another problem relating to the identification of the *hujar* is caused by one writer listing the same *hijrah* as belonging to two separate tribes, as does al-Rihani, for example, in the list appearing in his English text, and the Arabic text of his different works. This is due in part to the fact that many of the *hujar* were mixed, hence if one asked a native of a given *hijrah* the tribal origin of it and he was a Harbi, he would be inclined to give Harb as the answer, although Shammar tribesmen may also reside there. Then again many *hujar* have the same name; Rawdah or Ruwaydah, for example, is very common, signifying as it does garden or small garden. If one writer lists Rawdah as belonging to one tribe, and another lists it as belonging to a different tribe, chances are they are both correct, but are referring to different *hujar*.

TABLE ONE

NAMES OF *HUJAR* BASED ON UM AL-QURA SOURCES [1]

Tribe:

MUTAYR
Al-Artawiyah, Al-Faruthi, Al-Tamariyah, Al-Ja'ala, Um Hazm, Mubaydh, Al-Haswa, Daban, Budha, Al-Ithla, Al-Artawi, Mulayih, Wadakh, Al-Mutaywi, Al-Shaflahiyah, Al-'Ammar, Qarba, Al-Tamariyah, Al-Qariyah Al-Sifli, Al-Qariyah Al-'Ulya

'UTAYBAH
Al-Dahnah, Al-Hufayrah, Al-Labib, Amsada, Sinam, Al-Ruwaydah, 'Usayla, Sajir, 'Arwa, Al-Rawdha, Kabshan, Al-Maklah, Al-Sauh, 'Arja, Nifi, Al-Hayd, Abu Jalal, Al-Qarara, Shabirma, Al-Qarayn

HARB
Al-Qarayn, Burud, Al-Ba'ayith, Al-Muhala'i, Al-Fawwara, Qatan, Al-Dulayfmyah, Biqiyah, Al-Shabakiyah, Al-Thibiyah, Al-Faydah, Al-Bid'a, Al-Dukhnah, Al-Khashibi, Al-Quwara, Al-Shubayhiyah, Al-Mahamalani, Al-Nahitiyah, Aqlah Al-Qasur, Al-Bamiri, Al-Dath, Al-Jirathamiyah, Ghasl, Al-Dulaymiyah, Al-Sam'uriyah, Thadiq, Al-Namariyah, Aqbah, Khashiba, Dhaida, Kuhaylah, Abu Mughir

SHAMMAR
Al-Ajfar, Al-Safra, Um Al-Qalban, Jibba, Al-Hufayr, Al-Taym, Al-Khabba, Al-Sina, Al-Nifi, Al-'Adhim, Al-Mak/hul, l-Sahway, Al-Shafiq, Al-Qasir, Al-Faydha, Al-Aqlah

'ANAZA
Khibar, Al-Faydhah, Baydha' Nathil, Al-Sha'abiyah, Al-Samli, Al-Sha'abiyah the second, Al-Balaziyah

QAHTAN
Al-Rayn Al-Asfal, Al-Rayn Al-'A'la, Al-Jufayr, Al-Hisah, Sabha, Al-Hayathim, Al-Hasa Al-Sifli, Al-Hasa Al-'Ulya, Al-Munaysif, Laban

DAWASIR
Al-Hamr, Mushirfah, Al-Washita, Al-Hamarmah

'UJMAN
Al-Sarar, Al-Kahfa, Al-Wanan, Nunayth, Yakha, Al-Zaghin, Al-Ari'arah, Al-'Ayyanah, 'Anwa, Al-Faradi, Al-Sahaf, Um Rabi'ah, Al-Barah, Matnanah

'AWAZIM
Atiq, Thaj

AL MURRA
Yabrin, Al-Sikak, Nibak, Al-Badu'

---

[1] Ummal-Qura, numbers 208 and 292.

HUTAYM
Niwan, Al-Rawdh, Al-'Amayir

SUBAY'
Al-Hissa, Al-Dhubiya', Al-Khidr

SUHUL
Al-Mashash, Al-Ruwaydah, Al-Bid'a

AL-ZAFIR
Al-Sha'iybi

BANI KHALID
Al-Dafi
Julmudah

BANI HAJIR
'Ayndar [2]
Yakrib
Fudah
Salasil

TABLE TWO

NAMES OF *HUJAR* BASED ON IBN NASIR SOURCES [3]

Tribe:

MUTAYR
Al-Artawiyah, Mubayidh, Budha, Furaithan, Mulaih, Al-Ammar, Al-Ithla, Al-Artawi, Miska, Dhariya, Qariyah Al-'Ulya

'UTAYBAH
Al-Ghat Ghat, Al-Rawdha, 'Arwa, Sanam, Al-Dahma, (Barqa) Al-Suh, 'Arja, Sajir, 'Usayla, Kabshan, Nifi

HARB
Dukhma, Shubikiyah, Dulaymiyah Al-Qurayn, Al-Saqiyah, Hulayfa, Hunaydhil, Al-Barud, Khusayba, Qibah, Al-Fawwara

SHAMMAR
Banwan, Al-Fautaym, Al-Hafira, Al-Balaziyah, Al-Khabba, Al-Taym, Al-Ajfar, Al-Kahfa, Al-Ghaydaha, Baidha, Natil

'ANAZA
Shuaiba, Umm Qalban, Al-Shaqiq [4]

QAHTAN
Al-Hayathim, Al-Jufayr, Al-Hasah, Al-Rain Al-Asfal, Al-Rain Al-'Ali

---

[2] Given by Ibn Nasir as Al Murrah.
[3] Ibn Nasir, *op. cit.*
[4] Given by Umm al-Qura as Shammar; by Philby as 'Anazah.

DAWASIR
  Mushairifa, al-Wasita

'AJMAN
  Sarar, Hanina, Al-Sahaf, Al-'Uqayr, Nita', 'Urayra

'AWAZIM
  Al-Hasi, Thaj, Al-Hannat, Utaiq

BANI MURRA
  Shibaq, Abiraq, 'Ayn Dar [5]

AL-KHARJ COLONIES
  Dhubia', Al-Bid'a, Al-Munaysif, Al-Akhdar, Tasm

BANU HUTAYM
  Khuraifat, Al-Masa', Al-Marir

TABLE THREE

NAMES OF *HUJAR* BASED ON PHILBY SOURCES [6]

Tribe:

MUTAYR
  Al-Artawiyah, Mubaidh, Budha, Furaithan, Mulaih Ammar, Ithila, Artawi, Miska, Dhariya, Qariyah

'UTAYBAH
  Ghat Ghat, Al-Raudha, Arwa, Sanam of the Barqa branch of the tribe; Dahina, Al-Suh, Arja, Sajir, Usaila, Kabshan, Nifi from the Ruqa branch of the tribe

HARB
  Dukhna, Shubaika, Dulaimiya, Qurain, Saqiya, Hulaifa, Hunaidhil, Barud, Khusaiba, Qiba, Fawwara

SHAMMAR
  Banwan, Futaim, Hafira, Ballaziya, Khabba, Al-Taim, Ajfar, Kahfa, Ghaidha, Baidha, Nathil

'ANAYZAH
  Shuaiba, Al-Qulban, Shuqiq [7]

HUTAYM
  Khuraifat, Al-Masa', Murair

QAHTAN
  Hayathim
  Jafar
  Al-Hasat
  Rain

---

[5] Given by Umm al-Qura as Bani Hajir.
[6] Philby, *Sa'udi Arabia*, p. 262; Philby, *Empty Quarter*, p. 60.
[7] Given by Umm al-Qura as Shammar.

DAWASIR
  Mushairifah
  Wasita

'UJMAN
  Al-Sarrar
  Hanina
  Al-'Uqair
  Nata
  Uraira

'AWAZIM
  Al-Hasi
  Thaj
  Al-Hannat
  Utaiq

MIXED COLONIES
  Shibaq
  Ubairiq [8]
  Ayn Dar [9]

AL-KHARJ AREA
  (mixed Suhul/Siba'i tribesmen): Dhubai'a, Bid'a, Al-Munaisef, Akhdar, Tasm, Al-Ruwaidha

TABLE FOUR

NAMES OF *HUJAR* BASED ON AL-RIHANI SOURCES [10]

Tribe:

MUTAYR
  Al-Artawiyah, Muabidh, Faritan, Malih, Al-'Amar, Al-Ithlah, Al-Artawi, Masikah, Dhariyah, Qariyah Al-Ulya, Qariyal Al-Sifla, Al-Sh'ib, Sudair, Nukair

'UTAYBAH
  Al-Ghat Ghat, 'Urway, Al-Sinam, Al-Rawdah (of the Barqa branch) Al-Dahna, Al-Suh, Sajir, 'Arja, 'Usaylah, Nifi of the Ruqa branch of the tribe

HARB
  Dukhna, Al-Shabikah, Al-Dulaymiyah, Al-Qurayn, Al-Saqiyah, Halifah, Hunayzil, Al-Burud, Qibah (pronounced Ajbah) Al-Fawwara

SHAMMAR
  Al-Ajfar, Banwan, Fatim, Al-Qasir, Al-Hafir, Al-Balaziyah, Al-Khabbah, Al-Ghaydah, Baydha Natil, Al-Taym, Umm Qalban, Al-Shaqiq, Rawdat Al-'Uyun

---

[8] Given by Ibn Nasir as Al-Murrah.
[9] Given by Umm al-Qura as Bani Hajir.
[10] Al-Rihani, *Najd*, pp. 404-406. Ibn Sa'oud, pp. 198-199.

QAHTAN
Al-Hiyathim, Al-Hiyathim-Badiyah, Al-Jafir, Al-Hisa, Al-Rayn Al-Asfal, Al-Rayn al-'Ala

DAWASIR
Mushirqah, Al-Wasita

'UJMAN
Al-Sarar, Hanidh, Al-Sahaf, Al-Uqayr, Urayrah

'AWAZIM
Thaj, Al-Hissi, Al-Hinnat, Al-'Utayq

MURRA
Al-Shabak, 'Ubayriq, 'Ayn Dar [11]

AL-KHARJ COLONIES [12]
Al-Dhabiy'ah, Al-Bid'a, Al-Munaysif, Al-Akhdar, Taybism, Al-Ruwaydah

TABLE FIVE

NAMES OF *HUJAR* BASED ON DICKSON SOURCES [13]

Tribe:

MUTAYR
Irtawiyah, Al-Faraithan, Imgaiyadh, Mulaih, Al-'Imar, Al-Ithlah, Jariya (Qariya 'Ilya), Jariya (Qariya) Sifla, Ingair (or Nuqir), Naqira, Al-Sha'ab, Dhuraiyah, Mishaa'

'UTAYBAH
Ghat Ghat, Al-Dahana, As Sawh, As Sajar, 'Arjah (or 'Al-'Arj), 'Usaila, Nifai (or Al-Nifi'), Al-Hijarat Khalid ibn Luwai', 'Arma (or Al-'Urma) Al-Ghaba, Al-Raudha, Al-'Urq, Al Jafr, Raudh al 'Aiyun

HARB
'Ajibba (or Ijibba) Dukhna, Ash Shubaikiyah, Al Dulaimah, As Sadiqah, Al Qurain, Huaidhil, Al Buruq, Abu Hulaifa

QAHTAN
Al-Hayadhin, Al Jufair, Al Hisat, Al Ghil, Al Hijarat Ibn Ghannam, Haif Zahran, As Sabha, Al 'Ibra, 'Arhaiyan (the upper) 'Arhaiyan (the lower)

DAWASIR
Mushairiyam, Al Wusaitah

'AJMAN
Sarrar, Al Shafi, Al Hanin, Awaina, Uraira, 'Uqair (or 'Ujair)

'AWAZIM
Thaj, Al Hinnat, Al Haisi, Al 'Atiqi

---

[11] In *Najd* al-Rihani identifies it as Al Murrah; in Ibn Sa'oud as Bani Hajir.
[12] Philby, Sa'udi Arabia, gives these hujar as Suhul/Subay'.
[13] Dickson, Kuwait, pp. 282-284; spellings as given in the text.

BANI MURRA
   Ambaq, 'Ubairiq

BANI HAJIR
   Adh Dhahra

BANI YAM
   Ahl Najran

HUTAIM
   Bin Wan

AL-KHARJ COLONIES
   Al-Munaisifa, Adh Dhubai'ha, Al Bida'a, Al-Akhdar, Al Taiyib Ism, Ar Ruwaidha

NAMES OF *HUJAR* BASED ON DICKSON SOURCES [14]

Hujar:

   Al Artawiya, Al Mubaiyidh, Ruwaighab, Al Hasi, Al Dulaimiyah, Al Shabikiyah,
   Al Nafi, Al 'Arja, Sajar, Vasit, 'Arwa, Sannam, Ar Riya Al Hadri, Al Khabra,
   Al Ghatghat, Al Khadhrah, Al Haiyathim, Al Wasla, Hajrat Bani Hafif, 'Awai-
   ridh, Hajrat Khalid, Hajrat Bani Sulul, Hajar Al Aba Al Gharb, Hajar Tashlith,
   Eairilshan, Ad Dhinah Al Soh, Al Ghawarah, Al Dakhnah, Al 'Araifja, Al 'Asai-
   lah, Al Thalah, Al 'Ammar, Al Ratawi, Ar Raudhah, As Sabla, Ar Rain Al Nauqi,
   Al Jufair, Librah, Al Bada', Al-Dhabi'ah, Al Munaisif, Al Ghil, Hajrat al Lawa,
   Hajrat Haif Zahran, Hajar Ahl Al Sabikhah, Hajar Ahl Najran

TABLE SIX

NAMES OF *HUJAR* BASED ON OTHER SOURCES [15]

Name:

Lina:
   Identified to this writer as a *hijrah* by Shaiykh Muhammad al-Sahabi, also in
   Futayih, Firqah, p. 43. It is located near the Kuwait-Sa'udi border.

Saghu:
   identified to this writer as a *hijrah* by a Dawasiri farmer who escorted this writer
   around the ruins of the village. It is located about 110 miles southwest of Riyadh.

Um Al-Rudhma:
   identified as a *hijrah* in *Firqah*, p. 43.

Al-Masdar:
   identified as a *hijrah* in 'Attar, *Saqr*, [16] p. 200 .

---

[14] Dickson, Memo to the Civil Commissioner, Baghdad, MSS, Foreign Office,
Vol. 5062.

[15] As indicated in the text.

[16] Attar, *Saqar*, pp. 200-201, provides a list which is almost identical with al-
Rihani's, *Najd* list. Saqr provides total estimate of population in the *hujar* according to
tribal breakdowns. Hamd Ibrahim al-Haqil, *'Abd-al-'Aziz Fi Al-Tarikh* (*'Abd-al-'Aziz
in History*) (Beirut: Mu'assisah al-Ma'arif, 1968), p. 64, provides a list of fifty-two
hujar but this list contains no names that are not found in al-Rihani or in Philby.

TABLE SEVEN

THE LOYALIST IKHWAN [17] WHWO FOUGHT THE IKHWAN REBELS

Tribe	Hijra	Amir
UTAYBAH	Nifi	'Umar ibn Rubay'an
	Al-Dahna	Ghazi al-Barak
	Usayla	Ghazi al-Thum
	Arja	Qatim al-Halil
	Sajir	Nasir ibn Muhyi
	Al-Hayd	'Aqad ibn Muhyi
	Mussadah	Khalid ibn Jami'
	Al-Ruwaydah	Jamal al-Mihri
	Abu Jalal	Mahmas al-Thaghar
	Al-Rawdah	Majid ibn Dhari ibn Fuhayd
	Al-Labib	'Abd-al-Muhsin
	Al-Hufayrah	Sajdi al-Haydhil
	Sanam	Sultan Aba Al-'Ali
	'Arwa	Ja'ja ibn Humayd (Sultan's brother)
	Al-Qarara	Sultan Abu Sanun
	Kabshan	Sultan Abu Khayshim
	Shubayrimah	Nasir ibn Razin
	Al-Qarayn	Khatim ibn Mas'ad
	Al-Suh	Sultan al-Gharbi
HARB	Al-Fawara	Hijab ibn Nahit
	Dakhna	Ayid ibn Buhaymi
	Al-Qarayn	'Abd-al-Mun'im ibn Naqi
	Al-Khashibi	'Ubayd Zuaybi
	Al-Quwara	'Ali ibn Hadib
	Al-Burud	Na'if ibn Madhyan
	Khasaiba	Tha'ar Hamad
	Al-Ba'ayith	Rijah ibn Mutlaq
	Al-Thibiyah	Shahir ibn Muraykhan
	Al-Shubayhiyah	Hindi al-Thuwaybi
	Al-Baqi'a	Duwayyikh al-Bishri
	Al-Mahalani	Rashid ibn Rashid
	Qatan	Ubayd al-Thiri
	Al-Nahitiyah	Dabbas Ibn Ghan
	'Uqlat al-Suqur	Sahat al-Shutayr
	Al-Bamiri	Ghazi Abi Kilab
	Al-Dath	Dar bin Alyiris
	Al-Jirdawiyah	'Uqab ibn Khurays
	Ghasl	Hays ibn Sulayman
	Al-Dulaymiyah	Zayn ibn Jadi'
	Thadiq	Bijad ibn Ghumaydh
	Thadiq	Bijad ibn Ghumaydh
	Al-Nimriyah	Muhammad ibn Thuwab
	Al-Baqi'iyah	Sa'd ibn Ghulayfis

[17] Umm al-Qura, number 292, (11 July 1930).

Tribe	Hijra	Amir
MUTAYR	Al-Faruthi	Mishari
	Al-Artawiyah	Na'if ibn Mizyad
	Al-Namiriyah	Ya'qub al-Humaydani
	Al-Ja'ala	'Ali Hazibit
	Umm Hazm	Awwad al-Mafiri
	Mubaydh	Lami al-Qurayfa
	Al-Haswa	Jami'an ibn Dhari
	Daban	Daghim ibn Hadba
	Budha	Mutlaq al-Hafta
	Al-'Ithla	Hawayil ibn Salman
	Al-Artawi	Salim ibn Rajjah
	Mulayih	Faysal ibn Suqayyan
	Wadakh	Turki ibn Dhamnah
	Al-Tatbuwi	Salim ibn Maznam
	Al-Shufaylihiyah	Qadan ibn Darwish
	Al-'Amar	'Abd-al-Muhsin ibn Jabrin
	Qaryah (Al-'Ulya)	Najib ibn Shuqayr
QAHTAN	Al-Rayn Al-Asfal	Khalil ibn 'Umar
	Al-Rayn Al-A'la	Hadhhal ibn Su'aydan
	Al-Jufayr	Nasir ibn Sadhan
	Al-Hisah	Funayyis ibn Huwayl
	Sabha	Sa'id al-Ruwayikh
AL-SUHUL	Al-Bid'	Sawwar ibn Ma'dal
	Al-Ruwaydah	'Abdullah ibn Mazhur
	Al-Mashash	Hasilim ibn Jal'ud
SIBA'I	Al-Hissi	Fidghush Dawlith ibn Shuwayyah
	Al-Dhubay'ah	Badri ibn Dayyah

TABLE EIGHT

IKHWAN LEADERS AT THE GENERAL ASSEMBLY [18]

Hujar of the 'Utaybah Tribe

Name	Amir	Headmen	Other
Al-Dahinah	'Umar ibn Rubay'an	Na'if and Khalid al-Hallaj; Majid al-Barraq; Badr ibn 'Alush; Al-Shuqayri ibn al-Zahnaf	
Al-Hufayyirah	Manahi al-Haydhil	Sultan ibn Hashr; Salal ibn Manas al-Haydhil	Mutawwa'/'Abdullah al-Samt
Al-Labib	'Abd al Muhsin ibn Bandar Al-Haydhil	Salah ibn Bandar; 'Umar Abu Raqabah	
Masadah	Khalid ibn Jami'	Matrak ibn Jami'	
Sanam	Sultan Aba al-'Ala'	Hazza' ibn Mughayriq	Qadi/Muhammad Al-Shawli
Al-Ruwaydah	Jamal Al Mahri		

---

18 Umm al-Qura, number 209.

Name	Amir	Headmen	Other
'Usayla	Ghazi Al-Tum	Dhayfallah Al-Tum; Dakhil Allah ibn Wasmi	Qadhi 'Abd-al-Rahman Ibn Awdan
Sajir	Dha'ar ibn Rubay'an	Na'if ibn Turki; Wasif Allah ibn Turki; Turki ibn Tayhan	
'Arwa	Hashr ibn Ma'ad ibn Humayd		
Al-Rawdha	Majid ibn Dhawi ibn Fuhayd	Fayhan ibn Fuhayd	
Kabshan	Sultan Abu Khashim	Ja'id ibn Bijad Abu Khushaym	
Al-Mukallat	Majid Abu Khashim		
Al-Sauh	Sultan al-Sharbi		
'Arja	Qatim al-Hubayl	Talq ibn Jazi'; 'Abdullah Al-Wutayr	Mutawwa'/Ibrahim Al-Siyyarti

Hujar of the Mutayr Tribe

Name	Amir	Headmen	Other
Al-Artawiyah	'Abd al 'Aziz al-Dawish	Nayif ibn Mazyid; Faysal ibn Shiblan; Muhammad ibn Badr; Haza' ibn Badr; Nasir ibn Mazyad	
Al-Qaryah Al-Sufla	Na'if al-Fughm	Sa'ud ibn Kuraydi al-Fughm; Bandar ibn Dhaidah al-Fughm	
Al-Qaryah Al-'Ulya	Turayhib ibn Shuqayr	Falah ibn Shuqayr; Faysal ibn Nayif ibn Shuqayr; Hazza' ibn Zarbiyan; Majid al-Asqah; Ghassab ibn Mandil	
Al-Furaythan	Mishari ibn Basis	Qa'id ibn Basis; Majid ibn Khasman; Turki ibn Busayyis; Khalid ibnB usayyis	
Al-Tamariyah	Ya'qub al-Humaydani	Muhammad Malik al-Humaydani; Bijad ibn Kan'an al-Humaydani; Tha'ar ibn Ya'qub al-Humaydani	Qadi/Umar Khalifa
Al-Hasu	Jami'an ibn Dhawi		
Budha	Mutlaq al-Hafta		
Mulayh	Alush ibn Suqayyan	Ghazi ibn Shaqyan	Mutawwa'/Muhammad Al-Bayz
Al-Ithla	Hawayl ibn Samhan	Muthadir ibn Samhan	
Wadhah	Manyif ibn Qutayim		
Maba'idh	Tami Al-Qurayfah		

Hujar of the Hutaym Tribe

Name	Amir	Headmen	Other
Niwan	Dalim ibn Barraq	Dha'ar ibn 'Umayr	
Al-Rawdh	Ghazi ibn Hadi		
Al-'Amayir	Shakir ibn Qalub		

Hujar of the Suhul Tribe

Name	Amir	Headmen	Other
Al-Mashash	Manahi ibn Jal'ud		
Al-Ruwaydah	'Abdullah ibn Mazhur		
Al-Bid'	Sawwan ibn Ma'dal		

Hujar of the Harb Tribe

Name	Amir	Headmen	Other
Al-Qurayn	'Abd al-Mun'im ibn Naqi	'Abdullah ibn Naqi Salah ibn Naqi	
Al-Burud	Na'if ibn Mudhayyan	Fayhan ibn Mudhayyan Falah ibn Sumay'ar	Mutawwa'/Wail ibn Yahya
Al-Ba'ayith	Rijah ibn Mutlaq	Mukhaymir ibn Mutlaq	
Al-Muhala'i	Rashid ibn Rashid		
Al-Fawwarah	Hijab ibn Nahit	Dhayfallah ibn Nahit; Zayd ibn Nahit; Hamud Abu al-'Aun; Sumayyih Al-Bishri	
Qatan	Shadid al-Dayrl		
Al-Dulaymiya	Z .ibn Juday'	Du'ayj ibn Juday'; Dhawi ibn 'Juday'	
Buqya'a	Misham al-Bishri		
Al-Shubaykiyah	Hindi al-Dhuwaybi	Fayhan Al-Thubi, Muhammad ibn Nahiq al-Dhuwaybi; Na'if ibn Nahiq al-Dhuwaybi	
Al-Dhibiyah	Tu'aymis ibn Muraykhan	Nasir ibn Muraykhah;	
Al-Faydah	'Aqil Al-Zuhayri	Hamud al-Zuhayri	
Al-Bid'	Jawan Al-Balhi		

Hujar of the Qahtan Tribe

Name	Amir	Headmen	Other
Al-Rayn Al-'Ulya	Hadhdhal ibn Su'aydan	Hizam ibn Musfir; Asha ibn Musfir Qablan Huwayri; 'Abd-al-'Aziz Labda; Faysal Al-Labdah	
Al-Rayn Al-Sufla	Sultan ibn Safran	Khalil ibn 'Umar; Sa'id ibn Julayghim; Turki ibn Sulaym; Baddah al-'Ajjaj	
Al-Hayathim	Fasal ibn Hishr	Khalid ibn Faysal; Fahid ibn Mariha; Faysal ibn Mijdal	
Al-Hasa al-Sufla	Funayyis ibn Huwayl		
Al-Hasa al-'Ulya	Sa'ad ibn Jalban		
Al-Jufayr	Nasir ibn Sadhan		
Al-Munaysif	Hilal ibn 'Abbud		
Laban	Rija ibn Nasir		

Hujar of the 'Anazah Tribe

Name	Amir	Headmen	Other
Khibar	Muhammad ibn Farhan Al-Ayda	Hazza' ibn Hays al-'Aydan; Hazza ibn Muhammad al-'Aydan	
Al-Faydhah	Jar Yibi'i ibn Suwaylim	Nasir Suwaylim	
Baydha' Nathil	Khalf al-Awaji		
Al-Sha'abiyah (1)	Shari' ibn Mijlad		
Al-Samli	'Abd al-Muhsin ibn Shaman		
Al-Sha'abiyah (2)	Farhan ibn Mashur		
Al-Balaziyah	'Abd-al-Rahman ibn Mu'aytik		

Hujjar of the Shammar Tribe

Name	Amir	Headmen	Other
Al-Ajfar	Deputy Amir/Ayyad ibn Nuhayyir	Hamdan ibn Jadi; Sultan ibn 'Ayish	
Al-Safra	Mughaylith ibn Jarallah		
Um Al-Qalban	Ghadhban ibn Rimal		
Jibba	'Adwa ibn Rimal	Mur'id ibn Rimal	
Al-Hufayr	Katib al-Nammas		Qadi/Hamd ibn Muzayd
Al-Tayyim	Farayih al-Hamzi		
Al-Khabba	Furaiyih al-Harbid		
Al-Sina	Sa'dun ibn 'Abass		
Al-Nifi	'Abd al Karim al-Zayd		
Al-'Adhim	Hathil ibn al-Faysim	Ghadhib ibn al-Faysim; Shabib ibn al-Faysim	
Al-Mak/hul	Marzuq al-'Adim		
Al-Sahwah	Manzal ibn Hayil		
Al-Shafiq	Dhafi ibn Ma'rif		
Al-Qasir	Hawwas ibn Khamsan	Muqbil ibn Khamsan	
Al-Faydha	Jadi ibn Famdil;	Khatham Fandil; Sultan ibn Fandil	
Al-'Aqlah	Hawwas ibn Tawwa Shammar	Muhammad ibn Dhari ibn Tawala Mis'hal ibn Salim ibn Tawala	

Hujjar of the Al Dhafir Tribe

Name	Amir	Headmen	Other
Al-Sha'iybi	'Ajami ibn Suwayt	Hazza' ibn 'Aqab ibn Suwayt; 'Abdullah ibn Ya'qub ibn Suwayt; Hamdan ibn Dhu-wayhi; and many of the chiefs of the Dhafir tribes	

Hujjar of the Harb Tribe

Name	Amir	Headmen	Other
Aqbah	'Abd al-Muhsin al-Farm	Nafi' ibn Fadliyyah	
Dukhnah	'Ayid al-Buhaymah	Dha'ar ibn Batla; Badr al-Mushaddaq; Ubayd ibn Afra	Qadi/'Abdullah ibn Zahim

Name	Amir	Headmen	Other
Al-Qawara	'Ali ibn Hadib	Falih ibn Hadib; Ayid ibn Makhlaf	
Al-Khushaybi	'Ubayd al-Zughaybi	'Abdullah al-Zughaybi; Ghanim al-Zughaybi	
Dhaida	Hathul ibn Hadib		
Khushayba	Dha'an ibn Hammad	Sultan ibn Hammad	
Kuhaylah	Na'if ibn Nahil	Shakir ibn Salaf	
Abu Mughayr	Sa'd ibn Rubayq		
Al-Nahitiya	Dayban ibn Ghadim		
Thadiq	Bijad ibn Ghumaydh	Mut'ib ibn Ghumaydh Bijad ibn Hawijan	

Hujjar of the Subay' Tribe

Name	Amir	Headmen	Other
Al-Hasi	Fadghush ibn Shuwayyah	Walid ibn Shuwayyah; Ghaytham Fahad; Mutlaq al-Sadifi	
Al-Dhubay'ah	'Ali ibn Hudayhid	Thunayyan ibn Hudayhid; Falih ibn Ghayda	
Al-Khidr	Al-Dhuwayri ibn Jafran	Sabi' Dharman Aba Thunayn Dhidan Aba Thunayn	

Hujar of the 'Ujman Tribe

Name	Amir	Headmen	Other
Al-Sarrar	Hizam ibn Hithlain		Qadi/'Abdullah ibn Hasan
Al-Kahfa	Fahhad ibn Hithlain		
Al-Wannan	Salid ibn Wathin		
Hanidh	Mansur ibn Shafi		
Bakha (not a *hijra*)	Muhammad ibn Hasah		
Zughayn	Khalid al-Mutlaqqim		
'Uray'irah	Mani' ibn Jum'ah		
Al-'Uyaynah (not a *hijra*)	Na'if ibn Hithlain		
'Anwa	Muhammad ibn 'Usaydan		
Al-Qarradi (not a *hijra*)	Khalid ibn Hithlain		
Al-Sahaf	Fahad ibn Bajjash		
Umm Rubay'an	Mulahhi ibn Qadh'an		
Al-Barah	Mutlaq Zunayfir		
Mitnanah	Muhammad ibn Zabyah		

Hujjar of the Bani Khalid Tribe

Name	Amir	Headmen	Other
Al-Dafi	Faris al-Hasan	Shahib al-Hasan	
Julmudah	Qarran ibn 'Ajran	Khalid ibn Harbi ibn 'Akla; Hizam ibn Thunnayan; Falah ibn Kulayb	

Hujjar of the Bani Hajir Tribes

Name	Amir	Headmen	Other
'Ayndar	Muhammad ibn Nasir ibn Khalifah	'Abdullah ibn Muhammad ibn Khalifah; Muhammad ibn Mubarak ibn Khalifah	Other
Yakrib	Shafi ibn Shafi	Muzhir ibn Shafi; Hamdun ibn Shafi	
Fudah	Muhammad ibn Fa'za	Sha'yi' ibn Suda	
Salasal	Ali Ibn 'Ayid	Hamd ibn 'Abid	

Hujjar of the Al-Murra Tribes

Name	Amir	Headmen	Other
Jabrin (Yabrin)	Hamd al-Mardhif	Salih al-Mardhif	
Al-Sikak	Hamd ibn Hanzab	Fadl ibn Fadl	
Niyal	Sa'ud ibn Naqawan		
Al-Badu'	Rashid ibn Nadila	Lahum ibn Sharim; Salih Abu Layla; Mut'ib al-Sa'af	

Hujjar of the Al-Awazim Tribes

Name	Amir	Headmen
Atiq	Fallah ibn Jami'	
Thaj	Musa'ith al-Mal'abi	

Hujjar of the Al-Dawasir Tribe

Name	Amir	Headmen	Other
Al-Hamr	Mathal ibn Waqyan	Amir of the Dawasir Shayban	
Mushirfah	Manaji ibn Hafith	ibn Quwayd, Saqr ibn	
Al-Wasita	Muhammad ibn Waqiyan	Dar'an; Muhamas ibn Suwaylimah	
Al-Hamarmah	Al-Sharif Abdullah ibn Nasir	Na'if ibn Hamlan; Hajid ibn Jaruh; Salal ibn Hamlan	

TABLE NINE

WARRIOR STRENGTH IN THE HUJAR

Tribe	Hijra	Rihani Arabic [19]	Rihani English [20]	Dickson [21]
Mutayr	Al-Artawiyah	2,000	2,000	1,000
	Muba'idh	1,000	1,000	900
	Furaythan	1,000	1,000	600
	Al-'Ammar	700	700	700
	Mulayh	700	700	700
	Al-'Ithlah	1,000	1,000	600
	Masika	800	800	600
	Dhariyyah	800	800	600
	Qaryah Al-'Ulya	1,500	1,500	1,800
	Qaryah Al-Sifla	1,000	1,000	1,600
	Nuqair	—	1,000	1,200
	Al-Sha'ab	—	400	300
	Mishaa'	—	—	400
	Sudair	—	700	—
	Al-Artawi	600	600	—
Total Mutayr		11,100	13,200	10,400
Qahtan	Al-Hayathim	1,800	1,800	1,800
	Al-Jufayr	300	300	800
	Al-Hasah	800	800	700
	Al-Rayn Al-Asfal	2,000	2,000	1,000
	Al-Rayn Al-'Ala	2,000	2,000	1,200
	Al-Ghil	—	—	500
	Hijrat Ibn Ghannam	—	—	500
	Haif Zahran	—	—	400
	As Sabha	—	—	500
	Al-'Ibra	—	—	600
Total Qahtan		6,900	6,900	8,000
Dawasir	Mushayrifah	1,500	1,500	1,500
	Al-Wusayta	800	800	800
Total Dawasir		2,300	2,300	2,300

---

[19] Al-Rihani, *Najd*, pp. 454-456.
[20] Al-Rihani, *Ibn Sa'oud*, pp. 198-199.
[21] Dickson, Kuwait, pp. 282-284.

Tribe	Hijra	Rihani Arabic [19]	Rihani English [20]	Dickson [21]
'Utaybah	Al-Dahna	2,000	2,000	800
(Al-Ruwaqah)	Al-Sauh	300	300	300
	Sajir	800	800	700
	'Arja	2,000	2,000	1,000
	Usaylah	300	300	300
	Nifi	1,500	1,500	900
	Hijrat Khalid ibn Luwai	—	—	400
	'Arma	—	—	700
	Al-Ghaba	—	—	200
	Al-'Urq	—	—	1,000
		6,900	6,900	6,300
'Utaybah	Al-Ghat Ghat *	5,000	2,000	700
(Barqa)	'Urwa	1,000	1,000	—
	Sanam	1,000	1,000	—
	Al-Ruwaydhah	700	700	700
Total 'Utaybah		14,600	11,600	7,700
Al-'Ujman	Al-Sarrar	2,000	2,000	1,600
	Hanidh	1,000	1,000	800
	Al-Sahaf	800	800	500
	Al-'Uqayr	700	700	500
	'Uray'irah	1,300	1,300	1,000
	Al'Uyaynah (not a *hijra*)	—	—	1,200
Total Al-'Ujman		5,800	5,800	5,600
Harb	Dukhnah	2,500	2,500	600
	Al-Shubaykiyah	1,000	1,000	900
	Al-Dulaymiyah	1,000	1,000	700
	Al-Qurayn	700	700	400
	Al-Saqiyah	600	600	600
	Halifah	300	300	900
	Hanaythil	700	700	500
	Al-Burud	1,000	1,000	1,000
	Qiba	2,000	2,000	1,000
	Al-Fawwara	1,000	—	—
Total Harb		10,800	9,800	6,400

---

* The difference in estimates for Al-Ghat-Ghat is most notable, and probably due to the general confusion as to the actual size and strength of the *hijra*. Certainly, 5,00 0warriors is an exaggerated figure while 2,000 would put it at the strength of Al-Artawiyah which is again unlikely since Al-Artawiyah was large,r than Al-Ghat Ghat. Although Dickson's figure of 700 may be an underestimate, it probably closer to the truth. Earlier in the paper it was shown that Al-Ghat Ghat probably did not exceed 4,000 persons. 700 warriors out of this figure would be about 20% of the population which is a reasonable figure.

Tribe	Hijra	Rihani Arabic [19]	Rihani English [20]	Dickson [21]
Al-'Awazim	Thaj	1,500	1,500	1,600
	Al-Hisi	1,000	1,000	1,000
	Al-Hannat	1,000	1,000	1,000
	Al-'Utayyiq	700	700	800
Total 'Awazim		4,200	4,200	4,100
Al-Murra	Al-Sikaka	1,000	—	—
	Al-Ambaq	1,500	1,500	900
	Ayn Dar (Bani Hajir)	1,000	—	700
	Nibak	—	1,000	1,000
Total Murra		3,500	2,500	1,900
Shammar	Baydha' Nathil	1,500	—	— [22]
	Al-Ajfar	2,000	2,000	2,000
	Banwan	1,500	1,500	1,500
	Al-Futayim	600	—	—
	Al-Qusayr	900	—	—
	Al-Hufayr	900	—	—
	Al-Khabba	800	—	—
	Al-Ghaydha	1,200	—	—
	Al-Taym	600	—	—
	Umm Al-Qalban	500	—	—
	Al-Shaqiq	400	—	—
	Al-Balaziyah	500	—	—
	Khrayfat	1,300	—	—
	Al-Masa'	700	—	—
	Al-Marir	400	—	—
	Rawdhat Al-'Uyun	—	1,000	1,000 [23]
Total Shammar		13,800	4,500	4,500
Kharj District	Al-Dhubay'ah	800	800	600
	Al-Bid'a	800	800	500
	Al-Munaysif	600	600	500
	Al-Akhdar	500	500	500
	Tayyib Ism	400	400	400
	Al-Ruwaydah	400	400	400
Total Kharj District		3,500	3,500	2,900
Yam	Ahl Najran (not a hijra)	—	—	4,000

[22] Dickson identifies this as an 'Utaybah tribe of the 'Ammar.
[23] Dickson identifies this as an 'Utaybah tribe of the 'Ammar.

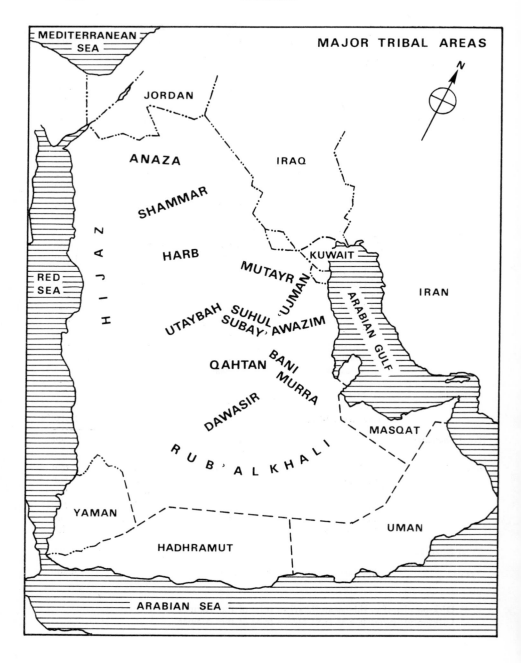

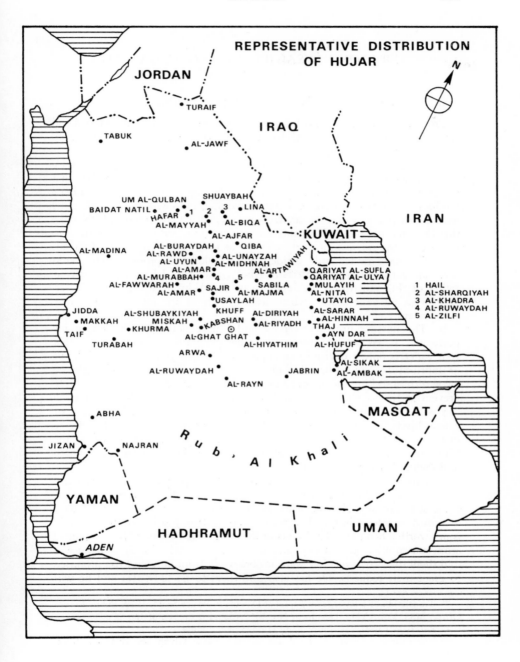

REPRESENTATIVE DISTRIBUTION OF HUJAR

LETTER FROM FAYSAL IBN SULTAN AL-DAWISH TO AMIR SA'UD [24]

In the Name of God the Most Merciful the Compassionate.

From Feisal bin Sultan Ed Doweisch to the respected brother Amir Sa'ud bin Imam Abd el Aziz ibn Abder Rahman Al Faisal, may God save him. Peace, Mercy and the Blessing of God be upon you always.

Your letter has been received and its contents noted. As for your advice to me to submit to the orders of your father the Imam, you will realize that my greatest desire is to comply with your orders especially after your father's kindness to me after the battle of Sabla. By God, I am willing to sacrifice my wealth and property for his satisfaction except for two reasons which make this difficult for me and beyond my power: first, my being compelled to bring back the missing property and the second, something more difficult.

a) We have raided only infidels and breakers of promises who build forts and encourage your subjects to rebel against you. I have informed your father of this and this is the reproach of the Akhwan against your father. Otherwise, all your actions when dealing with us are agreable (sic), may God reward you.

b) The missing property is gone and I have nothing of it left in my possession. It has occurred to me and other people have convinced me, that your order is only a device to entangle me and that you will either kill me or imprison me. Saud, I have left my desert, and my Sheikship, and sacrificed my wealth in seeking the gifts of God and fighting the infidels. If you wish to prevent us from fighting them and if when one of us commits an infraction you will either imprison or kill him, this is a calamity and oppression of your subjects, who may desert you, doubt your belief and irrevocably decide that you are hindering them in their religion, and indulging that of the Christians, and the Christians and their follower Faisal [25] have not failed to do what they can.

Anyone who goes over to them from the Nejd people is encouraged and favoured, and told to disobey Saud and that he will be given so and so. Since last year Abu Huneik [26] has been advising me and others and I have informed you accordingly. The ready proof is that you know Ibn Sabah [27] is not worth a hen to the Christians or the Arabs. He has given Ibn Mashun [28] arms, ammunition and money, and has communicated with the Ajman and told them that whatever they want is obtainable from him, and has promised to grant their requests. He has also told them to go to Wafra and he will

---

[24] Translation of a letter from Faysal al-Dawish to Prince Sa'ud, 1929, Public Record Office, MSS, Vol. 13736, Document No. 3457 (Sa'ud is the son of Ibn Sa'ud).

[25] Refers to Faysal, the son of King Husayn of the Hijaz.

[26] The nickname given by the Arabs to John Bagot Glubb, the British Political Officer in Iraq. It means "father of the little jaw".

[27] Refers to the Sheikh of Kuwait.

[28] A prominent leader of the Al-Ruwalah tribe.

keep Saud from them and that in case Saud should come after them, his territories are free for them to enter, and that he will speak to the Christians on their behalf.

You must understand that if the Christians were not only deceiving you and not only intending to seduce your subjects so that they may overpower you, the man of Koweit would not have disagreed with them; it is because he is under them that in these days I receive notices from Iraq and Koweit making me specious promises if I leave you. You have also prevented me from raiding the Bedouins. So we are neither. Moslems fighting the unbelievers nor are we Arabs and Bedouins raiding each other and living on what we get from each other. You have kept us away from both our religious and our worldly concerns. It is true that you have not failed to do what you can for me and my people but where are the rest of my tribes to go? They will perish and how can we be contended with this? In the past you used to forgive any of us who committed a sin, but now you treat us with the sword and pass over the Christians, their religion and the forts built for your immediate destruction, Saud.

So I have become frightened and have left Artawia for Lasafra. If you want us as your subjects you should look into our case. We want from you three things, which we wish your father to promise us if the Sheikhs 29 approve, and which you, Al Saud, should undertake: firstly, to wipe out the past, secondly, to release your prisoners and each of us for his part will guarantee to do the same, and thirdly, to be allowed to fight the infidels, with one of you, sons of Abd el Aziz, accompanying us. We will do other work for you, we the people of Nejd. If we are killed, it does not matter, and if succeed it will be for your benefit, just as our brethren the Ghut Ghut took the Hejaz and it became yours in your name.

If you agree to these points I promise to be your servant and slave and to allow you a free hand over our lives and property. Our brethren the prisoners will promise you the same. Your people of Nejd, do not be deceived by those near you. As regards the Bedouins, if they see your treatment of us, and see how the infidels receive those who go from you to them, by God, none will remain. You know that the best of them as regards religion, and the nearest to you are those whom you have killed and imprisoned. So if you want us, let some well-known learned man come to us and release the prisoners at Riyadh and I swear by God in this meeting held by the Ajman, Mutair and others that we will attack the infidels before we go to you or as God may guide you. I am still hopeful and I know how your father loves his subjects and likes to forgive them. He is the politician of us Arabs. So give us a special guarantee securing the safety of the Ajman and Ibn Mashur and those who are with him, and forgiving their past.

We ask you by God not to send us away disappointed or deprived of your friendship and of the religion of Islam, and compelled to go to the Christians whom we dislike and who dislike us.

---

29 Ibn Sa'ud was called *al-shayukh* (the sheikhs) to distinguish him from the others holding the title, sheikh. It is possible that the Arabic word meant Ibn Sa'ud, and hence the tranlation as Sheikhs may be misleading.

If you agree, by God, you may test us in anything you will and see what we will do. If a second incident occurs, you may do whatever you like. By God, we have left all the old folk weeping, the women weeping and we are weeping. Saud, my brother, do not give up your friend for your enemy. Please send the reply quickly anything happens and note one thing namely the enemy of your religion does not help you.

Abd el Aziz [30] sends his compliments.

Please convey my compliments to the Sheikhs and the sons.

(Sealed) Feisal ed Doweisch.

---

[30] Refers to al-Dawish's son, who was also known by the diminutive, 'Azayiz.

LETTER 31 FROM AMIR SA'UD TO THE SHEIKH OF KUWAIT

From Sa'ud bin 'Abd-al-'Aziz bin 'Abd-al-Rahman Al-Faysal to His Excellency the honorable, brother, Sheikh Ahmad Al-Jabir Al-Sabah, May God protect him and keep him well, amen.

After extending greetings and requesting the blessings of God and his mercy on you always, and inquiring about your well being, hoping that you are well and happy, we thank God for his blessings, benevolence, for through the generosity of God we are all well. May God keep you. You are aware of the matter of bin Bijad and Al-Duwish and their followers regarding their insubordination, disobedience, and contraventions of the *shari'a*. For four years we tried to facilitate the matter so that it would not be public and cause harm to everyone, since our intention and objectives is the comfort and well being of the Muslims, as well as their security. But things are limited by time. We thought that their raid was directed only against the fortresses and their inhabitants, and did not know that their intention was against Ibn Ramal and his followers, as well as the people of Qasim, whom they slaughtered and stole property to which they had no legal right. We became angry, as did others, as well as the people of Najd, and we leaped against them like one man. After that a meeting of all the Muslims took place in the Qasim, and after destroying them we moved toward Zilfi and those aforementioned [32] were at Sbila, about two hours away. We asked them to arbitrate the matter through the *shari'a*, but they continually refused, and insisted on not accepting it, so on the 19th of last month the Muslims marched against them and killed them, wreaking on them a terrible lesson. They lost a large number of men, but as for the Muslims, thanks be to God, all of them returned safely, except ten who were killed. This is usually what happens to those who contravene God's law and do not obey the *shari'a*. As for Al-Duwish, he was wounded, and God only knows if he will die from his serious wounds; we have captured his son and all of the chief people of Artawiyah, and bin 'Ashwan with the important bedouins of Mutayr, and bin Bijad as well and all the important 'Utayba.

When we saw what God did for us and the Muslims, we wanted to inform you, and we hope that God will bless us with gratitude for his blessings, and continue to do this for the Muslims. This is what we wanted to tell you. The children and the Brothers here, my Lord, send you their regards, as well as His Majesty the King and the Brothers send you their best wishes.

18 April 1929

---

[31] The original letter is in the possession of Haan al-Shaykh Khaz'al, the historian, resident in Kuwait. Original seen by this writer in Riyadh on 8 May 1969; a copy of this letter was given to him by Khaz'al.

[32] Refers to Ibn Bijad, al-Dawish, and their followers.

BIBLIOGRAPHY

PUBLIC DOCUMENTS

Great Britain. Public Record Office. *Telegram for Sir Percy Z. Cox*, 9 July 1913. Vol. 1820, Document No. 31610.

Great Britain. Public Record Office. *Letter from Viceroy to Foreign Office*, 20 December 1913. Vol. 1848, Document No. 57883.

Great Britain. Public Record Office. *Cable to Sir R. Wingate from the Government of India*, 7 January 1918. Vol. 3389, Document No. 4423.

Great Britain. Public Record Office. *Decypher of Telegram from Sir R. Wingate*, Cairo, 8 January 1918. Volume 3389, Document No. 4067.

Great Britain. Public Record Office. *Letter from King Husayn to the Acting British Agent, Jidda*, 18 Septemebr 1918. Vol. 3390, Document No. 161898.

Great Britain. Public Record Office. *Letter from King Husayn Under Cover of a Letter sent by Wingate to Balfour*, 3 October 1918. Vol. 3390, Document No. E 177596.

Great Britain. Public Record Office. *Letter to the Rt. Honorable Arthur James Balfour from Reginald Wingate, British High Commissioner*, 3 October 1918. Vol. 3390, Document No. 177596.

Great Britain. Public Record Office. *Note on the Cover Sheet of a report*, Vol. 3390, Document No. 161898.

Great Britain. Public Record Office. *Telegram from the Secretary of State for India to the Civil Commisioner, Baghdad*, 1 October 1918. Vol. 3390, Document No. 169854 .

Great Britain. *Report by Lt. Col. R. E. A. Hamilton, Political Agent*, Kuwait, 7 December 1918. Vol. 3390. Document No. 20419.

Great Britain. Public Record Office. *Letter from Sir Reginald Wingate*. 3 October 1918. Vol. 3390. Document No. 177596.

Great Britain. Public Record Office. *Sir F. Humphrey's Report on Ibn Rafida rebellion.* 15 August 1932. Vol. 4101.

Great Britain. Public Record Office. *Cable from Sir R. Wingate in Cairo to the Foreign Office.* 6 January 1919. Vol. 4144. Document No. 3663.

Great Britain. Public Record Office. *Dispatch from Colonel Wilson and a Letter from King Husayn.* 15 December 1918. Vol. 4144. Document No. 1181 .

Great Britain. Public Record Office. *Letter and Enclosures from Reginald Wingate to Arthur James Balfour.* Vol. 4144. Document No. 3059.

Great Britain. Public Record Office. *The Ikhwan and the Wahabis.* 1919. Vol. 4144. Document No. E 7615.

Great Britain. Public Record Office. *Arabia: The Nejd-Hijaz Feud.* 11 January 1919. Vol. 4144. Document No. 5815.

Great Britain. Public Record Office. *Telegram of Sir R. Wingate, Cairo, to Foreign Office.* 15 January 1919. Vol. 4144. Document No. 9710.

Great Britain. Public Record Office. *Cypher Telegram to Sir R. Wingate*, Cairo. 17 January 1919. Vol. 4144. Document No. 2390.

Great Britain. Public Record Office. *Telegram from Wilson.* 19 February 1919. Vol. 4144. Document No. 27283.

Great Britain. Public Record Office. *Cable from A. T. Wilson.* 4 March 1919. Vol. 4144. Document No. 34661.

Great Britain. Public Record Office. *Telegram from King Hussein for Emir Feisal.* 18 January 1919. Vol. 4144. Document No. 10448.

Great Britain. Public Record Office. *Cypher Telegram to Wingate.* 1918. Vol. 4144. Document No. 2390.

Great Britain. Public Record Office. *Secret Summary of the Najd-Hejaz Feud.* 11 January 1919. Vol. 4144. Document No. 5815.

Great Britain. Public Record Office. *Ditpatch on Conversations with Cavaliere Bernabei.* 8 January 1919. Vol. 4144. Document No. 12831.

Great Britain. Public Record Office. *Report from the Assitant Political Officer,* Basra. Vol. 4146. Document No. 94390.

Great Britain. Public Record Office. *Letter from Prince Faysal to Sir General Allenby.* Cairo. No date given. Vol. 4146. Document No. 108194.

Great Britain. Public Record Office. *Note by Captain Garland of the Arab Bureau.* Vol. 4146. Document No. E 91521.

Great Britain. Public Record Office. *Letter from 'Abd-al-'Azziz Al-Faysal to Sa'ud ibn 'Abd-al-'Aziz Al-Rashid.* Vol. 4146. Document No. 117487. 2 August 1919.

Great Britain. Public Record Office. *Telegraph from Political Agent, Baghdad, to Secretary of State.* 14 June 1919. Vol. 4146. Document No. 90222.

Great Britain. Public Record Office. *Telegram from Wilson.* 10 June 1919. Vol. 4146. Document No. 86896.

Great Britain. Public Record Office. *Translation of a Memorandum on the Wahabite Crisis from H.R.H. The Emir Feisal.* Vol. 4146. Document No. 108194.

Great Britain. Public Record Office. *From Secretary of State to Civil Commissioner.* Baghdad. 30 May 1919. Vol. 4146. Document No. 83242.

Great Britain. Public Record Office. *Telegram from General Allenby to Foreign Office.* 10 June 1919. Vol. 4146. Document No. 86805.

Great Britain. Public Record Office. *Telegram from India Office.* Whitehall. 13 June 1919. Vol. 4146. Document No. 88374.

Great Britain. Public Record Office. *Decypher of Allenby Telegram from Cairo.* 9 June 1919. Vol. 4146. Document No. 85980.

Great Britain. Public Record Office. *Report on the Ikhwan.* 13 May 1919, Vol. 4146, Document No. E 94390.

Great Britain. Public Record Office. *Dispatch from Colonel C. E. Wilson to Major Young.* Vol. 4147. Document No. 152998.

Great Britain. Public Record Office. *Letter from the Political Officer, Muntafik Division, Nasariyah, to the Civil Commissioner, Baghdad.* 12 May 1918. Vol. 4147. Document No. E 118698.

Great Britain. Public Record Office. *From Officiating Civil Commissioner of Baghdad.* 9 May 1918. Vol. 4147. (No Document No. given.)

Great Britain. Public Record Office. *Letter from Captain Bray to the India Office.* 28 July 1919. Vol. 4147. Document No. E 129678.

Great Britain. Public Record Office. *Translation of a letter from Shaykh Sir Abdul Aziz bin Abdur Rahman Al-Faisal As Saud From Colonel Bassett.* 3 June 1919. Vol. 4147. (No Document No. given.)

Great Britain. Public Record Office. *From General Officer Commanding, Egypt to the Secretary of the Government of India.* 1 June 1919. Telegram No. 892. Vol. 4147.

Great Britain. Public Record Office. *Letter from Ibn Sa'ud.* 1919. Vol. 4147. Document No. 21809.

Great Britain. Public Record Office. *From Captain Bray to India Office.* 28 July 1919. Vol. 4147. Document No. 129678.

Great Britain. Public Record Office. *Message From Political Officer Baghdad.* 1919. Vol. 4147. Document No. 8195.

Great Britain. Public Record Office. *Cable From Foreign Office to Colonel Wilson.* 1 December 1919. Vol. 4147. Document No. 156742.

Great Britain. Public Record Office. *Arabia Series, Part X, Memo from Officiating Civil Commissioner, Baghdad.* 10 May 1919. Vol. 4147. (No Document No. given.)

Great Britain. Public Record Office. *Report by Major Courtney to the Director of Military Intelligence.* No date given. Vol. 4146. Document No. 108194.

Great Britain. Public Record Office. *Report on the Operations of the Najd Mission.* 29 November 1918. Vol. 4144. Document No. 4370.

Great Britain. Public Record Office. *Ahmad Thuneyan Denial.* 1920. Vol. 5060. Document No. 1154.

Great Britain. Public Record Office. *Ditpatch from Major H. R. P. Dickson, Political Agent, Bahrain to the Civil Commissioner, Baghdad.* 5 March 1920. Vol. 5062. (No document No. given.)

Great Britain. Public Record Office. *Ditpatch to the Civil Commissioner, Baghdad.* Vol. 5062. (No Document No. given.)

Great Britain. Public Record Office. *Transmittal of Bin Sa'ud Message.* 17 August 1920. Vol. 5064. Document No. E 11890.

Great Britain. Public Record Office. *Dispatch from Major H. R. P. Dickson, Political Agent, Bahrein to the Deputy Political Resident in the Persian Gulf, Bushire.* 1920. Vol. 5065. Document No. E 12852.

Great Britain. Public Record Office. *Ditpatch to the Deputy Political Resident in the Persian Gulf,* Vol. 5065. (No Document No. given.)

Great Britain. Public Record Office. *Diary of Faziluddin.* 1920. Vol. 5184. Document No. E 12528.

Great Britain. Public Record Office. *Extract of a Report by Major W. Batten, Acting British Agent in Jidda.* No date given. Vol. 5243. Document No. 11363.

Great Britain. Public Record Office. *Report from Rear-Admiral, Egypt.* 20 February 1920. Vol. 5243. Document No. 11363.

Great Britain. Public Record Office. *Confidential Memo from the Political Agent, Bahrain to the Civil Commissioner, Baghdad.* 23/26 April 1920. Vol. 5261. Document No. E 8538.

Great Britain. Public Record Office. *Neutral View on Alleged French Treaty with Ibn Saud.* 20 September 1922. Vol. 7714. Document No. E 9565.

Great Britain. Public Record Office. *Telegram from the High Commissioner for Palestine.* 28 July 1922. Vol. 7714. Document No. 8278.

Great Britain. Public Record Office. *Despatch from Mr. Philby on the Wahabi Movement.* 3 August 1922. Vol. 7714. Document No. 40733.

Great Britain. Public Record Office. *Despatch from Consul Palmer in Damascus.* 3 July 1922. Vol. 7714. Document No. E 7361.

Great Britain. Public Record Office. *Transmittal of Documents by Field-Marshal Viscount Allenby to the Marquess Curzon of Kedleston.* 17 October 1922. Vol. 7715. Document No. E 11186.

Great Britain. Public Record Office. *Appreciation of the Wahabi Movement by the French Army.* 31 August 1922. Vol. 7715. (No Document No. given.)

Great Britain. Public Record Office. *Dickson to Political Agent Kuwait.* 27 October 1930. Vol. 11452. Document No. E 5776.

Great Britain. Public Record Office. *Glubb Report from Busaiyah.* 1929. Vol. 13713. Document No. E 114.

Great Britain. Public Record Office. *Relations with Najd.* 1931. Vol. 13736. Document No. E 3273.

Great Britain. Public Record Office. *English Translation of a letter from Feisal bin Sultan Ed Doweisch to Amir Saud.* Vol. 13736. Document No. E 3457.

Great Britain. Public Record Office. *Dispatch from Lt. Colonel H. R. P. Dickson, Koweit to the Policial Resident in the Persian Gulf.* 2 September 1929. Vol. 13740. Document No. 5154.

Great Britain. Public Record Office. *Bond to Henderson*. 29 August 1920. Vol. 13740. Document No. E 4586.

Great Britain. Public Record Office. *Cable from Colonel Biscoe*. 9 January 1930. Vol. 14449. Document No. E 164.

Great Britain. Public Record Office. *Cable from Colonel Biscoe*. 9 January 1930. Vol. 14449. Document No. E 275.

Great Britain. Public Record Office. *Consul General Biscoe to Lord Passfield*. 26 February 1930. Vol. 14451. Document No. E 1081.

Great Britain. Public Record Office. *Attachment on Number and Type of Booty Found in Ikhwan Tents*. 16 April 1930. Vol. 14451. Document No. E 1991.

Great Britain. Public Record Office. *Extract from Glubb Report*. 20 May 1930. Vol. 14451. Document No. E 2578.

Great Britain. Public Record Office. *Sir F. Humphrey's Report on Ibn Rafida rebellion*. 31 December 1932. Vol. 16017. Document No. 6943.

Saudi Arabia Ministry of Foreign Affairs. *Majmu'a Al-Mu'ahidat min 'Am 1922-1931*. (Collection of Treaties for the Years 1922-1931.) Um Al-Qurah, Mecca. 1931.

Saudi Arabia Government. *Al-Kitab Al-Akhdar Al-Najdi (The Najdi Green Book.)* Printed by order of the Sultan of Najd.

BOOKS

'Abd-al-Wahab, Muhammad ibn. *Al-Usul Al-Thalatha wa Adillatuha (The Three Principles and their Proofs)* Cairo: Dar Al-Tiba'a Al-Yusifiyah, no date given.

Al-'Ajlani, Munir. *Tarikh Al-Bilad Al-'Arabiyah Al-Sa'udiyyah. (History of Sa'udi Arabia.)* Beirut: Dar Al-Kitab Al-'Arabi, no date given, only Part I published.

Armstrong, R. C. *Lord of Arabia*. Beirut: Khayats, 1966.

Asad, Muhammad. *The Road to Mecca*. New York: Simon and Schuster, 1954.

'Attar, Ahmad 'Abd-al-Ghafur. *Saqr Al-Jazirat (Falcon of the Peninsula.)* 2nd edition. Jidda: Al-Mu'assisah Al-'Arabiyah Lil Tiba'a, 1964.

Benoist-Mechin, Jacques. *Arabian Destiny*. Translated from the French by Denis Weaver. London: Elek Books Limited, 1957.

Ibn Bishr, 'Uthman. *'Unwan Al-Majd fi Tarikh Najd. (Chapters of Glory in the History of Najd.)* Riyadh: Dar Banna lil Tiba'ah wa Tajlid, 1953.

Brouche, Jeanne. *L'Empire Arabe D'ibn Seoud*. Brussels: Librairie Folk Fels, 1929.

Cheesman, R. E. *In Unknown Arabia*. London: Macmillan Company, 1926.

Al-Dabbagh, Mustapha Murad. *Al-Jazirat Al-'Arabiyah (The Araiban Peninsula.)* Beirut: Dar Al-Tali'a, Part I only published, 1963.

De Gaury, Gerald. *Arabia Phoenix*. London: George Harris & Co. Ltd., 1946.

Dickson, H. R. P. *Kuwait and Her Neighbors*. London: George Allen and Unwin, Ltd., 1956.

——. *The Arab of the Desert*. London: George Allen and Unwin Ltd., 1949.

Ibn Ghanam, Husayn. *Tarikh Najd. (History of Najd.)* First Edition. Riyadh: Matba'a Al-Ahliyah, 1949.

Glubb, John Bagot, Sir. *War in the Desert*. London: Hodder and Stoughton, 1960.

Graves, Philip P. (ed.) *Memoirs of King 'Abdullah of Transjordan*. London: Jonathan Capte, 1950.

Hamza, Fu'ad. *Qalb Jazirat Al-'Arab. (Heart of the Arab Peninsula.)* Cairo: Al-Salafiyah Press, 1933.

——. *Al-Bilad Al-Arabiyah Al-Sa'udiyah (Sa'udi Arabia.)* Second Edition. Riyadh: Maktaba Al-Nasr Al-Haditha, 1968.

——. *Fi Bilad 'Asir. (In the Asir Country.)* Second Edition. Riyadh: Maktaba Al-Nasr Al-Haditha, 1968.

Al-Haqil, Hamd Ibrahim. *'Abd-al-'Aziz Fi Al-Tarikh.* (*'Abd al-'Aziz In History.*) Beirut: Mu'assisa Al-Ma'arif, 1969.

Ibn Hathlul, H. R. R. Sa'ud. *Tarikh Muluk Al Sa'ud.* (*History of the Sa'ud Kings.*) First Edition. Riyadh: Riyadh Publishing Company, 1961.

Hitti, Philip K. *History of the Arabs.* New York: The Macmillan Company, 1951.

Hogarth, David George. *The Penetration of Arabia.* Beirut: Khayyats, 1960.

'Issa, Ahmad. *Mu'jiza Fawq Al-Rimal.* (*Miracle Over the Sands.*) Beirut: Al-Matabi' Al-Ahliyah Al-Lubnaniyah, 1965.

Al-Jasir, Hamd. *Madina Al-Riyadh 'Abr Atwar Al-Tarikh.* (*The City of Riyadh in History.*) First Edition. Riyadh: Dar Al-Yammama 1966.

Kelley, John B. *Eastern Arabian Frontiers.* London: Faber and Faber, 1964.

Al-Khatib, 'Abd al-Hamid. *Al-Imam Al-'Adil.* (*The Just Imam.*) Cairo: Maktabah wa Matba'ah Mustapha Al-Bana Al-Halabi, Part I, no date given.

Kiernan, Reginald Hugh. *The Unveiling of Arabia.* London: George C. Harris & Co. Ltd., 1937.

Lipsky, George A. *Saudi Arabia.* New Haven: Hraf Press, 1959.

Lorimer, J. G. *Gazetteer of the Persian Gulf, 'Oman and Central Araiba.* 2 volumes. Calcutta: 1908-1915.

Al-Madani, Muhammad Mughayrabi Futayih. *Firqat Al-Ikhwan Al-Islamiyah bi Najd.* No publisher given, 1923.

Al-Mukhtar, Salah Al-Din. *Tarikh Al-Mamlakat Al-'Arabiyah Al-Sa'udiyah Fi Madiha wa Hadirha.* (*History of the Kingdom of Sa'udi Arabia, Past and Present.*) First Edition. Beirut: Dar Maktabah Al-Hayat, 1958. 2 volumes.

Musil, Alois. *Northern Negd.* American Geographical Society. Oriental Explorations and Studies, No. 5. New York: 1928.

Nasr, 'Abd-al-Rahman. *Ahil Al-Jazirah.* Cairo: Matba'ah Misr, no date of Publication given.

Palgrave, William Gifford. *Central and Eastern Arabia,* 2 volumes.

Philby, H. St. John. *Sa'udi Arabia.* London: Earnest Benn Limited, 1955.

——. *Arabia.* New York: Charles Scribner's Sons, 1930.

——. *Arabian Days.* London: Robert Hale Ltd., 1948.

——. *Arabian Jubilee.* London: Robert Hale Ltd., 1952.

——. *Arabia of the Wahhabis.* London: Constable and Company, 1928.

——. *The Empty Quarter.* New York: Henry Holt and Company, 1933.

——. *A Pilgrim In Arabia.* London: Robert Hale Ltd., 1946.

Al-Rihani, Amin. *Muluk Al-'Arab.* (*Kings of the Arabs.*) Beirut: Dar Al-Rihani Lil wal Nashr, 1960. Two volumes.

——. *Najd wal Mulhaqatihu.* (*Najd and its Dependencies.*) Beirut: Dar Al-Rihani Lil Taba'a wal Nashr, 1964.

Rihani, Ameen. *Ibn Sa'oud of Arabia: His People and His Land.* London: Constable & Co. Ltd., 1928.

Sa'id, Amin. *Tarikh Al-Daulat Al-Sa'udiyah.* (*History of the Sa'udi State.*) Three volumes. Beirut: Dar Al-Kitab Al-'Arabi, 1965.

——. *Sirat Al-Imam al-Shaykh Muhammad ibn 'Abd-al-Wahhab.* (*Biography of Muhammad ibn 'Abd-al-Wahhab*) Jidda: Shirkat Al-Sahafa wal Matbu'at Al-Muttahida 1964.

Al-Sa'idi, 'Abd-al-Mut'al. *Shabab Al-Quraysh Fi Bad' Al-Islam.* (*The Quraysh Youth at the Beginning of Islam.*) Third Edition. Cairo: Dar al-Fikr Al-'Arabi, 1960.

Salama, Bulus. *Malhami 'Id Al-Riyadh.* Beirut: Dar Al-Shamali Publishing Co., 1963.

Smith, Wilfred Cantwell. *Islam In Modern History.* Princeton: Princeton University Press, 1957.

Van Der Meulen, D. *The Wells of Ibn Saud.* New York: Frederick A. Praeger, 1957.

Wahbah Hafiz. *Jazirat Al-'Arab Fi Al-Qarn Al-'Ashrin,* (*The Arab Peninsula in the Twentieth Century.*) Cairo: Matba'ah Al-Nahdat Al-Misriyah, 1961.

———. *Khamsun 'Amma Fi Jazirat Al-'Arab.* (*Fifty Years In the Arab Peninsula.*)
First Edition. Cairo: Matba'ah Mustapha Al-Babi Al-Halabi, 1960.
———. *Arabian Days.* London: Arthur Barker Ltd., 1964.
Weintraub, Stanley and Rodelle. *Evolution of a Revolt: Early Postwar Writings of
T. E. Lawrence.* London and University Park, 1968.
Winder, R. Bayly. *Saudi Arabia in the Nineteenth Century.* London: Macmillan, 1965.

ARTICLES

Calverly, E. E. "The Doctrines of the 'Arabian Brethren,' " *Moslem World,* Vol. XI,
1921, p. 364.
Harrison, Paul. "Al-Riyadh, the Capital of Nejd," *Moslem World,* Vol. VIII, 1919,
pp. 412-419.
Lewis, C. C. "Ibn Saud and the Future of Arabia," *Royal Institute of International
Affairs,* Vol. XII, 1933, pp. 418-534.
Philby, H. St. John B. "Arabia 1926-1929: Three Years of Wahhabi Rule," *Contem-
porary Review* (London), Vol. CXXXVII, January-June 1929, pp. 714-719.
Smalley, W. F. "The Wahhabis and Ibn Saud," *Moslem World,* Vol. XXII, July 1932,
no. 3.
Toynbee, A. J. "A Problem of Arabian Statesmanship," *Journal of the Royal Institute
of International Affairs,* Vol. VIII, 1929, pp. 367-375.
Wahba, Hafizh. "Wahhabism in Arabia: Past and Present," *Journal of the Central
Asian Society,* Vol. XVI, Part IV, 1929, pp. 458-467.
Von Weisl, Dr. Wolfgang. "Islam's Iconoclasts at Mekka's Gates," *The Living Age*
(Boston), Vol. CCCXXIII, October-December, 1924, pp. 318-321.
London Times Clippings (Arabia), July 1920 to April 1926, "Pilgrims' Accounts of
the Taif Massacre," October 1924.
London Time Clippings (Arabia), July 1920 to April 1926, "The Wahabis At Taif,"
16 Septemebr 1924.
Umm al-Qura, No. 111, 28 January 1927. Editorial.
Umm al-Qura, No. 126, 10 May 1927. The Riyadh Conference.
Umm al-Qura, No. 208, 18 December 1928. The Riyadh General Assembly.
Umm al-Qura, No. 211, 11 January 1929. Editorial.
Umm al-Qura, No. 212, 18 January 1929. Editorial.
Umm al-Qura, Uo. 218, 1 March 1929. The *Hujar* in the Arabian Peninsula.
Umm al-Qura, No. 222, 29 March 1929. Editorial.
Umm al-Qura, No. 239, 31 July 1929. Meeting at Dawadimi.
Umm al-Qura, No. 240, 26 July 1929. Editorial.
Umm al-Qura, No. 242, 9 August 1929. Education Mission Abroad.
Umm al-Qura, No. 252, 18 October 1929. Sha'ra Conference.
Umm al-Qura, No. 287, 6 June 1930. War Readiness in Najd.
Umm al-Qura, No. 289, 30 June 1930. Editorial.
Umm al-Qura, No. 291, 4 July 1930. The Bedouin.
Umm al-Qura, No. 292, 11 July 1930. Subsidies.
Umm al-Qura, No. 293, 18 July 1930. Names of Loyal Ikhwan.
Umm al-Qura, No. 302, 19 September 1930. Types of Battle Among the Arabs.
Umm al-Qura, No. 303, 26 September 1930. War Equipment Among the Arabs.

UNPUBLISHED MATERIAL

Mutlaq ibn Salih, *Shath Al-Nad Fi Tarikh Najd.* Xerox copy in possession of John
S. Habib.
'Abd al-Rahman ibn Nasir, *'Unwan Al-Sa'd Wal Majd.* Xerox copy in possession of
John S. Habib.

OTHER SOURCES

Al-Ghat Ghat, Saudi Arabia. Personal interview with Sheikh/Majid ibn Khathila. March 1968, and various interviews since that time up until October 1969.

Al-Ghat Ghat, Saudi Arabia. Personal interview with Sheikh/Muhammad ibn Majid bin Khathila. March 1968 and various interviews since that time up until March 1969.

Al-Artawiyah, Saudi Arabia. Personal interview with Sheikh/'Abd-al-Rahman al-Dawish. March 1968, and in Riyadh in March 1969.

Riyadh, Saudi Arabia. Personal interview with Sheikh Muhammad/al-Sahabi, 20 November 1967, and several others in Riyadh since that date.

Riyadh. Saudi Arabia. Personal interview with Muhammad ibn Jaba' al-Dawish, November 1968, and several since that date.

Riyahd, Saudi Arabia. Personal interview with 'Abd-al-Rahman al-Maghrabi, October 1968.

Riyadh, Saudi Arabia. Personal interview with HRH Prince 'Abd-al-Rahman ibn 'Abdullah ibn 'Abd-al-Rahman Al Sa'ud.

Riyadh, Saudi Arabia. Estimate of Christos A. Antachopoulos, December 1968.

London, England. Personal interview with Sir John Bagot Glubb, June 1968.

INDEX